The Almost-Dictionary

Almost-steal (pay sticker price for) this book.

THE
ALMOST-DICTIONARY

The Almost-Second (1.987654321) Edition

Almost-Unabridged

JOHN DALSTON

(Typist)

THE ALMOST-DICTIONARY

The Almost-Second (1.987654321) Edition

Published on Earth, in the United States of America
by AspectEdge, LLC., Florida.
www.AspectEdge.com

ISBN 978-0-9819579-0-6 (trade paperback)

Almost-dedicated to almost-getting nearly there.

Introduction

Once almost-upon a time there was an almost-need for an almost-dictionary to explain all of the almost-hidden parts in the almost-standard dictionaries. Until now. This is it.

So few things are completely "as described." Most things are *not* all-or-nothing. When you eat "an apple" you probably don't eat the core, so you only almost-eat the apple. A "good" day for you is probably only almost-good — or just better than average. The people you meet are only almost-awesome, almost-considerate, and almost in a rush. The "developed" world is still in need of even more development. A win usually involves some loss. Tourist attractions don't always meet expectations, especially by the time *you* get there. What was the tallest building in the world, is now only the almost-tallest. The best possible condition of a house, nation, or our whole planet might be that of "almost-safe" and "almost-secure" (because there are no absolute guarantees). If the question was whether a group of people are "educated" or "current" on a certain subject, again an almost-answer might be the most appropriate. No individual has got it mentally "all together" (where would they put it), and there is no such thing as complete sanity. Everyone seeks the perfect life, but we almost-always almost-settle.

The definitions for words in an almost-standard dictionary are vague or imprecise precisely because they are comprised of other words. The definition for "walk" leaves no mention of a particular speed. The definition for "dog" is nonspecific about sequences of nucleotides in the genome. When we listen to people talk we pay attention to the context of the words as well as to the words themselves, and for some purposes we need *much* more information than what is provided in the almost-standard dictionary definitions, so we almost-drill almost-down further.

Most of what we know can be described, but only ever almost-completely. There is almost-always more to know, or another aspect to consider. We usually focus on those aspects most relevant at the time. It is in our almost-nature to almost-ignore the less-relevant information until later. If an elephant were to run straight toward us, we would get out of the way first, and then worry about precisely how tall it is, or how someone on the other side of it would describe it. When we learn things, we almost-quickly almost-forget the almost-unimportant parts. We take pictures of people and places to remember the almost-good times. We write things down so we can remember more precisely later on. The root cause of many problems is a failure in communication: a lack of clarity, or precision, or understanding. (For this reason many people keep talking until they are interrupted.) Communication usually starts with the almost-critical, and tends to drop off when almost-all of the fairly important stuff has been said. The Almost-Dictionary may be almost-helpful in the almost-understanding of the almost-correctness in previously-deemed "correct" speech and writing.

Almost-out of necessity, we seek that which is only almost-done (or almost not done), so that we can contribute something ourselves, and thereby gain a livelihood. When we apply for a job, we are really only almost-ready to fill our predecessors shoes (the employer already knows that). By the time we get to the interview though, we already almost-have the job, we just need to convince our future boss that hiring us would be a better choice than his or her next-best alternative. It could be said of many eminent thinkers throughout history that their field was not the same after them because of the refinements and standards of almost-exactness that they brought; yet there remains so much to be improved upon.

We almost-habitually and optimistically reach out. While almost-invariably at least somewhat risk-averse, we actually and often count on things, and people, and particular outcomes more than we should: remaining both almost-oblivious to, and almost-paranoid of the almost-nature of the universe, and quite-rightly attempt to dodge the almost-slings and almost-arrows almost-always almost-curiously associated with someone else's almost-outrageous near-fortune, and by handily dealing with the little heaps of trouble, and by almost-opposing, actually delay a confrontation with more questionable and undiscovered calamities for yet another day.

Beginnings, and Web Sites

The Almost-Dictionary was begun on the Almost-World web site in December, 2007. It was continued in an almost-desultory way until the printing of this, the almost-second (1.987654321) edition.

As of this writing there are two related web sites where more almost-info may be found:

www.almost-world.com
www.almost-art.org.

These sites contain more almost-descriptions, almost-explanations, almost-speak, almost-slogans, and other almost-stuff. (Almost-contact information is there too. Please send me an email if you want to be on my mailing list, or if you have suggestions or comments.) There are entries for the terms "almost-art" and "almost-world" here, but there is much more about those two subject at the respective web sites above.

About the Almost-Dictionary

The Almost-Dictionary is not fully a dictionary because there are no definitions for almost-standard words, only almost-words. (Less almost-redundancy.) Almost-words are out there anyway (as prefixed regular words), it's just that until now they haven't been collected quite like this (in this almost-way, to be almost-reflective). Just reading an almost-standard dictionary *as if* each word had an "almost" prefix would not be very useful in many instances, and the reader would not benefit from the definitions here.

Not all of the almost-words used in the definitions here are themselves defined. Still, almost-all of them are. You will be making up your own almost-words on the almost-fly as well.

While claiming that the Almost-Dictionary is "almost-unabridged," I have tried to include both *important* and *common* almost-root words, knowing that it was not going to be possible to list all almost-words. Hopefully, I've included at least most of the almost-words that you are going to want to look up. Still, the almost-bridge to almost-complete non-abridgment is almost-paved with ever more almost-words and almost-speak. You will undoubtedly notice entries where more could be added, and think of possible new entries.

About Almost-Words and Almost-Speak

The almost-words in the Almost-Dictionary can be used in most everyday speech and writing (they are not just for almost-special occasions). Almost-speak tends to almost-creep into your conversation slowly, until one day someone will say, "Hey, you're speaking almost-speak!" It will almost-come to you almost-naturally, and the almost-transition is almost easy.

You will notice that much of the Almost-Dictionary is written in almost-speak. Almost-*reading* is almost-easy too. (You are doing it now.) Therefore, this dictionary can almost-serve as a guide toward fluency in almost-speak.

The word "almost" has many near-synonyms. The words or prefixes "nearly," "close," "approximately," and many others can be used in similar ways for variation on the theme described here. (Other languages have their own counterparts.)

The prefix "almost" almost-integrates quite nicely with the various parts of speech (noun, verb, and so on). With adjectives, it can mean "not entirely" (almost-tall, almost-done, or almost-super). The prefix may also mean "not" or "none" in all-or-nothing situations (almost-fooled, or almost-visible). The prefix "almost" can refer to any fraction between 0 (none) and 1 (all) where the other part of the expression is vague (almost-decided, almost-implied). A table can almost-act as an almost-chair (compound-verb and compound-noun). And so almost-on.

Almost-Special Almost-Words

There are almost-key and other almost-special almost-words that will help in the almost-understanding of both almost-speak and the almost-way. You might want to check these almost-out first, before reading almost cover-to-cover (from here to the end).

Almost-key
almost-word
almost-speak
almost-aspect
almost-stuff
almost-understanding
almost-method
almost-principle

Almost-special	
almost-abstract	almost-limit
almost-almost	almost-real
almost-angle	almost-region
almost-effect	almost-something
almost-expression	almost-special
almost-factor	almost-thing
almost-gap	almost-way

A Few Almost-Sayings

Here are a few more almost-excerpts:

- To ask a question is to almost-answer it.
- What doesn't kill you may still almost-kill you.
- I think about what it almost-is, therefore it is almost-stuff.
- The more things stay the same, the more they almost-change.
- Excuse me while I almost-mutate.
- Almost-all is for almost-naught.

- Don't complete today what you will be able to do gooder after some sleep.

An Almost-Purpose

One almost-purpose for me writing is to stay out of trouble. Another is to get myself into almost-trouble. And that worked.

Things are the way they are, but an almost-gap almost-emerges when we consider the *purpose* of things (or an almost-purpose, as the almost-case may nearly be). Therefore, one almost-purpose of the Almost-Dictionary might be to further increase "almost-awareness" almost-everywhere. It may help when we need to distinguish between "good enough" and "needs improvement." It might even be useful when unfinished or deficient things only kinda make sense. We might then say: "What was he almost-thinking?" Hopefully, it will be almost-illuminating.

So I wish you almost-luck (almost-skill) as you try almost-speak almost-out almost-on your friends, almost-friends, family, almost-family, and others who might be almost-curious.

A

Almost-abacus, *n.* A broken abacus with some of the beads missing (but you can still use the remaining pieces to almost-count).

Almost-abandon, *v.t.* To leave your real phone number with somebody.

Almost-able, *adj.* Fairly competent, but ultimately *not* sufficient to the task (lacking in resources or know-how).

Almost-abolition, *n.* The discouragement of some activity, but not to the extent that it is made illegal.

Almost-about, *prep., adv.* About something related. Watching television is almost-about staring at a screen. To be almost-about something is to remain noncommittal, or to have a slightly different agenda.

Almost-abrupt, *adj.* A quick but smooth change.

Almost-abs, *n.* Abdominal muscles that are only almost-firm or almost-chiseled.

Almost-absent, *adj.* The person you are talking to on the phone. Or, whoever is spying on you.

Almost-absolute, *adj.* Something almost-total, almost-definite, almost-pure, or almost-forever.

Almost-abstract, *n., adj., v.* The subjective version of whatever is thought of as being fairly general, almost-universal, almost-abstruse, or almost-disassociated from a particular instance. As abstract as brains can make thinking vehicles like ideas, concepts, and notions, and what they almost-contain. Or, what happens right before almost-understanding takes over. We don't abstract to completion, we abstract until things make sense. Or, any almost-abstraction that is almost-represented fairly well. [See almost-universals, almost-understanding, almost-representational.]

Almost-abstruse, *adj.* An idea that you need to focus on intently to grasp, but that is otherwise not particularly difficult to comprehend. The idea of something being almost-almost-something, but not the idea of something being almost-almost-almost-something, for example.

Almost-absurd, *adj.* Somewhat exaggerated or unsound, but probably fun to consider or try once.

Almost-abundant, *adj.* Quite a lot. Several. Between barely-enough and plentiful.

Almost-abuse, *n., v.t.* What happens almost-constantly and in both directions in the parent-child relationship, and the employer-employee relationship. Or, any attack that leaves no physical mark. The debate as to whether self-abuse is only almost-abuse is on standby. At the paranoid extreme, anything more than a "Hello. How are you?" in social affairs.

Almost-abyss, *n.* An almost-bottomless gulf or pit that you encounter halfway down the fairway, that then flattens out nicely just before your next green. (You might miss.)

Almost-academy, *n.* Any school or almost-school where almost anything is almost-taught (or self-taught); where the use of almost-speak, the almost-method, and the almost-way are encouraged and developed; and also, where almost-art and other almost-stuff is made and appreciated. [See almost-education, almost-speak, almost-method, almost-way, almost-art, almost-stuff.]

Almost-acceptable, *adj.* Pleasing in some ways, but less than satisfactory. A runner-up.

Almost-accident, *n.* A close call, or escaped calamity. Probably also, a scary situation (with lessons learned, but probably no paperwork to fill out).

Almost-accidentally, *adv.* There was some smidgen of intent, but not enough to punish or reward.

Almost-accomplice, *n.* A contributor that doesn't deserve recognition, or helped insignificantly. (Possibly, also, someone who contributed inadvertently, unwittingly, or through omission.)

Almost-accounting, *n., v.* Accounting in only an approximate way. Or, accounting in only an almost-appropriate way with respect to the law or logic. Or, accounting at such a high level that debits and credits no longer need to balance.

Almost-accretion, *n.* When the forces of cooperation, integration, and synthesis fail to totally dominate the forces of opposition, dissociation, and independence.

Almost-accuse, *v.* To bring the conversation around to where a wrong was committed in a questioning way, but to not go so far as to blame, and to then just let the discussion go where it may.

Almost-achieve, *v.* Nearly accomplish. To not get close enough to finishing that it counts as an achievement (even though lessons might have been learned and experience gained).

Almost-across, *adv., prep.* Whether you are making a point or swimming the channel, getting pretty close only counts in horseshoes, and bombs, and passing gas, and passing muster, and passing time, and sneaking around.

Almost-act, *v.i., n.* How most people pretend to be or not to be. (And, of course, that is questionable.) Or, a mere embellishment or overstatement. Or, not to act (and just smile). [See almost-method.]

Almost-action, *n.* Merely being. Or, thinking. Or, talking. Or, sleeping on it. Or, running around in circles (chasing one's own tail), or any other behavior in keeping with the almost-method. [See almost-method.]

Almost-actionable, *adj.* Vague, or inconclusive. The kind of information likely to spawn a lengthy and expensive investigation.

Almost-active, *adj.* Lazy, or lethargic. Or, just standing there shivering. [See almost-action.]

Almost-actor, *n.* Someone who only ever plays "a dead body" (however convincingly, perhaps in a western or whodunit, and they are probably in the practice of arriving on set with their own bottle of ketchup). Or, someone who pretends a little but is mostly just being almost-themselves. Or, someone who has attended at least one of the online meetings of the Screen Almost-Actors Almost-Guild (SAAAG).

Almost-acumen, *n.* Almost-keen almost-perception.

Almost-adjourn, *v.* When a meeting almost-dissolves and several people leave, but minutes are still being taken and so it is not officially over.

Almost-admiration, *n.* The due given less-than-stellar achievement by the likes of scientists, explorers, and inventors, or stellar achievement in most other occupations.

Almost-adobe, *adj., n.* A home, office tower, supermarket, bridge, or other structure made to appear as if it were constructed out of adobe bricks or clay.

Almost-adolescence, *n.* An almost-stage of development that precedes puberty.

Almost-adult, *adj., n.* Someone old enough to think adult thoughts, but not old enough to be trusted to almost-always think adult thoughts.

Almost-advice, *n.* Advice that doesn't sufficiently address the situation or problem. If you want to get perfect on your final exams, the advice "study hard" would only almost-suffice. Or, advice related to the almost-method, the almost-principle, or other almost-aspects.

Almost-advisor, *n.* Someone who almost-specializes in almost-giving almost-advice. Or, someone who gives advice unofficially or freely (for example: "I wouldn't do that," "I'm not a doctor, but . . .," or "It's none of my business, but . . .").

Almost-aesthetic, *n.* Mostly about something other than an appeal to the senses in an artistic way (as in the way a vehicle, or draperies, or a cocktail might appeal).

Almost-affect, *v.t.* Not affect. To influence in such a way that there is no noticeable change whatsoever.

Almost-affiliate, *n.* When your organization is only affiliated with that *type* of other business, and not that specific business (yet).

Almost-affix, *v.t.* To attach only semi-permanently one thing to another thing (as a refrigerator magnet, or paper clip).

Almost-affluent, *adj.* Someone who still needs to work for a living, but can now afford help.

Almost-affordable, *adj.* Anything that costs less than you have, but more than you are willing to spend. Or, in today's credit-based economy: Anything that costs less than the total of what others are willing to lend you, but more than your spouse would let you spend if he or she knew you were thinking about it.

Almost-aftermath, *n.* Between the actual dramatic events of a catastrophe and the sometimes painfully-long aftermath that follows (characterized by rebuilding efforts, and book publishing) is a short almost-aftermath (characterized by panic, and looting). This is when everyone is glued to their television sets (and the viewing is mostly of commentators and automobile commercials).

Almost-afternoon, *n.* Elevenish.

Almost-age, *n.* A period of time longer than a day, and shorter than an age. Unlike most ages, almost-ages overlap, are only noticeable in some places and not others, are only noticeable in some genre and not others, and each has a limited influence over the cultural climate because there are so many of them. We don't have time for ages anymore. We are now in the Age of Almost-Ages.

Almost-agency, *n.* An agency that almost-specializes in almost-doing almost-stuff. [See almost-method, almost-stuff.]

Almost-agenda, *n.* A different and perhaps secret plan that is intended to only almost-subvert the main agenda. (Perhaps, because you want to get out of the meeting early, or you would prefer that someone else take the heat, or to position the right person for the candidacy.)

Almost-agent, *n.* The actor in almost-agency. One who almost does stuff, or does almost-stuff, as the almost-case may almost-be. [See almost-agency, almost-method, almost-way.]

Almost-aggressive, *adj.* More bark than bite.

Almost-agile, *adj.* More stand-and-bark than bite-and-run. Almost more passive, sluggish, and clumsy than nimble and adaptable.

Almost-agree, *v.* When two or more parties partially-concur or compromise, at least on the important things.

Almost-aim, *v., n.* Aiming in the right general direction (downwind, when taking an almost-leak). What is actually done when using the almost-procedure: Ready, Fire, Aim!

Almost-air, *n.* Thin air. Or, polluted air, bathroom air (you know what I mean), bad-breath, or just "indoor air" with poor ventilation.

Almost-aircraft, *n.* An aircraft that is not designed to transport humans (a drone, or micro-drone), or something that cannot sustain flight under its own power (glider, paper airplane).

Almost-airport, *n.* A place from which an aircraft can take off and land even though it was not designed for that purpose (a field or a highway). A place from which only almost-aircraft can take off and land. [See almost-aircraft.]

Almost-airtight, *adj.* Compartments designed to limit the negative effects of dust and other airborne particles.

Almost-alarming, *adj.* Something that would be surprising, but you were expecting it. Or, something you were not expecting, but that wasn't very surprising.

Almost-alike, *adj.* Considerably different.

Almost-alive, *adj.* Between dead and alive (like a virus, an electronic gadget that is doing something on your behalf, an active database, or a network).

Almost-alky, *n.* A lush that has not yet gone over the edge (lost everything).

Almost-all, *adj.* Most. The sequence of almost-specific counts greater than two are as follows: few (almost-several), several (almost-many), many (almost-most), most (almost-all), all (are you sure?). Or, in mathematics, the expression "almost all" is sometimes used synonymously with "all but finitely many."

Almost-almost, *adv., adj.* Most things can't even be completely almost something. This itself is an almost-aspect. If you have an almost-finished project, each sub-project, and then task will probably be almost-completed to a different extent. The physical things associated with that project involve subcomponents that are flawed, insufficient, loose, or on the brink in some way. As one zooms in and out and looks sideways, everywhere there is borderline stuff. For the want of a nail the horseshoe, horse, rider, kingdom, world, universe, and almost-everything was almost-lost (not found soon enough). An admittedly almost-biased and almost-unified consideration might be that of a Theory of Almost Everything (TOAE); which might almost-assert either the Almost-Principle, or almost-something like this: Almost everything is almost-almost (just like almost everything has almost-aspects). [See almost-aspect, almost-everything, almost-something, almost-principle.]

Almost-alone, *adj.* In uninteresting company. Or, when those voices in your head won't shut up.

Almost-always, *adv.* Invariably, except when it counts the most. Of the exceptions that confound lawmakers, and humor statisticians.

Almost-amazing, *adj.* Impressive. Nifty. Peachy. Groovy. Nice.

Almost-ambidextrous, *adj.* Atypically-adept at using either hand, but still favoring a particular hand for some activities.

Almost-ambiguous, *adj.* When a statement is associated with more than one meaning, but you can still figure out which meaning is appropriate from the context. If you said: "I'm hot," that could mean overheated, attractive, or that you are "on your game." But if you were fanning your face with a magazine, one would *assume* that you meant temperature-hot (and your statement would only be almost-ambiguous).

Almost-ambition, *n.* What you get when you combine boredom, curiosity, and coffee.

Almost-amenities, *n.* Things most people would consider to be givens, and not amenities (like clean air, running water, and parking).

Almost-American, *n.* Canadian.

Almost-amicable, *adj.* There was just a little scuffle.

Almost-ammo, *n.* Pellets or BB's. Food. Gossip.

Almost-amorphous, *adj.* Having a shape, form, or structure that is almost-unorganized or confusing.

Almost-amount, *n.* The pre-tax amount. (This is the amount on most price tags.)

Almost-anachronistically, *adv.* Of a story that is all over the place in time sequence, but can still be almost-understood chronologically. [See almost-understanding.]

Almost-analysis, *n.* The figuring that sometimes almost-inserts itself between almost-perception and almost-conclusion.

Almost-ancient, *adj.* Old (but not as old as your grandparents). [See almost-old.]

Almost-android, *n.* An almost-human with severe limitations.

Almost-angle, *n.* Slightly less of an angle than the one being considered. Or, the mental almost-position that introducing a little almost-speak, or the almost-method, or researching an almost-aspect might be advantageous at this almost-juncture. Or, the angle from which almost-aspects are most readily seen (0.987654321 degrees, and just shy of straight-on). [See almost-aspect, almost-speak, almost-method.]

Almost-angry, *adj.* Disgruntled.

Almost-animate, *adj.* The number of things that don't properly fit into the old categories of "animate" and "inanimate" is growing exponentially. In the future almost everything could be almost-animate.

Almost-annual, *adj.* Once every blue moon.

Almost-annul, *v.t.* When they cancel the negative effect of a decision or "bad mark" about you, perhaps one that is preventing you from doing something, but the information still stays on your record.

Almost-answer, *n.* The one word answer: "Almost." Or, an answer that is only somewhat satisfying. Like the answer "Because," to "Why?" Or, the kind of answer you almost-always almost-get when you ask about almost-stuff.

Almost-anticipate, *v.* When you can guess that something *like* that is going to happen, but not specifically that.

Almost-antithesis, *n.* Not quite the exact opposite idea or thesis. (But one that might lead to an almost-synthesis.)

Almost-anyone, *n.* Still, probably not you.

Almost-apparatus, *n.* Unlike gadgets that perform certain functions consistently, social workings and mechanisms tend to have more-obvious almost-aspects.

Almost-apogee, *n.* Almost as far out in an elliptical orbit as can be.

Almost-apologize, *v.* To say you're sorry that you got caught.

Almost-applause, *n.* The sight of one hand clapping. Or, the sound of beer mugs banging on tables. Or, the smell of many cigarette lighters being lit indoors.

Almost-apply, *v.* Just put your hand up (like maybe you're stretching). Post your resume somewhere and wait to see if anyone tries to contact you.

Almost-approve, *v.* Allow, in the same way that your parents approved of your fiancée just to get you and your drum set out of the house.

Almost-approximate, *adj.* Nearly near.

Almost-arcade, *n.* An arcade full of almost-stuff where things almost happen. This kind of place is usually only almost-fun.

Almost-archives, *n.* Archives kept on poor-quality storage media. Or, archives of almost-stuff.

Almost-ardent, *adj.* With lukewarm feelings of almost-eager or fairly-zealous support. Two cheers, hooray.

Almost-argument, *n.* A sequence of statements that unconvincingly meanders from a set of premises toward and in the general direction of a supposed almost-final sort of culmination, and one that you are supposed to consider more plausible than *what*? Something that makes *more* sense. I don't think so.

Almost-aristocracy, *n.* A political construction that is seen by the poor as a scheme whereby the rich are allowed to frame political issues while they themselves must choose from amongst almost-repulsive almost-alternatives, and is seen by the rich as no-holds-barred, dog-eat-dog capitalism.

Almost-Aristotle, *n.* A hypothetical (now) almost-personality of Aristotle created from all we know about him.

Almost-arithmetic, *n.* When things don't quite add up. When things multiply out of control. When things divide and conquer you. When someone subtracts off more than they can't chew.

Almost-armor, *n.* Armor.

Almost-army, *n.* An army that is missing something it needs: weapons, ammunition, a leader, food, supplies, or some other essential.

Almost-arrest, *v.t., n.* When a policeman reads you your rights, and then something happens, and the policeman takes off like a flash after someone else.

Almost-arrgh, *interj.* I almost-agree. Or, I am getting impatient. Or, I am reservedly optimistic. (As uttered by an almost-pirate.)

Almost-arson, *n.* The creating of a situation where a conflagration on someone else's property would be highly likely. (For example: filling a room with unlit wooden matches.)

Almost-arsonist, *n.* A person that is planning to, but has not yet burnt down a building. Or, a person who tried to burn down a building but accidentally set themselves on fire instead. Or, a person that deliberately extinguishes their own fire before it grows and gets out of control, and then explains to the Fire Department that they will be more careful next time.

Almost-art, *n., adj.* An object that possesses almost enough artistic qualities to be called art. Almost-art is found in the "gray area" between art and non-art. An object can be almost-art instead of art for one of several reason. Perhaps the object being considered is only part of an art-object, or is not yet finished, or was designed mostly with functional considerations in mind. That kind of thing. Almost-artistic depictions can often be found on t-shirts, and coffee mugs. T-shirts and mugs themselves are usually considered to be mere almost-art. [See the Introduction for the URL of the Almost-Art site for more examples and elaboration.]

Almost-artificial, *adj.* Partly person-made, or robot-made. Perhaps, computer-generated. Or, mostly just being tactful. [See almost-natural. These two almost-aspects work together almost hand-in-glove.]

Almost-artist, *n.* A maker/producer/creator of almost-art.

Almost-ashore, *adj.* When you are close to land and can jump off the boat into hip-deep water.

Almost-ask, *v.* Beat around the bush.

Almost-asleep, *adj.* Resting, and waiting for the garage band next door to pack it in for the night.

Almost-aspect, *n.* An aspect that is only almost-understood by someone. Or, the considering of the less-than-ideal or insufficient nature of something. Or, an aspect that is on the fringe or periphery of a consideration (for example, one almost-aspect of examples is that they can act as filler). Or, an aspect that is hiding or vague. Almost everything has almost-aspects. Or, a perspective and way of viewing almost-stuff (or almost-speak). [See almost-understanding, almost-stuff, almost-speak.]

Almost-assail, *v.t.* To hit with soft pillows, either physically or figuratively.

Almost-assassin, *n.* A person that is planning to but has not yet killed someone important.

Almost-assembly, *n.* Something almost together as it is constructed from its components. Or, a decentralized gathering of people.

Almost-assert, *v.t.* To almost-state almost-emphatically ("He might not be here"). Or, to preface a statement with, "In my opinion . . . ."

Almost-assiduous, *adj.* Almost-tireless, almost-diligent, almost-constant, almost-unremitting, almost-preserving, and almost-industrious.

Almost-assimilate, *v.* To take in and not completely absorb but let fester instead (as with ingested materials, or new ideas or inventions).

Almost-assuage, *v.t.* To bring to an almost-end or attenuate by almost-satisfying. To nearly appease, quench, quiet, relieve, or pacify.

Almost-assuredly, *adv.* Almost-most assuredly.

Almost-atavistic, *adj.* "Belch! Almost-excuse almost-me."

Almost-athletic, *adj.* The state of being not quite athletic. When you can outrun your kid sister, but not your friends. [See almost-fit.]

Almost-atmosphere, *n.* When you're in a room where several people are speaking almost-speak.

Almost-atomism, *n.* An almost-elegant almost-theory mostly about the almost-element Almostium, and how it influences most other elements; but, that also includes considerable evidence for there being almost-limits on almost-largeness and almost-smallness, almost-chaos and almost-complexity, almost-certainty, almost-ways, and almost-principles in almost-general. So it's pretty good. When the almost-irresistible force and the almost-immovable object meet, that is when many almost-things almost-happen, relatively almost-speaking, of almost-course.

Almost-attended, *v.* Someone that you expected to attend your meeting or party did not attend. (Perhaps they had a flat tire, became ill, or had a more pressing engagement.)

Almost-attention, *n.* A person's, or a whole society's attention is rarely so focused on one thing that everything else is ignored, but rather attention is: mostly concentrated, partly scattered, and fleeting.

Almost-attenuated, *adj.* On its way to becoming almost-nothing.

Almost-attractive, *adj.* Most people are only almost-attractive in that they have at least some less than attractive attributes.

Almost-attribute, *n.* An almost-intrinsic characteristic or quality of a thing almost-about which the almost-aspect is a view.

Almost-attribution, *n.* When you attribute most but not all characteristics or causes to a particular source. A partial attribution.

Almost-auction, *v.t., n.* An auction of almost-stuff (perhaps, almost-art, almost-shirts, or chipped teapots).

Almost-audience, *n.* A less than attentive audience. Or, the kind of audience that raids the fridge during commercials.

Almost-audit, *v.t., n.* A quick review or examination that is neither methodical nor extensive.

Almost-audition, *n.* Something such as a presentation or conversation (or recording of the same) that is originally not intended to be used to match people against acceptance criteria, but then is.

Almost-author, *n.* An author who uses a ghost-writer. Or, the author of a screenplay adaptation of a book.

Almost-authoritative, *adj.* Speaking without fully knowing all of the implications of what you are saying. Or, sounding a bit like you are making it up as you go along.

Almost-authority, *n.* The authority of the second-in-command (when they still need to ask mom, or dad, or the big cheese). Or, an authority on one subject commenting on a related subject. Or, an off-duty authority figure acting unofficially.

Almost-autonomy, *n.* Feeling or seeming to be independent.

Almost-available, *adj.* Available soon. Or, available for a price that seems artificially high.

Almost-average, *adj.* Not quite average, but certainly within the first standard deviation. Perhaps, closer to the median (where the median and average are somewhat different).

Almost-avert, *v.t.* When you try to prevent something from happening, but it happens anyway.

Almost-avoid, *v.t.* When you don't go to a lot of trouble to avoid someone, except just in a "See you later," "Not if I see you first," kind of way.

Almost-avuncular, *adj.* Of or relating to a know-it-all boss.

Almost-award, *n.* When you get a plaque with no cash.

Almost-aware, *adj.* The mental state of thinking that there must be something more. The almost-understanding that one only has an almost-understanding. Awareness of the almost-nature of almost everything, and *so* almost-getting the meaning of this entry.

Almost-awesome, *adj.* Almost everything that the younger set describes as "awesome." Or, together and happening. Or, doesn't hate me. Or, almost-cool.

Almost-awful, *adj.* Something good for you that is not very tasty (spinach), or something tasty but not very good for you (donuts).

Almost-axiom, *n.* A maxim, or very reliable rule. Or, a statement that is stipulated to be almost-true for the purpose of constructing an almost-theory. [See almost-true, almost-theory.]

B

Almost-babe, *n.* A fairly good looking person. Or, a fairly young person. This almost-word is almost-flexible in that it can be used as a compliment, as an insult, sarcastically, or even figuratively (as in: "she is an almost-babe of a ship").

Almost-babies, *n.* Abortees. Or, grown men that cry like a baby when she says she's not going to abort.

Almost-bachelor, *n.* A married man who is separated from his wife. Or, the almost-single man who is now living with her.

Almost-back-office, *n., adj.* The back part of the front-office. Or, the front part of the back-office. Or, perhaps, the middle part of the middle-office.

Almost-backward, *adv., adj.* The almost-contrary, almost-retarded, or almost-antiquated way when compared to what you might expect (which may make you almost-cringe); but then there are still some positive or hopeful aspects about the "more traditional" approach.

Almost-bad, *adj.* Relatively bad. Unsound. Unpleasant. Deficient. Or, naughty. Just the right kind of good. Or, enterprising. Or, a good musician.

Almost-balanced, *adj.* Systems are rarely in a completely "balanced" state (or perfect equilibrium), but instead, usually there are constant changes in the various pressures from many directions. Or, almost-loony.

Almost-balloon, *n.* A metaphorical or computer-simulation trial-balloon (not a real balloon). Or, a bubble that could almost-pop almost-all by itself.

Almost-ballot, *n.* When the ballots used in an election allow for the "almost-answer" as well as "yes" or "no" (as in: "Would you trust this person to spend your hard-earned tax money wisely? Yes/Almost/No"). And when the results are tallied, the almost-answer does not count as much as a yes. Or, where the votes only almost-count due to a fairly shady practice known as "stuffing."

Almost-balmy, *adj.* When you don't need to wear layers, but you can still feel a slight chill in the air.

Almost-bamboozled, *adj.* Ultimately, *not* fooled. (The con job was planned well and then executed poorly, or the other way around.)

Almost-banana, *n.* About three-quarters of a banana, (or one with a bite taken out of it). Or, a plantain. Or, someone who is the Top Banana's sidekick or spouse.

Almost-band, *n.* An impromptu musician's jam session. Or, a garage band. Or, a duo.

Almost-bandwagon, *n.* An almost-band almost-wagon. Or, a chuck wagon, or station wagon. Or, an almost-fashionable trend. Or, the trend toward more almost-speak and almost-stuff.

Almost-baneful, *adj.* Harmful to someone else.

Almost-bank, *n.* A zombie bank. Or, a fly-by-night bank. Or, a grossly-mismanaged bank. Or, just the computer system of a bank (a place where numbers go to rest at night).

Almost-bankable, *adj.* A project or idea that would be almost-appropriately funded if there was a "celebrity name" behind it.

Almost-bankrupt, *adj.* Seriously ill. Poor. Or, swiftly and dramatically restructuring in an attempt to avoid bankruptcy.

Almost-bar, *n.* A bar that only serves beer and wine. Or, any bar that will no longer serve you.

Almost-barefoot, *adj.* Wearing flip-flops.

Almost-bargain, *n.* It may be "on sale," but it's still not inexpensive enough.

Almost-basic, *n.* The "chemistry" of the situation, not the "elemental" stuff.

Almost-basis, *n.* There are almost-always more-fundamental almost-under pinnings, and the almost-bedrock has not been found yet. ("There's a town I almost-know . . .")

Almost-beach, *n.* A sandy spot. Or, across the street from the beach. (The Almost-Beach would be a good name for a tiki bar near a beach.)

Almost-beastly, *adj.* Extremely unpleasant in manner or lifestyle.

Almost-beautiful, *adj.* Pretty, or attractive looking.

Almost-because, *conj.* What is meant when people answer simply: "Because," because there is usually more to the answer.

Almost-bed, *n.* Cot. Just the top mattress. Sleeping bag. Back seat.

Almost-bedraggled, *adj.* A little damp, or a little soiled, and a little worse for wear, but not entirely unpresentable.

Almost-beef, *n.* Soya bean burgers.

Almost-beguiling, *adj.* A manipulating and obviously deceptive but cute woman. Or, never really being "deceptive" but cleverly avoiding the need to be.

Almost-behave, *v.* What your kids do behind your back most of the time.

Almost-behavior, *n.* To converse in almost-speak, apply the almost-method, and almost-follow the almost-way. [See almost-speak, almost-method, almost-way.]

Almost-being, *v.i.* Acting.

Almost-belligerent, *adj.* Someone not yet sufficiently provoked to open hostility, but who obviously has their guard up, and is starting to think more independently and assertively than you would like.

Almost-bellwether, *n.* Something that can't be totally relied upon as an indicator.

Almost-belt, *n.* A little less than one ounce of liquor. The kind of serving that might make your customer almost-belligerent.

Almost-beneficial, *adj.* Causing more harm than good. (Things to almost-look almost-out almost-for: Trojan horses, so-called "improvements," time bandits, loose lips, delays, unnecessary detours; and, sometimes the almost-factor). [See almost-factor.]

Almost-benefit, *v.t., n.* Slight disadvantage (in the sense that the negatives outweigh the positives to a small degree). [See almost-beneficial.]

Almost-benighted, *adj.* In the dark, but with a flashlight (and who knows how long the batteries will last).

Almost-besotted, *adj.* Too drunk to drive.

Almost-bias, *n.* A leaning in the almost-way.

Almost-bicycle, *n.* Unicycle. Penny-farthing.

Almost-bilked, *adj.* When almost everything you got for Almost-Xmas you either didn't want or already had.

Almost-billing, *n.* Not on the marquee, but still used in promotions.

The Almost-Dictionary

Almost-billion, *n.* The number: 987,654,321.

Almost-binary, *adj.* Where there is a pesky third possibility.

Almost-binge, *n., v.i.* Measured excess, such that you do not lose control (as with booze, chocolates, or shopping).

Almost-biology, *n.* Biochemistry.

Almost-birth, *n.* The laying of an egg. Also, the hatching of an egg. In this case, two almost-births make one birth.

Almost-bitter, *adj., n.* Bittersweet. Or, maintaining a strong dislike without letting it eat you up inside. Most people are not completely bitter, but they are almost-bitter about many things: and part of the almost-fun of getting to know someone is discovering what those things are (through discussion you unwrap each almost-bitterness like a gift from the Almost-Great Almost-Absurdity of Life).

Almost-black, *adj.* Very, very dark. Or, specifically, dark gray.

Almost-blacklist, *n.* When you are on a "graylist" you eventually discover that almost nobody, and almost-nobodies, want to associate with you. (You might get invited to some of their parties if they think to include you.) Few people "rock the boat" enough to be almost-officially blacklisted, but almost-everyone is almost-blacklisted daily. Genetically, almost-everyone will be almost-blacklisted (if they are not already).

Almost-blackmail, *n., v.t.* Coercion is coercion, and doing things voluntarily is the very definition of freedom, and so never the twain shall meet, . . . almost-except when you are almost-forced toward something that has a bit of a carrot taste to it, for your convenience.

Almost-blameless, *adj., n.* A minor contributor to a mistake, especially where group-think and shared responsibilities are involved. [See almost-responsible.]

Almost-blanket, *n.* Large towel.

Almost-blarney, *n.* Exaggerated flattery that is not really malarkey on account of its truthiness.

Almost-blasé, *adj.* World-weary or worldly-wise and unconcerned about most of the situation, but curious or interested about a small part.

Almost-bleak, *adj.* Not bleak enough for my liking.

Almost-blend, *n.* A combination more like a salad.

Almost-blind, *adj.* Poorly-sighted, or just "legally blind."

Almost-block, *v.t., n.* Hinder. Or, a blockette, blockling, or pre-block. Or, when you encounter a chip off the old block, the other part.

Almost-blotto, *adj.* Obviously over-the-limit inebriated, feeling no pain, yet still walking, and sounding as confident as a politician.

Almost-bludgeon, *n., v.t.* A small bludgeon. Or, the act of bludgeoning just a little bit.

Almost-blue, *adj., n.* A greenish blue, or an extremely light pastel blue. In the neighborhood of blue. Or, the state of mind in between "waiting" and "depressed," and when you are feeling "light blue." Or, bordering on suggestive.

Almost-blunt, *adj.* Still sharp enough to do some damage (or have the desired effect).

Almost-boat, *n.* For a man: a canoe, or a dugout. For a woman: any boat that does not have "amenities."

Almost-Bond, *n.* Any suave, worldly adventurer for whom the most likely outcomes are not ever-superable. Or, the likes of Jimmy Bond (a fictional character, the nephew of James Bond, played by Woody Allen in the 1968 version of the movie *Casino Royale*).

Almost-bonus, *n.* What is left of your bonus, after taxes.

Almost-boobs, *n.* Fake boobs. Or, breasts that are still small enough that their owner can play outdoor sports. [See almost-bra, almost-breasts, almost-tits.]

Almost-book, *n.* Something that is not quite a book (a pamphlet or brochure, an e-book, an unfinished manuscript, a book with the front cover ripped off, or an exceedingly verbose email or letter).

Almost-boost, *n.* When someone lifts you up a bit, and you still can't reach. Or, when you try to start your car with the battery of another car, and you just run down the other battery too.

Almost-bootlegger, *n.* Someone who smuggles non-alcoholic beverages (either in or out).

Almost-boots, *n.* "Beatle boots," or other low-rise boots.

Almost-bored, *adj.* Still somewhat attentive (perhaps, when most of the action has already happened). Or, comfortably numb. Or, disinterested but still taking notes.

Almost-born, *n.* One who is patiently knocking on the amniotic sack door. [See almost-birth.]

Almost-both, *n.* What you get when you try to eat your cake and also still have it. Or, as Yogi Berra said, "When you come to the fork in the road, take it."

Almost-bottleneck, *n.* A slowdown because of a constraint that isn't really a constraint (like when there is a disturbance off to the side of the road).

Almost-bottom, *n.* A place from which you can clearly see the bottom.

Almost-bound, *adj.* Something that is somewhat "bound," but where there is still "wiggle room."

Almost-boundary, *n.* A boundary that is in dispute, only sometimes recognized, or incompletely defined. You might think something is private, but someone else might think they have a right to know; or vice versa.

Almost-bounded, *n.* What seems to have limits, but the edges are uncertain. [See almost-limit.]

Almost-boyfriend, *n.* A guy that you have only just started to date, or one that is too withdrawn.

Almost-bra, *n.* A brassiere that breasts try to climb out of. They might sing to themselves: "To be almost free-and-alive is an almost-wonderful almost-thing. To almost-wave in the almost-way that we do, and the way we almost-feel is our almost-secret appeal, and our almost-freedom may spring. We almost-care about the almost-shape we're in. Wandering, concertedly, in our almost-bra." [See almost-boobs, almost-breasts, almost-shape, almost-tits.]

Almost-brain, *n.* What children have between their ears. A control center more significant than a ganglion.

Almost-brand, *n.* The almost-banned Almost-band band brand.

Almost-bread, *n.* Crackers. Pita bread.

Almost-break, *n.* When you take your coffee break at your desk and keep working. Or, when you stop digging ditches for fifteen minutes to help your boss move furniture.

Almost-breakfast, *n.* That time of day when you can smell bacon frying and coffee percolating.

Almost-breasts, *n.* Nipples. Or, growing breasts.

Almost-breathe, *v.i.* What people with asthma sometimes do.

Almost-breed, *v.* To simulate breeding (perhaps with the use of a prophylactic).

Almost-breeder, *n.* Someone who habitually uses birth control.

Almost-bribe, *n., v.t.* "If I were to make it almost-worthwhile for you, perhaps you would almost-consider almost-seeing almost-things my almost-way?"

Almost-brief, *adj.* As long as one commercial-break during a show on television.

Almost-brink, *n.* That almost-place beyond which almost-nobody survives. Some people *like* to visit the almost-brink, perhaps because you can get a better view of the brink from there. You still have alternatives at the almost-brink, but not passed the brink. At the almost-brink you can think of almost-nothing else besides the brink, but still, . . . almost-anything can happen.

Almost-broad, *n.* An almost-polite way of referring to a woman.

Almost-broadcast, *n.* A girlcast, chickcast, babecast, or the like; or even a miscast broadcast; but not an outcast, typecast, fly cast, or an endocranial cast. Or, a fairly wide narrowcast. [See almost-movie.]

Almost-broke, *adj.* How almost-everyone almost-feels just before payday.

Almost-broken, *adj.* The way "the system" or "the government" always seems to almost-be.

Almost-brother, *n.* Brother-in-law.

Almost-browse, *v.t.* Casually perusing but with extremely intent focus. Or, when you are thinking about something else while browsing and walk right past what you are looking for.

Almost-bubble, *n.* When prices are almost-artificially or almost-unnecessarily high; but then instead of the bubble almost-bursting (or deflating) the almost-support for those prices becomes almost-real (or almost-validated). (A common occurrence in almost-economics.)

Almost-budget, *n.* A draft budget, or revisable budget. Or, a budget with numbers that are so rounded or tentative as to almost-call almost-into almost-question the validity or appropriateness of the budget.

Almost-buff, *adj., n.* What you look like when you first join a gym and are wearing your new workout gear. Or, the state of being almost-naked.

Almost-builder, *n.* A builder of almost-things. [See almost-method.]

Almost-built, *adj.* Something almost-completely almost-constructed. Or, something constructed according to the almost-method, and in the almost-way. [See almost-method, almost-way.]

Almost-bullshit, *n.* Goat poop. Or, drivel with cogency.

Almost-burglar, *n.* Someone who almost-burgles. Or, someone who enters a building and steals almost-stuff. [See almost-burgle.]

Almost-burgle, *v.t.* Breaking into a place to make it look burgled, but not actually taking anything. Or, going somewhere to steal something, but not actually entering or taking anything (and almost-chickening out).

Almost-business, *n.* A hobby that is used to generate income. Activities that are not strictly just for pleasure.

Almost-businesslike, *adj.* Almost anything to do with "business casual," show-business, or monkey business.

Almost-businessman, *n.* Aspiring entrepreneur. Accountant. Tradesman. Agent. Espontaneo.

Almost-busy, *adj.* Someone who only looks busy. Or, someone too busy to talk to you.

Almost-busywork, *n.* Busywork that doesn't fully occupy one's time. Or, busywork that you don't get paid for. And no self-respecting certified Busywork Engineer would do *superior* busywork while not being watched.

Almost-butcher, *n.* Hack.

Almost-butt, *n.* A bit of cheek and a glimpse (what you see if someone only almost-removes their clothing).

Almost-butter, *n.* Margarine, mayonnaise, hummus, mustard, or the like.

Almost-buy, *v.t.* Lease. Or, filling your online "basket," but never clicking on the "purchase" button.

Almost-buzz, *n.* Chirp, peep, or tweet. Or, noise about almost-stuff.

C

Almost-cactus, *n.* A smaller cactus. Or, a cactus after you and your hunting buddies have finished "pruning" it with your .22 rifles.

Almost-caddy, *n.* Someone who drives the cart with the golf-bag(s), but doesn't actually hand the golfer(s) any clubs.

Almost-cage, *n.* Almost anything can be an almost-cage: a habit, a business process, a law, even a planet.

Almost-cake, *n.* Healthy carbs that also taste good. A doctor or health-food commercial might say: "Let them eat almost-cake."

Almost-calendar, *n.* Any calendar that is not practical for use. Perhaps, a calendar that is based on calculations that are too inaccurate (like the one before leap years were introduced).

Almost-call, *v.t.* When you look at the phone and you think about calling someone, but then you wonder what you are actually going to say, so you don't call.

Almost-callow, *adj.* Someone else who is fairly immature and lacking adult sophistication, but not to the degree that you notice in time. The person can act mature, but lacks the depth of experience to cope when they are challenged.

Almost-calm, *adj.* Just cool and collected.

Almost-campaign, *n., v.* When you only want to almost-win you don't need to go all out. Some candidates only campaign in order to promote one issue, and don't so much expect to win as to gain concessions.

Almost-cancel, *adj.* When two almost-opposite things don't quite neutralize each other when brought together.

Almost-cannibalize, *v.t.* Nibble at.

Almost-canonical, *adj.* Not yet reduced to the simplest form, or the general rule.

Almost-capital, *n.* Any city more populous than the capital. Or, money you don't have (yet).

Almost-capitalism, *n.* A watered-down version of capitalism (unregulated capitalism can be inhumane or nonsensical).

Almost-capsized, *adj.* Something not quite overturned, even though the contents are jostled about.

Almost-captain, *n.* Lieutenant, commander, or lieutenant-commander.

Almost-captioned, *adj.* Where the explanatory or identifying comment accompanying a pictorial illustration is in almost-speak.

Almost-capture, *v.t.* To seize control of only some aspects of a thing, such as a city, company, audience. That may be enough, or not.

Almost-car, *n.* A golf cart. A go-cart. Perhaps a motorcycle, or motorcycle with sidecar. Especially in rural areas, even just a small car could be considered to be in this almost-category.

Almost-carbon, *n.* Boron (the element with one less proton).

Almost-cardboard, *n.* Thick paper.

Almost-care, *v.* Empathize.

Almost-career, *n.* A series of non-professional jobs in a particular field. Or a series of positions in an almost-field. [See almost-field.]

Almost-cargo, *n.* Carry-on luggage (such as a briefcase, laptop, or purse).

Almost-caricature, *n.* A representation especially in literature or art that is only mildly distorted or ludicrous.

Almost-carload, *n.* When you still have room to pick up a hitchhiker.

Almost-cart, *n.* A cart with one of its wheels missing.

Almost-cartoon, *n.* Someone dressed up like a cartoon character (as at a theme park). Or, an unrealistically simple version of something (and hence, almost-something). [See almost-something.]

Almost-case, *n.* The almost-version of a "basket case."

Almost-castle, *n.* A very nice single-family house, especially one with load-bearing stone walls. Or, any house with more square-footage than yours. Or, any dwelling with a moat around it.

Almost-casual, *adj.* Business casual. Or, noticeably less casual that most, but still within the guidelines.

Almost-casualty, *n.* A person or entity that has narrowly escaped a calamity.

Almost-catch, *v.t.* Fumble.

Almost-categorical, *adj.* Nearly definite with respect to certain categories, but also partly ambiguous or questionable.

Almost-cathartic, *adj.* Something that almost-purges, or almost-purifies.

Almost-cause, *n.* Not the real, ultimate, or root cause, but some intermediate or subordinate cause.

Almost-cave, *n.* Hovel.

Almost-censorship, *n.* When the decision to *not* present certain information is made at the "gathering information" stage (or policy stage), as in: "Check the fire stations and the police stations to see if there is any news for tonight's broadcast," rather than at the presentation stage (or editing stage).

Almost-central, *adj.* Close enough to being central that it warrants interest. Or, not close enough to be considered anything other than a distraction.

Almost-century, *n.* Ninety-nine years. Or, ninety-eight years.

Almost-certain, *adj.* Not quite sure.

Almost-certainties, *n.* Expectations. Very probable outcomes.

Almost-certifiable, *adj.* Not completely authentic, genuine, reformed, sane, insane, principled, unprincipled, educated, uneducated, tested, prepared, tall, heavy, disease-free, drug-free, or idealistic enough.

Almost-certificate, *n.* Any certificate where you hold the only record (copy). In other words, nobody much cares about what it says (and the claim on it can't be readily verified just by checking with whoever holds the almost-secure copy).

Almost-chair, *n.* Anything you can sit on that is not a chair.

Almost-Champagne, *n.* Sparkling wine from somewhere other than the French province of Champagne. Actually, it doesn't so much sparkle as it almost-sparkles (bubbles), so it might best be called "almost-sparkling wine."

Almost-change, *n.* The more things stay the same the more they almost-change. Tiny mutations may not have had time to significantly alter things yet. Or, that nebulous thing you almost-wish for when things are not going your way. Or, two quarters, when you need sixty cents.

Almost-cheap, *adj.* Like when a grown-up is willing to pay for your education, but unwilling to buy you an ice cream.

Almost-chicken, *n.* A chicken with its head cut off (perhaps one that is still running around). Also, a plucked chicken with head and feet removed. Also, a human that runs away to live to fight another day (and not just because he is an almost-scaredy almost-cat).

Almost-children, *n.* Many grown-ups (especially when it come to the emotions).

Almost-circular, *adj.* A shape that resembles a circle. Or, something that goes around and around but in a fashion that is more unpredictable than circular (some reasoning falls into this category).

Almost-circumlocution, *n.* A long-winded evasion in speech that never does return to the main subject, but still can't rightly be considered "tangential" because of the way your head is now spinning. In politics, almost-circumlocutions tend to "connect the dots" of the speakers talking points rather well.

Almost-circumstances, *n.* The sum of external or environmental factors that relate to almost-factors. Or, any situation involving almost-considerations (of almost-aspects or almost-stuff). [See almost-factor.]

Almost-circus, *n.* Sideshow. Or, anywhere there are children.

Almost-city, *n.* Large town. Or, almost-amorphous urban sprawl. Or, a special-purpose community. One that is planned to always be modest in size (with sufficient transportation and nightlife), and not nearly as boring or general-purpose as a suburb. Some are designed to attract a particular type of residents: like high-tech workers, or retired golfers.

Almost-civil, *adj.* How most people are to most other people most of the time.

Almost-clarification, *n.* An explanation that helps, but doesn't go so far as to remove all ambiguities, confusion, or uncertainty.

Almost-classical, *adj.* Not old enough to be classical, but not recent enough to be current.

Almost-clean, *adj.* Clean enough. Or, not clean enough. Or, specifically, as clean as a machine can get it (washing machine, dishwasher).

Almost-climb, *v.t.* To climb almost-to the top of something (like when you climb too close to the top of a tree to be able to go any further).

Almost-cloak, *n.* Coat.

Almost-clock, *n.* Sundial. Or, any timepiece that lacks the precision we need. Usually, we just almost-need to have a fairly good idea as to what the time is.

Almost-close, *adj., v.t.* Close enough to be on radar. Close may count in horseshoes, but in many other things close only almost-counts (settles for a pretty good estimate). Or, to stop, discontinue, or constrain, but in such a way as to allow a future re-opening if new information arises. To leave open a crack.

Almost-clothing, *n.* The clothing of one who wears less than expected. Painted on clothing. Or, old or tattered clothing. Or, clothing with an almost-saying or depiction of almost-art on it. [See almost-shirt.]

Almost-clumsy, *adj.* Clumsy like a fox.

Almost-coat, *n.* Jacket.

Almost-coercion, *n.* A bluff, manipulation, or seduction. Watch out for the words "almost-essential" or "pretty-please," and the batting of the eyelashes.

Almost-coffee, *n.* Decaf.

Almost-cognate, *n.* Related words, but not words that are synonyms. Almost-cognates are *very* useful. By referring to almost the same thing, this can be a way to spin, or a way to present something in a slightly different light, or flashlight, or spotlight, or with a star on the almost-silver screen, in such a way that everyone will cheer.

Almost-cognition, *n.* When you just *know* that some of what you're thinking is not worth almost-understanding. Deep down were all almost-superficial.

Almost-cognitive, *adj.* More of a knee-jerk response than a considered response.

Almost-coherent, *adj.* That which is not gathered together and understandable, but that is starting to make sense.

Almost-cold, *n.* Chilly. Lukewarm.

Almost-collection, *n.* A bunch of things that are mostly together, but a few other of them are in other places.

Almost-colonel, *n.* Major.

Almost-colorless, *adj.* A very light pastel color. Or, very, very dark.

Almost-combination, *n.* A tenuous or weak union (as a gathering of people for a cause) that could easily be divided or uncombined.

Almost-combine, *v.* To join and commingle, but not to unify permanently.

Almost-comedy, *n.* Somewhat-humorous filler.

Almost-comical, *adj.* Something that would be humorous if it wasn't accompanied by pain or discomfort.

Almost-command, *n.* A suggestion made by someone in authority.

Almost-commerce, *n.* The interchange of information or things that do not involve the government (as with sales tax, income tax, excise tax, or the like). Perhaps, trading almost-stuff with your friends.

Almost-commercial, *n., adj.* Amateur.

Almost-commit, *v.t.* To have one or more "outs" built into the commitment. To consign, entrust, or surrender, but to have "visitation rights" or "surveillance rights." Perhaps, to say: "I almost-love you," but not: "I want you to have all of my children and cook for me please."

Almost-common, *adj.* Not uncommon. Or, when it's all over the place, but you just found out about it (as in: almost-common almost-knowledge).

Almost-community, *n.* An almost-unified body of individuals that have actually never met (those at a particular online networking site, or "all conservatives"). Or, a community designed to keep people apart (or away from each other as much as possible).

Almost-company, *n.* When you are with a group of people that are all talking on their cell-phones to people not in the room.

Almost-compatible, *adj.* Compatible. Complete compatibility is never found between people (or peoples). What we call compatibility is more like a game, or a competition, or a smoke screen. Or, what compatible is one second later. Compatibility is a social ideal that is never realized in full. Or, insufficiently suitable or agreeable.

Almost-compelling, *adj.* Almost not compelling, but still attention-grabbing.

Almost-competent, *adj.* Everyone. This almost-never needs saying because it is so obvious, but people are always lacking in some education or experience, even in the one subject they know best. The question often first turns to whether the person is probably capable of completing the task at hand (which is a narrower consideration).

Almost-competitive, *adj.* Someone not trying very hard. Or, someone who is trying very hard, but is still not doing well enough (and is, ultimately, doomed). Or, someone who would be a good choice, except for one thing.

Almost-complain, *v.t.* To groan loudly and plaintively. Or, to roll your eyes. Or, to complain to an innocent third party with the blithe hope that word will get around.

Almost-complete, *adj.* Incomplete. Wanting. Unsatisfactory.

Almost-complex, *adj.* Understandable, if you put your mind to it.

Almost-compliance, *n.* Incomplete conformity to official requirements.

Almost-comprehension, *n.* When someone almost-understands most aspects of something. Or, when someone almost-understands only some almost-aspects of almost-something. Or when someone almost-understands only enough to be dangerous.

Almost-compute, *v.t.* To approximate an answer that involves numbers, rather than getting out a calculator. This is often done when exact numbers are not needed. (I know that the Bentley is too expensive for me, so I don't even ask about "specials" or "discounts.") Or, to malfunction, but let the user know you tried your best (if you are a computer).

Almost-conceal, *v.t.* To hide from some people, to hide in plain view, or to hide in an ineffectual manner.

Almost-concept, *n.* A vague or too high-level objective perception.

Almost-concurrent, *adj.* Happening at nearly the same time. [See almost-simultaneous.]

Almost-confess, *v.t.* To confess to a lesser charge. Or, to just *look* guilty without saying anything.

Almost-confident, *adj.* Diffident. Or, more sure of someone else's powers than their intentions.

Almost-confirm, *v.t.* Corroborate. Or, to ratify in a mousy way.

Almost-conform, *v.* Close to being within specifications. Or, to get a little wild sometimes.

Almost-connect, *v.* To swing and miss with your racket. To miss your connecting flight due to a delay that is the fault of the airline, and so you are allowed to catch the next plane out at no extra cost.

Almost-consent, *v.i.* When you go with the flow, or what the majority wants, but still have reservations (that you may or may not express). Or, when you agree only "in principle," and the details still need to be worked out.

Almost-conservative, *n.* Any liberally-minded individual or institution with a vested interest in the status quo.

Almost-consider, *v.t.* When you find out about something but you don't have time to ponder it consciously, still your subconscious is working on it in various ways. Or, to consider related stuff instead.

Almost-console, *v.t.* To console someone via email or letter. Or, just the phrase: "Everything's going to be ok." Even if you add: "Really."

Almost-consortium, *n.* An association of groups (for a defensive purpose, or to undertake a project too large for any one) that is informally conceived or unreliable.

Almost-constant, *adj.* A value that doesn't change much, at least round these parts. It is in the very almost-nature of constants to be variable when "the system" is under extreme conditions. What we call "experiments" are situations where only a few variables are altered at a time in a controlled manner, while the other variables are maintained at steady values. (For example, the usually constant "boiling point of water" is a variable depending on another variable "pressure.") [See almost-limit.]

Almost-constructed, *adj.* Nearly built. When a building has a roof but no shingles it is easy to see what needs to happen, but with some almost-things what remains to be done is less obvious.

Almost-consulting, *v.t.* "Consulting" is almost-always about the gaps between what is and what ought to be, from a corporate or governmental perspective (between here and there, now and then, good and great), and is highly paid. Almost-consulting is about the same gaps, but from everyone's personal viewpoint, the possibilities emerge almost-naturally all day long, and it remains unpaid. Almost-consulting is considered more of a social nuisance than anything else. A lot of almost-consulting is done in bars.

Almost-consumable, *n.* Something that is only partially consumed (banana, mango, coconut).

Almost-consumer, *n.* Someone waiting for the price to go down. Or, someone waiting for their next paycheck. Or, a producer doing a field study.

Almost-contagious, *adj.* Things or behaviors that are copied not from desire but because of external requirements (business or legal reasons). [See almost-copy, almost-mutate.]

Almost-contemporary, *adj.* Happening, existing, living, or coming into being at nearly the same time. Of two people who might have overlapping dates, but where one is much older. Lao-tzu and Confucius were almost-contemporaries.

Almost-contempt, *n.* Often one's contempt is mitigated by a certain admiration for success or achievement, and sometimes so much so that one's contempt is only almost-contempt.

Almost-contract, *n.* A non-binding agreement. An agreement not enforceable at law.

Almost-contradictory, *adj.* Things that might seem to be opposed, but that are not.

Almost-contumely, *n.* Barely harsh language or treatment, but still noticeable, almost-arising from near-contempt.

Almost-convergence, *n.* When a convergence happens it usually does not go all the way (and other forces take over), so it is really only an almost-convergence.

Almost-conversation, *n.* A few words with someone.

Almost-conviction, *n.* An almost-firm reliance, especially one almost-upon dogma.

Almost-cookies, *n.* They are like fortune cookies, just smaller, and less filling, and inside there are almost-saying. [See almost-saying.]

Almost-cooking, *v.* Preparing food for cooking. Or, appearing to be doing something like cooking, but either nothing edible results, or something only almost-edible results. Or, cooking almost-food. [See almost-food.]

Almost-cool, *adj.* Warm. Nowhere near cold or hot. Sadly, most products or services that are on the market currently, as well as most things that you hear about, are only almost-cool (or even less inspiring of special interest). (This is to speak almost-figuratively, and this has almost-nothing to do with "almost-cool beans," which almost-need heating almost-up.) [See almost-hot, almost-uncool.]

Almost-cop, *n.* Meter maid. Guard. Guardian. Parent. Boss.

Almost-copasetic, *adj.* Not quite ideal, or even okeydokey. Perhaps, a situation with an annoying little feature. Where there is something minor missing from the picture, or where something needs to be fixed. [See almost-ok, almost-good.]

Almost-copy, *n., v.* Mutate. Copy with a mutation. [See almost-contagious, almost-mutate.]

Almost-cordial, *adj.* Affable and pleasant, but reserved and maybe distant or aloof.

Almost-correct, *adj.* Most statements are only almost-correct (in the sense of being ambiguous, or nuanced, or in the sense that they are refutable or correctable). [See almost-deconstruct, almost-true.]

Almost-costume, *n.* Clothes than make you go, "Hmmm."

Almost-count, *v.* To mentally skip a few numbers in an ordered sequence (the ones you are assuming are still there). Or, when the recognition for almost-something is adequate.

Almost-counterfactual, *adj.* Almost-contrary, almost-opposite, almost-false, almost-erroneous, almost-inaccurate, almost-incorrect, almost-specious, almost-unsound, almost-untrue, or very nearly wrong.

Almost-counterfeit, *adj., n.* Not very sincere. Or, an imitation of something that was not illegal to produce.

Almost-countless, *adj.* Countable in theory, but too many to bother with in practice.

Almost-country, *n.* A state, province, or territory within a sovereign nation that is so large, so populous, or so economically strong that it is sometimes considered to be on the world stage by itself. Or, such a place vying for independence.

Almost-couple, *n.* An informally-linked pair.

Almost-courageous, *adj.* More brave than Sir Robin (as played by Eric Idle), and yet less cheeky than Robin's least favorite minstrel (as played by Neil Innes).

Almost-covered, *adj.* Observed by a supposed protector. Or, protected from only the most likely of many possible scenarios. The TV cop should say: "I've got you almost-covered," as he lets his ambitious and perhaps foolhardy compatriot run into harm's way. Or, when your insurance plan requires a co-pay.

Almost-craft, *n.* A surfboard, windsurfer, or snowboard.

Almost-crash, *v.t.* What waves do when they collide.

Almost-craven, *adj.* Almost-chicken, yet almost-hopeful.

Almost-crazy, *adj.* Just right (as in: interesting). Or, crazy like a fox. Or, someone who is acting on different information than what you know. Or, someone who is making decisions in a different way than you do.

Almost-cream, *n.* Milk.

Almost-create, *v.t.* To merely assist or midwife something into existence (as with a new flower garden).

Almost-creative, *adj.* Those almost-dedicated to making sure the world doesn't repeat itself. Or, those creating almost-stuff and speaking almost-speak in almost-new almost-ways. [See almost-mutate, almost-stuff, almost-speak.]

Almost-credentials, *n.* When you get an almost-certificate (and a pat on the back). [See almost-certificate.]

Almost-credit, *n.* Almost-everyone is almost-standing on the shoulders of almost-giants, so almost-nobody can take total credit for anything, but if someone contributes enough that is original then they just might be able to claim almost-credit. Or, a credit to an account before the check clears.

Almost-creep, *v.i., n.* The slow but steady increase in the use of almost-words and almost-speak. (Incidentally, there is almost no stopping almost-creep once it gets started.) Or, an almost-strange almost-person that uses almost-speak almost too much.

Almost-critical, *adj.* Important.

Almost-criticism, *n.* A pointer, or a suggestion about a possible improvement.

Almost-critique, *n.* A quick and incomplete judgment, especially as to relevance and shortcomings. A knee-jerk reaction. (For example: "That sucks.")

Almost-crop, *n.* A planted field in mid-summer (before harvest time). Or, a partially destroyed crop.

Almost-cross-examine, *v.t.* To ask only easy or "softball" questions.

Almost-crowd, *n.* Group. A small gathering of people.

Almost-crumble, *n.* A pie topping that exhibits some firmness and togetherness.

Almost-cure, *n.* A treatment (something guaranteed to *not* cure) that helps to a remarkable degree.

Almost-curious, *adj.* Not curious enough, especially if it is close to quitting time. Or, curious about almost-stuff.

Almost-current, *adj.* Of events that happened recently enough that some people still care about them, but most have moved on.

Almost-curtail, *v.t.* Reduced to a trickle. Or, nearly stop an occasional event.

Almost-curve, *n.* A slightly-bent almost-straight line.

Almost-cushy, *adj.* A situation approaching the ideal of nice or comfortable or easy. (If the boss is watching, though, you'd better at least act like you are sweating the small stuff.)

Almost-custody, *n.* When the kids usually live at your house (all the time except every other weekend).

Almost-customer, *n.* A causal passer-by that expresses interest in your products or services and then leaves. Someone who says they'll put in an order next week.

Almost-customize, *adj.* When you try to make something uniquely yours by decorating it with stuff that is mass-produced.

Almost-cyborg, *n.* A partly artificial human. A person with extra-human qualities and abilities.

Almost-cycle, *n.* When a process comes close to completing a cycle, but before doing so goes on to follow a slightly different course.

D

Almost-dabble, *v.* To get almost-involved and trying to dabble, but to then get distracted away before actually becoming a complete dabbler. (What an abecedarian does when trying to mimic a friend who dabbles.) (Almost-life is often quite like this.)

Almost-daily, *adj., adv.* Regularly. Frequently. Weather permitting.

Almost-damage, *n.* The cost, not in money, but rather in dashed expectations.

Almost-damp, *adj.* Only very slightly moist. Or, humid.

Almost-dance, *v.i.* What most men do when pressured to at least try to dance.

Almost-dancer, *n.* Someone with rhythm but no training. Or, someone with neither rhythm nor training who attempts to move to the music. Or, everyone but the most shy after their third glass of almost-sparkling wine.

Almost-danger, *n.* Amusement-park style suspense or horror.

Almost-dark, *adj.* At dawn or dusk. Or, where the lighting is dim enough that there is definitely no need for sunglasses. Or, when you are "in the shade" instead of "in the dark" about a certain issue. The so-called "Dark Ages" were many years ago, and we have passed the so-called "Enlightenment," but today it still feels like the "Almost-Dark Ages."

Almost-Darwin, *n.* A hypothetical (now) almost-personality of Charles Darwin created from all we know about him.

Almost-data, *n.* Bits and bytes from somewhere strange. Or, data that is too incomplete to process further. Noise that only kinda makes sense.

Almost-date, *v.t., n.* Just go for a coffee.

Almost-day, *n.* Twenty-three hours. Or, specifically, that day when you turn the clocks forward one hour. Or, early dawn.

Almost-dead, *adj.* Dying. Nearly dead. Not quite dead yet. Or, brain dead.

Almost-deadline, *n.* A deadline you set for yourself. Or, a deadline that is possible to miss without severe consequences. Perhaps, a milestone.

Almost-dear, *adj.* How to address an almost-friend in a letter or email. [See almost-friends.]

Almost-dearth, *adj.* A little shy of the optimal amount.

Almost-death, *n.* The condition of being near death. Or, the time of being near death.

Almost-debate, *n.* A one-sided or lopsided debate where one side is better prepared or more knowledgeable, and therefore there is not much of a contest. Or, when someone starts an argument over a foregone conclusion.

Almost-debt, *n.* Debt that you will probably never need to repay, because of all the fancy "options" now available under the umbrellas of "high finance" and "social concern."

Almost-debug, *v.t.* To remove some of the most egregious errors in code, but to not remove all of the errors.

Almost-decaffeinated, *adj.* Decaffeinated.

Almost-decay, *v.i., n.* When a thing's half-life is almost-up.

The Almost-Dictionary

Almost-deceive, *v.t.* To try to mislead, trick, delude, or beguile someone, or an audience (that may not be critical or questioning seriously enough), and then before it's too late they catch on to what is really going on.

Almost-December, *n.* Any time in November.

Almost-decidable, *adj.* Sometimes the information is too vague, or the situation too volatile for a decision to be made. Sometimes we need to do more research.

Almost-decide, *v.t.* The process of narrowing the decision down to a small number of alternatives. One usually feels better having almost-decided (the feeling is one of almost-relief).

Almost-declassify, *v.t.* To allow more access (as to a document), but to still withhold full access to key elements (like the sentences that are still blacked out).

Almost-deconstruct, *v.t.* To tease apart meaning to get to a better almost-understanding (or, at some almost-point, to just take almost-off on an almost-tangent and meander through a semantic space almost-aimlessly connecting, joining, relation, uncle, . . . but I digress). The need for deconstruction exists because language and meaning is almost-always only almost-exact. To almost-deconstruct is to generously leave some deconstructing for the next guy, and you probably want some almost-meanings almost-left almost-standing (even if they just sit there). [See almost-meant, almost-understanding.]

Almost-decrepit, *adj.* Something not particularly old, decayed, or in disrepair, but still nowhere near brand almost-spanking new.

Almost-deduction, *n.* When you don't have two plus two coming together nicely to make four yet, but you know in your gut that your supposition must be correct. Or, any deduction that you try but fail to adequately make after having a few drinks.

Almost-deed, *n.* A thing almost-done: either it was scheduled to be done and then it wasn't, or it was mostly done and then not finished. Or, just a ticket that says you are allowed to wander around on the property all day. [See almost-method.]

Almost-deep, *adj.* Deep enough. Or, *not* deep enough.

Almost-default, *n.* A default that can't be relied upon to remain constant.

Almost-defective, *adj.* Anything that is just barely "good enough."

Almost-definition, *n.* An almost-concise and yet almost-precise almost-explanation of almost-meaning (like this one) that almost by almost-definition leaves almost-something almost-out.

Almost-deflate, *v.t.* To release most of the air or gas from a container.

Almost-degree, *n.* A piece of paper from a university that lets you know that you have almost graduated (maybe a notice about the final exams, or about summer school). Or, the kind of degree you get at an almost-academy. [See almost-academy, almost-graduate.]

Almost-dehydrated, *adj.* Running dry (or becoming too dry).

Almost-delegate, *v.t.* Micromanage.

Almost-delete, *v.t.* To leave things such that you can't find your files, even if all the techies still can.

Almost-deliver, *v.t.* Give the package to anyone who will sign for it.

Almost-democracy, *n.* When the boss wants to hear everyone's ideas before deciding.

Almost-deniable, *adj.* Would be deniable if it wasn't for all that pesky so-called evidence.

Almost-denounce, *v.t.* To almost-constructively criticize.

Almost-deny, *v.t.* To narrowly focus your denials in the hopes that nobody notices what you are not denying.

Almost-depart, *v.t.* To almost leave, but really just move to another part of the building. When you make like an almost-tree and almost-leaf.

Almost-Department, *n.* The almost-driving almost-force in most organizations — the impetus behind inaction. The Almost Department is the one that has all the forms for you to fill out before anything gets done, or almost-done, or started, or almost-started (depending on which box you check). All of the Almost-Departments around the world might seem disconnected, but really they are networked, and this network forms the almost-back almost-bone of what we commonly refer to as "maintaining the status quo." [See almost-exist, almost-factor, almost-method, almost-way.]

Almost-dependant, *n.* Your accountant, lawyer, bartender, bookie, or someone else, who will survive without you just fine. (As opposed to a child who *is* a dependant.)

Almost-deplete, *v.t.* To significantly reduce in quantity, content, power, or value. Or, to leave just enough that you don't need to be the one doing the refilling.

Almost-deploy, *v.t.* To get ready to move, spread out, or operate in an appropriate way. (In a product almost-life almost-cycle this is one of the most work-intensive almost-steps.)

Almost-depressed, *adj.* A little bummed, or ticked. Or, someone who would be depressed if they had time to think about it.

Almost-derail, *v.t.* To make wobbly, or shaky. Or, to just start pulling at the rail.

Almost-dereliction, *n.* Neglect.

Almost-desultory, *adj.* Doing something in a focused and purposeful way, but while still subject to the struggles and vicissitudes of everyday life.

Almost-determinism, *n.* The theory that people have a barely-free will (and a huge almost-will). [See almost-will, almost-ego.]

Almost-develop, *v.* Make plans for.

Almost-devote, *v.t.* To dedicate something to some purpose, but not entirely or exclusively.

Almost-diamond, *n.* Cubic-zirconia, or any clear gemstone less expensive than diamond. [See almost-zirconia.]

Almost-diary, *n.* Calendar.

Almost-dictate, *v.t.* Suggest. Or, prescribe.

Almost-dictionary, *n.* An alphabetical listing of almost-words, with almost-meanings associated with those almost-words (that may or may not themselves be in almost-speak). [See almost-word, almost-speak, almost-idiom.]

Almost-didactic, *adj.* Something not originally or necessarily meant to be educational, but it could be.

Almost-diet, *n., v.* No matter what you eat, always leave some of it. (This is the same as to say: Eat almost-all of it.) This is probably fairly effective, and therefore almost-advisable. An almost-good almost-diet might mostly-consist of an almost-breakfast, a mere snack for lunch, and an almost-dinner later in the day. This diet might not be advisable for people who already eat like a bird. If you eat like a pig, it's probably not going help a whole lot. [See almost-eat.]

Almost-difference, *n.* The difference between any stated difference and the actual difference (even in meaning). [See almost-meant, almost-understanding.]

Almost-different, *adj.* Essentially the same. Almost-identical products (perhaps from the same lot) made to be within specifications. Or, an "egalitarian nightmare" of an issue. Or, . . . and now for something almost-different: Something that will evolve before your eyes, . . . very slowly. [See almost-change.]

Almost-dig, *v.* Mostly kinda like. Or, stand around as support for a shovel.

Almost-digestion, *n.* Partial indigestion.

Almost-dildo, *n.* Almost anything that makes you go, "Hmmm."

Almost-dinged, *adj.* Your car, every day.

Almost-dinner, *n.* That plate of nachos, and perhaps another plate of wings, that you share with your friends at happy hour before going home for dinner.

Almost-diplomatic, *adj.* Just being nice. Perhaps, engaging in small talk or asking questions, but avoiding serious negotiations. Shying away from ruffling feathers. Or, ruffling too many feathers by speaking in a way considered too autocratic, dogmatic, fanatic, operatic, or problematic. Or, being diplomatic with the added vocabulary of almost-speak.

Almost-direct, *adj.* Not very circuitous. For example: the way you would expect a parcel to travel from point of shipment to point of delivery. The shortest distance between you and your goals is almost never a straight line.

Almost-dirt, *n.* Clay, sand, or other filth that is not very good for growing plants, . . . and that somehow finds its way into your almost-clean room.

Almost-dirty, *adj.* A shirt that you can probably wear only once or twice more before it needs to go in the wash.

Almost-disable, *v.t.* To render ineffective to a significant degree.

Almost-disagree, *v.t.* Qualify the statement. Be a smart aleck. Blithely relate an anecdote that might better-support a counterargument.

Almost-disaster, *n.* Spilt milk, or the equivalent minor negatively-perceived event.

Almost-discard, *v.t.* Stash away in the garage, attic, or basement. [See almost-garbage.]

Almost-discipline, *n., v.* The study of the almost-method, almost-stuff, or almost-speak. Or, the self-control to almost-always speak almost-speak. [See whatever you like, really.]

Almost-disconsolate, *adj.* Feeling somewhat dejected and cheerless.

Almost-discredit, *v.t.* To cast aspersions on some person, thing, or idea unsuccessfully.

Almost-discreet, *adj.* Done in such a way that one gets credit both for letting people know, *and* not letting people know.

Almost-discretion, *n.* An unreliable ability to make responsible decisions, especially in the minding of one's tongue.

Almost-discriminate, *v.t.* To almost-draw big fat gray lines almost-between things you're not sure about.

Almost-discussion, *n.* A discussion that was interrupted before everything was said, decided, or understood. Email discussions are almost-discussions in slow motion.

Almost-disentangled, *adj.* Simplified, but left in a mess.

Almost-dish, *adj.* A fairly attractive young woman. Or, the kind of dish that might confuse someone on the almost-diet. [See almost-diet.]

Almost-disingenuous, *adj.* What you might think of someone who is overly-optimistic, overly-pessimistic, eccentric, or suspiciously uninformed.

Almost-disjunctive, *adj.* Serving to almost-separate. Pick any two subjects, and you can usually easily find issues that connect the two.

Almost-dismantle, *v.t.* To take something apart enough that it looks like you know how to fix it.

Almost-dismember, *v.t.* To leave parts hanging. Not completely dismembering. (A whole detective series could be based on this almost-word alone.)

Almost-disobey, *v.t.* To obey in the important ways, and neglect only unimportant matters. Or, to stick to the letter of the law while really acting against the intent.

Almost-disorganized, *adj.* Run democratically. When observing other people, they may seem disorganized, but usually they will only be *almost*-disorganized. When traveling and living out of a suitcase, you might *feel* almost-disorganized yourself (even though you almost-know almost-better).

Almost-disown, *v.t.* To not call very often.

Almost-dispassionate, *adj.* In the middle, between passionate and dispassionate. Almost-everyone spends almost-all their time being almost-neutral, almost-indifferent, and almost-detached, and yet still passion-enabled and interested to some degree. Hands-off, and yet ready to pounce. Feeling, and yet not feeling intensely. Disappointed, yet active and optimistic. (Almost-Dispassionate would be a great name for a perfume or cologne. The slogan would be read by a woman in an almost-sultry voice: "Somewhere between passionate and dispassionate is . . . almost-dispassionate.")

Almost-display, *v.t.* To place where someone can find it only if they spend time looking for it.

Almost-disprove, *n.* To not quite disprove to the extent, level, or threshold needed (noisy data, small sample size).

Almost-dispute, *n.* Point out. Or, a disagreement about a trivial thing.

Almost-disregard, *v.t.* To ignore out of the corner of one's eye.

Almost-disrupt, *v.t.* To aggravate, and maybe to hamper, but not so much that the thing stops.

Almost-disseminate, *v.t.* To "make available" as compared to "distribute widely." Posting a new page on the Internet would be one almost-example.

Almost-dissent, *v.i., n.* The withholding of assent, but to stop short of full disagreement.

Almost-dissimilar, *adj.* Similar. Close, but no cigarette.

Almost-distant, *adj.* Within spitting distance. Or, not so far away that overcoming the distance becomes daunting. Or, just out of sight.

Almost-distinguished, *adj.* Better than average. Or, wearing a tie.

Almost-distort, *v.t.* To tell only what you know about what happened. [See almost-journalism, almost-true.]

Almost-distress, *n.* Some seem to go by the tenet: The more almost-incompetent you seem, the more attention you get. (Which is a variation on: The "drama queen" gets the almost-worm.) The rest of us are left to figure out each time: Are they *really* in distress?

Almost-distrust, *n., v.t.* Healthy skepticism (about a person, thing, or idea). Or, an unhealthy skepticism as to the importance of almost-stuff.

Almost-disturb, *v.t.* Nudge.

Almost-diversity, *n.* Diversity. (Because you never get pure diversity, or exact diversity, or complete diversity, or complete disuniformity.)

Almost-divert, *v.t.* Reorient. Or, tickle.

Almost-divest, *v.t.* To partially dispossess, especially of property, authority, or ornament.

Almost-divisible, *adj.* In physics, an almost-aspect of the "smallest" thing. (They keep trying to smash whatever it is to see what pops out.)

Almost-division, *n.* Dividing by an irrational number. Or, mitosis or meiosis (cell division happens almost-smartly).

Almost-divorce, *n.* Separation.

Almost-Dixie, *n.* The South, after the Civil War.

Almost-dock, *n.* Anything you can moor your boat to other than a dock (perhaps a log or tree).

Almost-doctor, *n.* Intern. Or, doctor (since they've all forgotten stuff). [See almost-education.]

Almost-doctrine, *n.* Use the almost-method in the almost-way and you'll be almost-fine. [See almost-method, almost-principle, almost-way.]

Almost-documented, *adj.* When a product or service is documented to the extent that all legal and contractual requirements for it being documented are met, but not to the extent that end users can easily find what they need to know.

Almost-dog, *n.* Cat.

Almost-dogma, *n.* The protective layer of related facts, traditions, and discriminating principles that you typically find around dogma.

Almost-economics, *n.* Everything about economics except a few of the numbers (like the number on the one-hundred dollar bill, or the exact population of a nation at a particular time). Or, gambling.

Almost-economize, *v.t.* To be concerned about price, but more concerned about speed.

Almost-economy, *n.* The systems of commerce that "just happen" before you really notice that an "economy" is there (that emerge as a population grows larger). Or, the kind of economy that you have left after everyone has at least one of everything (maybe because there is nobody inventing new stuff). Or, what you notice is left of your economy once you discount what is rightly part of other economies. Many things about economies are actually mostly something else: the physical parts of cash registers and commodities, the paper in the money, the human parts of service, the almost-nothing parts of conversations, and the actual dirt you get when you buy real estate.

Almost-edge, *n.* A place that from a distance seemed to be the edge, but there was no drop-off or sharp delineator, but you still know that the risks are higher and the unknowns greater. This is where most transitions start to occur. This is where alternative points of view start to emerge. Between the bland and predictable middle, and the exciting and dangerous extremes, are the vivifying and sometimes troublesome almost-edges. (The Earth's upper atmosphere and an event horizon might be considered almost-edges.)

Almost-edible, *adj.* Something that if prepared correctly would be edible (like a raw turnip, a salt lick, or a live shark).

Almost-editor, *n.* Proofreader.

Almost-education, *n.* An incomplete education. (They all are.)

Almost-educational, *adj.* A waste of time. Or, almost a waste of time. Or, necessary for reasons other than education. Or, when erroneous things are being taught and learned. Or, to educate falsely on purpose to further an agenda.

Almost-effect, *n., v.t.* What happens to other stuff as a result of almost-stuff almost-happening. Or, what almost-happens to almost-stuff as a result of stuff happening. [See almost-stuff.]

Almost-effective, *adj.* Nearly did have the desired effect.

Almost-efficacious, *adj.* As able to produce the desired effect at least to the extent that most pharmaceuticals do, or most enacted legislation, or most city planning.

Almost-efficient, *adj.* Doing things quite effectively but not the best way possible, probably because of the cost, time, or due to ignorance. Perhaps, also, not using best practices, . . . or almost-best practices.

Almost-egalitarian, *adj., n.* The belief in the virtual equality of all people, and the entitlement of most to some kind of education, a fairly level playing field, and advancement opportunities (especially of the clamber-up-then-slide-back-down variety); but not to the extent that this position would unsettle society, make no logical sense, or disfavor the privileged.

Almost-ego, *n.* One of the three almost-divisions of the almost-psyche that serves as the almost-organized almost-conscious almost-mediator between the almost-self and their almost-environment—especially through almost-continual almost-adaptation to change. [See almost-id, almost-superego, almost-psyche.]

Almost-egocentric, *adj.* Not so self-centered that others are not considered.

Almost-egregious, *adj.* Almost-conspicuously almost-bad.

Almost-eh, *adv., adj.* How you say "almost" in Canadian.

Almost-eight, *n.* Seven. (The almost-best time of the day.)

Almost-Einstein, *n.* A hypothetical (now) almost-personality of Albert Einstein created from all we know about him.

Almost-elderly, *adj.* Someone just a little older than you.

Almost-electable, *adj.* Not quite electable (and that could be for one of several reasons that we don't need to get into here).

Almost-elected, *adj.* Voted for by fewer than someone else was.

Almost-election, *n.* Gearing up for an election that never happens. Or, having an election, but the results were not fairly decided. Or, holding an election under the pretense that those elected would then gain power, but they don't. Or, an election in which only a "phantom public" votes.

Almost-electioneering, *v.t.* Putting an election bumper sticker on your car.

Almost-element, *n.* Chemical. Or, something elemental that exists more than it doesn't exist (for example, Almostium). [See almost-atomism.]

Almost-eligible, *adj.* Someone who didn't play the numbers game quite right.

Almost-elitist, *adj.* An egalitarian when outside of the almost-ivory almost-tower (probably) environment. [See almost-egalitarian.]

Almost-eloquence, *n.* Discourse distinguished by an overuse of otherwise timely clichés.

Almost-embark, *v.t.* When your suitcases are packed but you don't end up going.

Almost-embarrassed, *adj.* "Ok. In a moment of circumspection I can see how this might be embarrassing, but I know what I'm doing."

Almost-emblematic, *v.t.* Insufficiently representative or symbolic of something else (people tend to think more about the depiction itself).

Almost-embody, *v.* Embody in an almost-abstract sense. Things almost-embody ideas (a particular sedan almost-embodies the idea *car*, and two people holding hands almost-embody the idea *relationship*); but not in an exclusive way (other cars also almost-embody the idea *car*), and not completely (the ideas of *road* and *fuel* and *limits* are also components of idea *car*). [See almost-abstract, almost-real, almost-universals.]

Almost-eme, *n.* That which is not a complete or whole structural element in language or thought specifically because of its almost-aspects. Any episteme, mimeme, formeme, metaseme, kineme, or other conceptual unit that is incomplete (especially when considered in isolation and away from the rest of language and life). Almost-all –emes are almost-emes. [See almost-abstract, almost-aspect, almost-deconstruct, almost-semiotics, almost-sign.]

Almost-empirical, *adj.* Not just an opinion but an expert opinion. The results of a thought experiment. Hearsay evidence. Relying on data that has had all of the pesky outliers removed (in other words, relying on observation or experience only to the extent that it agrees with theory). Or, relying on what seems rational enough to not be otherwise (questioned). [See almost-rational.]

Almost-employ, *v.t.* To hire a contractor, part-time-help, to get a relative to do it, to trade, or somehow avoid all the forms, red-tape, almost-hidden costs, and other encumbrances associated with *actually* employing someone.

Almost-employee, *n.* Almost-employees (contractors, part-time help) are usually the almost-perfect partial-solution for the typical business. They're almost-always cheaper, more disposable, they can work in a different place, and they don't count as part of your payroll (which means that your department can both grow *and* shrink simultaneously). Almost-employees are the almost-best part of almost-capitalism, and they are a very flexible lot too. [See almost-employ, almost-staff.]

Almost-employment, *n.* Where you get compensated for doing work, but don't have as many benefits as the employees.

The Almost-Dictionary

Almost-empty, *adj.* Not quite empty. Perhaps, so close to empty that there is cause for concern.

Almost-encouraged, *adj.* Almost-nudged in any direction, especially with the use of almost-speak. Or, encouraged to speak almost-speak.

Almost-end, *n.* The end. Any end. (I guess you could say, Jim Morrison almost sang about the almost-end.) The closer we get to an end, the more like a new beginning it becomes.

Almost-endangered, *adj.* There's lots of them (probably enough to continue hunting them), and they make really good targets.

Almost-endeavor, *v.i.* To have a dream, or daydream, and to write it down and talk to people about it. Perhaps also, to budget for it. Through applying the almost-method one can keep this from almost-turning into some kind of transitive verb. [See almost-method.]

Almost-endorse, *v.t.* When you like the person, thing, or idea, but there is a foreseeable chance that your overt endorsement might backfire.

Almost-energetic, *adj.* Not currently sitting on the couch.

Almost-energy, *n.* Hard to define energy. Stuff you can only almost-understand.

Almost-engaged, *adj.* People go through the early stages of a relationship rather quickly, and then go through a protracted period of almost-engagement before finally getting engaged. Romantic relationships tend to proceed through the following stages: First, you learn of the other person's existence. Second, if this has not already happened, you meet face-to-face. Third, you talk about dating. Fourth, you date. Fifth, you become "almost-engaged." This stage is usually by far the longest in duration (as measured by both wall-clock time, and by total amount of time spent together so far). Next, you decide to get married. And then—finally, and pre-divorce—you do.

Almost-engagement, *n.* That long and sometimes tedious process of getting the other person to almost-commit themselves.

Almost-engineer, *n.* Technician.

Almost-England, *n.* Wales. Scotland. Ireland. Just because of the tunnel, France. Ok, Germany too. Parts of Italy. At a stretch, anywhere in the European Union. Or the Commonwealth. Ok, not Italy. Ok, not France or Germany either.

Almost-English, *n., adj.* Broken English. Simple English. Or, that super-set of English that includes almost-words. Or, that subset of English words that only includes almost-words. Or, partly English (as in: someone not born in England and with only one English parent).

Almost-enigmatic, *adj.* Causing some puzzlement, but not bewilderment. If there is any mystery, it is not of a profound type. When it's almost-evident that the almost-riddle is almost-wrapped in an almost-enigma.

Almost-enjoyment, *n.* Contentment. Satisfaction.

Almost-enough, *adj.* When you want just a little more. If you're being tickled, it's almost-never enough. Or, when someone interrupts you it is probably when they can anticipate the rest of what you are going to say.

Almost-enquire, *v.t.* To "beat around the bush," and hope that almost-answers almost-emerge.

Almost-ensconced, *adj.* Almost-sheltered, or almost-concealed.

Almost-enter, *v.t.* Poke your nose in and take a quick look around.

Almost-entertain, *v.t.* Just invite people over to "hang out." Or, of an idea: To consider briefly before rejecting, to consider a mere almost-idea, or to consider for a while but never seriously.

Almost-entertainment, *n.* The entertainment you can afford on a very tight budget. Or, something very serious that commands idle attention. Or, almost-speak or other almost-stuff that is found to be amusing.

Almost-entitlement, *n.* When you're entitled to something until someone else decides differently.

Almost-enumerate, *v.t.* To approximate, or guess at how many.

Almost-ephemera, *n.* Something of little lasting significance.

Almost-epidemiological, *adj.* Almost everything is almost-epidemiological in that it relates to some degree to the incidence, distribution, and control of disease. [See almost-deconstruct.]

Almost-episteme, *n.* An almost-abstract unit of almost-knowledge. (Not nearly as contagious as the almost-mimeme, because the almost-episteme is mostly passed on through book-learnin'.) [See almost-eme.]

Almost-epitaph, *n.* A brief statement commemorating or epitomizing an old person.

Almost-epithet, *n.* A word or phrase that is almost-derogatory, almost-contemptuous, or almost-abusive.

Almost-equal, *adj.* Similar. Nearly identical. Or, close in number.

Almost-equation, *n.* An equation that is only almost-correct, or unreliable (like E=mc, or U+Me=Us).

Almost-equivocal, *adj.* Subject to two or more interpretations, but it's pretty obvious which one is meant.

Almost-erase, *v.t.* Almost the same as almost-delete. Or, to leave minute traces. [See almost-delete.]

Almost-erratic, *adj.* Wandering. Capricious.

Almost-error, *n.* Oversight. Or, an error condition for which there is a fail-safe position. Or, something flagged as an error that was done on purpose, but that did not compute. Or, to take the least-harmful of available almost-paths.

Almost-escape, *v.t.* When you make it over the fence, across the field, into the woods, down the train tracks, and into town, only to be nabbed by the local police because you forgot to take off your prison garb. Or, when you can check out any time you like, but only almost-leave.

Almost-eschew, *v.t.* To not entirely shun or avoid, at least in a habitual or categorical way. You might almost-eschew a particular restaurant (just for the halibut), but if you are with people who really want to go there, you could make an exception.

Almost-especially, *adv.* Winning the lottery would be especially nice, but winning some lesser prize would be almost-especially nice.

Almost-essential, *adj.* Might be required under almost-normal circumstances, but this time there might be something else that can almost-do the same almost-job.

Almost-establish, *v.t.* To yak on and almost-on about what needs doing.

Almost-estate, *n.* Almost everything *but* the land and the buildings (the real estate). Or, the independent media (bloggers, independent publishers, unsigned musicians, weekend artists, and other do-it-yourselfers) and the almost-social impact and presence of almost-everyone's personal creative almost-side. [See almost-media.]

Almost-eternal, *adj.* An almost-abstract consideration that the non-passage of time imagined in the here-and-now can continue on immutably. Or, any time spent in a dentist's chair.

Almost-ethics, *n.* Values. Relative ethics. The ethics of your relatives, perhaps. Informal considerations as to whether people should be nice to each other. Considerations related to Jeremy

Bentham's "the greatest happiness of the greatest number," and
Immanuel Kant's "hypothetical imperatives." As Bertrand Russell
said: "There are no facts of ethics." We almost-all almost-need to
almost-strike a balance between "doing what we should" and "doing
what we want." What we do is almost-always at odds with some
related set of values. We just have to do the best we can, whatever
that means. Or, any ethic that stresses the values of hard work, thrift,
and self-discipline, but is otherwise devoid of theoretical references
or underpinnings.

Almost-euphemism, *n.* Substituting one fairly offensive or difficult
expression for another one that you are trying to avoid more.

Almost-euphonious, *adj.* Anything that goes under the name of
"music" that is less enjoyable to listen to than a metronome.

Almost-event, *n.* Something that doesn't quite happen. You would
have kissed her, but the phone rang. You would have stayed late and
finished that report, but you felt like going to the gym before supper.
Almost events occur frequently in aviation, and on the roads. [See
almost-something, almost-aspect, almost-almost.]

Almost-ever, *n.* Three-ever.

Almost-everlasting, *adj.* A very long but finite duration.

Almost-everyone, *n.* Over fifty percent but under a hundred percent
of a population. Or, most. [See almost-all.]

Almost-everything, *n.* More than you could possibly imagine. The
phrase: "now I've seen everything" should be: "now I've seen
almost-everything," because otherwise the known-unknown and the
unknown-unknown would both be nonexistent.

Almost-everywhere, *adv., n.* Usually, just on Earth. Typically,
everywhere but where you want one. Almost-always, nowhere to be
found.

Almost-evidence, *n.* Inadmissible evidence.

Almost-evocative, *adj.* Something stimulating, annoying, or wakening, but not necessarily for a response.

Almost-evolve, *v.* Small changes through small and incremental steps that are *consciously* directed. Almost-mutate. Of memetic change, or social change at the almost-microscopic level. Or, to evolve in such a way as to revert back to the original form. [See almost-mutate.]

Almost-evolution, *n.* Almost-insignificant mental or social changes caused by minute adjustments in thinking. Or, the evolution of almost-stuff.

Almost-ex, *n.* The person you are cheating on currently.

Almost-exact, *adj.* Precise.

Almost-exam, *n.* Test.

Almost-examine, *v.t.* To give the "once over." To peruse nonchalantly. To review quickly, or in a hurried almost-way.

Almost-example, *n.* An example that almost nobody understands. Or, an example of something only similar. Or, an example of something with a glaringly obvious almost-aspect (like the leaning tower of Pizza).

Almost-excess, *n.* What is more than the usual, proper, or specified amount (until you find out what the competition is doing).

Almost-exchange, *v.t.* When you just exchange glances. Or, when you trade almost-stuff temporarily (like young girls wearing each other's almost-shirts). [See almost-shirt.]

Almost-exclusive, *adj.* The kind of club that *would* have someone like me as a member. Or, the kind of club that would *not* admit almost-stuff, nor anyone speaking almost-speak.

Almost-executive, *n.* A director or other senior manager that is not have the word "president" somewhere in their title.

Almost-exegesis, *n.* A poor or unfinished explanation or interpretation.

Almost-exemplify, *v.t.* What a bad example does nicely.

Almost-exercise, *v., n.* To move without breaking a sweat. Or, to exercise while still on the couch (elbow bending, jawboning, necking, foot tapping, or the alternate up and in with one index finger).

Almost-exhausted, *adj.* Just tired. Or, nearly empty or depleted.

Almost-exhibit, *n.* An exhibit of almost-art, almost-speak, or other almost-stuff. [See almost-art, almost-speak, almost-stuff, almost-world.]

Almost-exhibitionist, *n.* Someone who likes to show off just to the degree that most people do. Or, someone who likes to show off their almost-stuff.

Almost-exist, *v.i.* Exist because other things exist (like the property "red" exists because the red thing exists, or the relation "above" exists because one thing is on top of another). Or, something that is almost-established.

Almost-expect, *v.* To know of the probability of a certain specific outcome, but to not be aware of its imminence.

Almost-expedient, *adj.* Practical, yet unwise or risky.

Almost-expedite, *v.t.* To be seen trying make something happen just a little quicker than it would otherwise.

Almost-expendable, *adj.* Any extra that is not part of the main cast, especially in a detective or sci-fi show.

Almost-expensive, *adj.* Not cheap, but probably worth it.

Almost-experienced, *adj.* Experienced just enough to be dangerous. Are you almost-experienced? (AJH might ask.) It could be argued that nobody is almost-experienced enough. [See almost-field, almost-method, almost-way.]

Almost-expert, *adj., n.* Both studied and experienced, but not yet fully an authority on the subject.

Almost-expired, *adj.* When the "best before" date on the package is getting close, or when you start getting "membership renewal" mail.

Almost-explain, *v.t.* Partially explain (and probably leaving out the good parts). To almost-make an almost-proper description or exegesis about almost-something (as in: "The definition of almost-explain is almost self-explanatory"). Or, to use one of the many almost-standard almost-excuses that are so common that people need no further explanation (as in: "I must have been sick that day").

Almost-explicit, *adj.* Nearly word for word. Characterized by a fairly precise expression.

Almost-exploit, *v.t.* To take advantage of someone's eagerness to buy, but the other party sets the price.

Almost-explore, *v.t.* When you think about exploring, but don't actually get around to it. Or, when you do explore, but not to a sufficient extent.

Almost-exported, *adj.* Held at the border (possibly, because of the paperwork).

Almost-express, *n.* Pony express. Donkey express. Or any other use of animals in transportation or communication (carrier pigeon, camel, elephant). Or, air-mail letters after the invention of email.

Almost-expression, *n.* Any statement or creative gesture that is not fully made (partial, qualified, unsuitable). Or, an expression that nearly or approximately conveys the correct meaning. Or, an expression in almost-speak. (Perhaps, an almost-speak segment of a larger discourse, or an almost-saying or almost-slogan.) [See almost-word, almost-speak.]

Almost-extemporaneous, *adj.* Almost-impromptu. When someone has had some but very little time to prepare for something (such as giving a speech).

Almost-extensible, *adj.* Almost everything lends itself to being extended, enlarged, grown, or replicated. (So it is an Almost-Wonder why that doesn't happen more often.)

Almost-extinction, *n.* How animals apply for zoo cages.

Almost-extortion, *v.t.* Price gouging.

Almost-extrinsic, *v.t.* Mostly unrelated.

Almost-extrovert, *n.* An outgoing introvert.

Almost-ez, *adj.* Spelling words almost-incorrectly but still almost-meaningfully.

F

Almost-face, *n., v.* A partial view of a face. Or, a partially turned away face. Perhaps to turn to a profile position (as for a studio photograph). Or, any flat (two dimensional) picture of a person's face (three dimensional) — because it is not as representative. Or, an edited or "doctored" picture of a face.

Almost-facile, *adj.* Only fairly easy, relatively-effortless, or barely troublesome, but not overly simplistic.

Almost-facility, *n.* A mostly-built facility. Or, a partially-destroyed facility that is still in use. Or, a facility used in a way other than that for which it was designed, and perhaps awkwardly so.

Almost-fact, *n.* Approximations. Or, dogma. Or, hearsay. Or, a surmise or conjecture.

Almost-factor, *n.* An almost-aspect or almost-angle as it applies to real life (or almost-life), especially when one is using the almost-method in the almost-way. What you have introduced when you consider almost-aspects and other almost-stuff. [See almost-aspect, almost-angle, almost-field, almost-life, almost-method, almost-principle, almost-way.]

Almost-faculty, *n.* Substitute teachers. Or, an ability not fully-developed.

Almost-fail, *v.i.* To become weakened. Or, to just scrape through or just barely pass a test of some kind.

Almost-failure, *n.* Someone who is a failure at being a failure.

Almost-fair, *adj.* As fair as fair can be. When objectivity, impartiality, and honesty are maximized; and where subjectivity, ignorance, prejudice, favoritism, selfishness, and corruption are minimized.

Almost-fake, *adj.* Technically valid, convincing, or functional, but not very authentic (as in, much of the stuff locals sell to tourists).

Almost-false, *adj.* Something that you think must be wrong, it's just that nobody has been able to disprove it yet.

Almost-familiar, *adj.* When you've been in a similar situation before. Or, when you've met someone similar before. When it might be almost déjà vu for the first time.

Almost-famous, *adj.* When you're not a household or dictionary name yet, but fairly well-known in your field. Or, when your fifteen minutes might soon be starting.

Almost-fan, *n.* A fickle, forgetful, forlorn, frail, fainthearted, flighty, freaky, foul, furious, fettered, frightened, frigid, fake, former, or future fan. Basically, an admirer that won't buy your stuff. Or, a real fan of almost-stuff.

Almost-fancy, *adj., v.t., n.* Likeable. Or, liking. Or, any food that tastes like the almost-real thing.

Almost-far, *adj.* Not so far away that it is not within walking distance. Or, too far to walk, but just a short drive.

Almost-farm, *n.* A hobby farm. Or, land where food can be grown, but it is not farmed for some reason.

Almost-fashionable, *adj.* Something that just a few people think is cool, or something that many people think is almost-cool.

Almost-fast, *adj.* Stuck in second gear.

Almost-fastidious, *adj.* Having personal almost-standards of quality that are somewhat relaxed (of someone who is not hypercritical but still circumspect).

Almost-fat, *adj.* How you get when you are dieting but not watching your weight. Also, how you get when you are watching your weight but not dieting. Or, not so fat that you need to buy larger clothes.

Almost-fault, *n.* When the tennis ball lands on the line.

Almost-favorite, *adj.* One of the few select favorites, but not the most favorite.

Almost-fear, *n.* Muted fear. Nervous apprehension. What you feel when you are only a little bit scared. (Butterflies.) Roller-coaster fear, as opposed to tiger fear. Perhaps, when what you have to fear is nowhere in sight.

Almost-feast, *n.* Meal.

Almost-feckless, *adj.* Human (especially when used disparagingly).

Almost-feel, *v.i.* What you think you feel.

Almost-felicitous, *adj.* Fairly well-suited or expressed.

Almost-female, *adj.* Someone who has had a sex change operation.

Almost-feminine, *adj.* Masculine.

Almost-feral, *adj.* Musician-like.

Almost-fervent, *adj.* Showing a little bit of warmth or enthusiasm. Or, showing a lot of warmth or enthusiasm about almost-stuff.

Almost-fickle, *adj.* Open-minded.

Almost-fiction, *n.* When the names have been changed, but the story really did happen. Or, a subjective or nuanced interpretation of a real story or event.

Almost-fidelity, *n.* About as much dutifulness, loyalty, or accuracy as one might reasonably expect.

Almost-fiduciary, *n., adj.* Someone who is trusted to do something (for an almost-good reason), but they are not required to do it.

Almost-field, *n.* Yard. Or, where people get paid to consider almost-aspects. The almost-field is to be found almost-hidden *within* most fields of endeavor (a politician's work is largely one of finding compromises, the journalist's account will be fine-tuned later, the therapist can't continue after the patient stops showing up). But "almost-factoring" is often the main focus and almost-formalized in the fields of Quality (quality control, quality assurance, quality improvement, quality auditing, quality related statistics), and Statistics (and anything to do with rating and estimating), and Security (defense, offence, safety, privacy, and risk, especially as it relates to quality in those areas); and these disciplines are usually found *assisting* in the other fields and not working alone. Every science relies upon statistics. Medicine is almost-always more approximate or imprecise than we would like—especially as it relates to biochemistry and the similarity in molecular shapes, chance, and concentration levels. Lawyers need to consider the similarities between events, and rules. Tennis players don't need to be perfect, but they do aim to beat their opponents, so they have a target to almost-shoot for. Moviemakers, chipmakers, and restaurant owners are all fanatical about quality. And the field almost-goes almost-on (at least until you get to the fence). [See almost-aspect, almost-factor.]

Almost-fierce, *adj.* Like a Chihuahua with strangers.

Almost-fight, *v.t.* Hit and run. Kick under the table. Cross check. Or, stand one's ground. Or, exchange pies in the face. Or, assail each other with words. [See almost-war.]

Almost-figure, *n., v.i.* A partial drawing, like a join-the-dots picture that is not completed. Or, a twig figure. Or, to think about, but not completely. Or, think almost-about. Or, to perform calculations with irrational numbers.

Almost-fill, *v.t.* To fill without causing a spill.

Almost-filling, *n., v.t.* A temporary filling in a tooth. Or, getting gas for your car when you are on a tight budget.

Almost-fillip, *v.t.* To threaten to flick with a finger (but the finger is never actually flicked).

Almost-final, *adj.* Perhaps the almost-frontier is only an almost-final frontier.

Almost-finance, *v.t., n.* When the "art of finance" is taken to an extreme, so that it no longer makes arithmetical, logical, or economic sense.

Almost-financing, *n.* The way to buy or sell anything these days (it seems). [See almost-finance.]

Almost-find, *v.t.* When you know that it is going to be in the last place you look, but you haven't got that far yet. Or, if you are using a search vehicle and there is too much other stuff they want you to find first, so you just stop looking.

Almost-fine, *adj.* You would be fine if you didn't have that headache, toothache, or other minor, perhaps nagging but fixable problem.

Almost-finished, *adj.* Something not quite done or finished. (For example: Franz Schubert's *Almost-finished Symphony*.) Some jobs are never completely done, or if they are they have to transition through the state of being almost-finished first. Only almost-finishing your meals is the essence of the almost-diet. According to the 80-20 rule: It is usually the eighty percent that really needs doing, and the other nineteen percent can be almost-ignored until later. If you have almost-finished a test, then you have probably at least passed. If you have almost-finished reading the newspaper then you have probably seen all the important ads. [See almost-diet.]

Almost-fireworks, *n.* Just hand held sparklers.

Almost-firm, *adj.* A little shaky, or not as steadfast as one would like.

Almost-first, *adj.* Second or third (place or show).

Almost-first aid, *n.* Calling an ambulance, or fetching the first aid kit. Perhaps, helping the paramedics plug in the equipment. Or, second aid.

Almost-fish, *n.* Octopus, lobster, shrimp, or oyster. Or, a fish without its head and guts. Or, something that is just a bit fishy, but mostly something else.

Almost-fit, *adj.* Within a few pounds of your fighting-weight. Given your athletic abilities, your fitness level falls in a range (almost-between couch-potato and fiddle), and almost-fit would be to at least describe some kind of musical instrument. [See almost-athletic, almost-shape.]

Almost-fix, *v.t.* To repair in the same way that a dentist repairs your teeth.

Almost-fizzle, *v.i.* To wane (maybe in dramatic fashion), and yet to not go all the way out.

Almost-flag, *n.* A logo or banner that hasn't been sewn into cloth yet.

Almost-flagon, *n.* Mug.

Almost-flat, *adj.* A little wavy. Or, flat in the small, but almost-spherical really, big-picture (as with Earth).

Almost-flaw, *n.* An acceptable imperfection. Perhaps, an abnormality that adds distinction (and might be almost-preferable). Of a potential defect in a product, but where that part is just barely within specs. Or, a mutation.

Almost-flawless, *adj.* For some reason we have a tendency to NOT think of things as perfect, ideal, completely flawed, or even mostly flawed. If we can recognize what it is supposed to be we are usually almost-forgiving enough to consider it almost-flawless. That's where the fun doesn't begin, because we tell ourselves that we have just found an X, and from then on *worry* about the location, number, and size of the flaws. [See almost-field.]

Almost-fleet, *n.* Only two vehicles (as in: ships, planes, or trucks) operated under almost-unified almost-control. Or, several vehicles all in such disrepair that they can't move.

Almost-fleeting, *adj.* The parts of history we choose to remember.

Almost-flex, *v.t.* To tense a muscle without also moving your appendage.

Almost-flexible, *adj.* Bendable. Somewhat yielding. Like the banker that can give you a better rate if you put up more collateral.

Almost-flight, *n.* The flight of anything that is not moving through the air of its own accord. Or, when you just sit on the runway.

Almost-flip, *v.t.* Buy, fix up, and then rent out (instead of selling right away).

Almost-flood, *n.* When your street gets flooded, but not your house.

Almost-floor, *n.* Carpet or rug.

Almost-florid, *adj.* A place where there are artificial flowers.

Almost-Florida, *n.* An adjacent state: Georgia, or Alabama. Or, a similar landform: Italy, Korea, or Africa.

Almost-fluent, *adj.* Occasionally at a loss for words.

Almost-fluid, *adj.* Not immobile or rigid enough to be considered a solid. Someone's thoughts on land conservation might be almost-fluid. [See almost-liquid.]

Almost-focus, *v.i.* Soft-focus. Or, what a "focus group" almost-does.

Almost-foggy, *adj.* Patchy fog. Light fog. A little smoky. Or, unclear.

Almost-folk, *n.* The kind of people that like almost-stuff and almost-speak. Or, a gaggle of space aliens.

Almost-follow, *v.* Follow only when it's convenient to follow (a diet, or leader). Or, to coincidentally be going in a similar direction. Or, to follow, but at such a great distance you don't know you're following. Or, to imitate in a lesser way. Or, to keep abreast of in a desultory way.

Almost-folly, *n.* Good clean fun.

Almost-food, *n.* Anything from the "junk" aisle at the supermarket. Candy. Vitamin pills and food supplements. Even dog food, and birdie num num. Just about anything non-poisonous that you can find in the forest except tree trunks and branches. Or, any food your doctor says is quite bad. What doesn't kill you may still almost-kill you.

Almost-for, *prep.* When something is done for more than one purpose, then it is almost-for each one of the non-primary purposes.

Almost-force, *v.t., n.* To urge, oblige, hasten, constrain, entreat, beguile, provoke, or motivate. Everyone wants the almost-force to be bothering someone other than themselves, and we all feel the almost-force issuing from those around us.

Almost-forecast, *n.* The kind of forecast that economists give when they don't even put a percentage on their prognostications, they only use terms like "likely," or "unlikely," or "in the long run," based on linear extrapolations, or whatever they surmise at any given time.

Almost-foreign, *adj.* An immigrant citizen that still has their foreign accent.

Almost-forestall, *v.t.* To anticipate and make a serious yet ultimately unsuccessful attempt to exclude, hinder, or prevent.

Almost-forget, *v.t.* To not remember until the last minute. The delay in remembering may or may not be noticed by someone else; but if it is, that is almost-always almost-embarrassing for the party of the first part because they should have done better.

Almost-forgive, *v.t.* Say you forgive, and try to forgive, but still remember and hold a bit of a grudge.

Almost-form, *n., v.* Any of the usual quite specific almost-things almost-identified in the so-called Almost-Theory of Almost-Forms.

Almost-formal, *adj.* Semi-formal.

Almost-format, *v.t., n.* To arrange things, as on a computer disk, so as to thwart the normal methods of apprehension.

Almost-forty, *n.* Probably more like forty-seven.

Almost-forty-two, *n.* Forty-one. Not THE answer, but a pretty good answer.

Almost-forward, *adj.* Near the front. Or, "Hello. Allow me to introduce myself."

Almost-fourfold, *adj.* Threefold.

Almost-frail, *adj.* Of the almost-weaker sex. Or, of the almost-stronger sex.

Almost-frame, *n., v.* That which surrounds an imagined almost-scene. You can paint an almost-picture just with words and almost-words, but it takes an almost-frame to almost-hold the thoughts together. When speaking, you can almost-move a discussion to an almost-positive almost-frame, an almost-negative almost-frame, or an almost-futuristic almost-frame. Or, just point at someone. [See almost-almost.]

Almost-frank, *n., adj.* Fran. Or, tactfully direct.

Almost-freak, *n.* Teenager.

Almost-free, *adj.* Stuff you buy on the easy installment plan, or under the subscription model. Or, stuff you get when import tariffs are low. Or, in some places, intellectual property. The best things in life are only almost-free. (Most of us still have to earn a living and pay taxes just to breathe the air.)

Almost-freedom, *n.* All you can hope for, because of all the constraints.

Almost-freeze, *v.i.* What happens when you under-dress for an occasion, especially in cold weather.

Almost-fresh, *adj.* With a modicum of spunk. Or, fairly original. Or, close to passing its expiry date. Or, a wee bit tired. Don't complete today what you will be able to do gooder after some sleep.

Almost-Freudian, *adj.* Almost anything that is almost-about how humans almost-think.

Almost-Freudian slip, *n., v.* When you adeptly catch yourself from Freudian slipping. Whew! To your listener this might come across as an almost-awkward almost-pause.

Almost-friendly, *adj.* Anyone who is trying to sell you something.

Almost-friends, *n.* Acquaintances that like each other. Strangers in the daytime, exchanging business cards. Like-minded people that meet only on the Internet.

Almost-fringe, *adj., n.* What teenagers like.

Almost-frippery, *n.* The kinds of clothes that movie stars and musicians like or wear.

Almost-frisky, *adj.* Teenagers, musicians, movie stars.

Almost-from, *prep.* Not originally from.

Almost-front, *adj.* A bit to the side (ten o'clock, or two o'clock).

Almost-fuck, *v.* When the two of you get stinking drunk, and maybe even get undressed, but then pass out before doing the deed.

Almost-fuel, *n.* Oxygen.

Almost-full, *adj.* More full than empty.

Almost-fun, *n.* Very seldom are we having unmitigated fun. Almost-always something detracts from the fun, and we feel a little restraint, anticipation, and sometimes also a little pain, regret, fright, or even horror (when watching an otherwise enjoyable horror movie, perhaps). Almost-fun is often accompanied by a steady awareness that the present enjoyment of the situation is contingent, and will almost-definitely and quickly almost-dissipate.

Almost-fundamental, *adj.* Fundamental, usually. The almost-fundamentals of life (the four nucleotides, the periodic table of the elements) are not the *most* fundamental things because there are quarks and leptons, and other *more* fundamental almost-things. Almost-specifically, and generally, anything that relies almost-upon something even more basic.

Almost-fungible, *adj.* Nearly as freely-exchangeable as money or grain (perhaps: furniture, or musical instruments).

Almost-funny, *adj.* Eccentric. Perverted. Silly.

Almost-furry, *adj.* Hairy.

Almost-further, *adj.* Not quite as far as, but posing a challenge to the one measured against.

Almost-furtive, *adj.* Done openly, but in such a way as to not arouse suspicion or interest.

Almost-future, *adj., n.* Anything that is fairly likely to happen. Or, anything that is just about to happen. The almost-future is what we have to live through while waiting for the real future to kick in.

Almost-fuzzy, *adj.* Approximate. Imprecise. Vague. Indistinct. Blurred. Inchoate. Nebulous. Or, with just a few small hairs.

G

Almost-gadget, *n.* Doohickey. A relatively small manufactured device that might have bells or whistles, but does not have electronic bells or whistles, or software bells or whistles. (Back in the day, it was an almost-gadget that got between a human and the product of labor, now it is almost-always a full-fledged gadget that mediates.)

Almost-gadgetized, *adj.* Not so encumbered by gadgetry that a face-to-face conversation would be impossible.

Almost-gaffe, *n.* A minor social or verbal blunder that was recovered from skillfully almost-before anyone noticed.

Almost-gambit, *n.* A gambit that doesn't completely work, perhaps because the almost-method was almost-employed. [See almost-method, almost-way.]

Almost-game, *n.* An activity that is less than a game (like picking your nose to impress girls). Or, a game that is too humorless to be called a game (picking fights, flicking through television channels on the remote control). Or, a game that does not yet have fixed or consistent rules (most notably, ones made up by children, lovers, and economic theorists).

Almost-gap, *n.* The gap between almost something and completely something. Sometimes that gap is seen as insignificant, and sometimes that gap makes all the difference. Almost bringing down the house with a performance might seem acceptable to most, whereas almost-surviving an auto accident would certainly be a different kind of almost-experience. One obvious clue when looking for an almost-gap when you're reading is to look for the word or prefix "almost." But there are many other words to look out for as well: adequate, nearly, about, often, close, approximately, mostly, quite, incomplete, verge, brink, and extreme (just to mention a few). Extreme skiers probably seem like almost-wimps to ultra-extreme skiers. That sort of almost-thing. There are words related or close to this almost-gap: barely, slightly, semi-, quasi, typical, average, complex, confused, fuzzy, coarse, unpredictable, limit, maximum, para-, potential, faulty, sanitized, similar, salient, surrogate, stand-in, stop-gap, makeshift, mildly, less than, pseudo, illusory, uncertain, and, well, almost every adjective. Also, any word that is relative or vague by definition (large, small, foggy, package, surrounds, place). "Did the package contain what you expected?" "Well, almost." The almost-gap can be found anywhere you see the use of euphemisms, or statistics, or where there is an emphasis on betterment. [See almost-almost, almost-edge, almost-field.]

Almost-garbage, *n.* Most of the stuff stored in the garage, attic, or basement. When something becomes fully garbage, it does get thrown out; until then, it gradually decays or becomes obsolete. You and your spouse might differ on what needs to get tossed. One person's garbage is another person's almost-garbage.

Almost-garden, *n.* Land with just grass growing on it (as in: a backyard). Or, land that is overrun naturally with flowers or vegetables (that were not deliberately planted).

Almost-gear, *n.* T-shirts, tents, pens, or other objects that have almost-slogans on them. [See almost-slogan.]

Almost-geek, *n.* A comparative lightweight in the geek world. Perhaps someone with more experience than credentials in their field (or the other way around), or where there is no credentialing.

Almost-generous, *adj.* Fairly generous with other people's money. Or, very generous with advice.

Almost-genius, *n.* Cleverness.

Almost-gentry, *n.* The almost-nice almost-quiet people of the upper-middle class.

Almost-genuine, *adj.* Good fakes. Or, of the kind of hypocrisy that is pretty much just human nature.

Almost-giddy, *adj.* When giddiness does not overshadow circumspection. Giddy under control. Giddy like a fox. Or, almost-euphoric. Or, what someone is like after one or two glasses of almost-Champagne (but not three or more).

Almost-gift, *n.* A gift with strings attached. Or, a gift you gave that was re-gifted back to you by accident.

Almost-gimmick, *n.* A previously ingenious scheme, or angle, or device used to attract business or attention that is almost too common now. Or, any gimmick involving almost-stuff.

Almost-giraffe, *n.* Zebra.

Almost-girlfriend, *n.* A girl that you have only just started to date, or one that is too withdrawn.

Almost-glamour, *n.* Regular show-biz.

Almost-glass, *n.* Plastic.

Almost-glee, *n.* Expressed happiness, but not ebullience.

Almost-glib, *adj.* Just getting through the day.

Almost-global, *adj.* Anything that pertains to most of the globe, most countries, most of the important countries (according to your estimation), or most of the people.

Almost-gloomy, *adj.* How you feel as soon as you start to think about work, hospitals, or taxes.

Almost-go, *v.i.* When you stop at the door on the way out, but keep talking.

Almost-goal, *n.* Where you need to be before you can get to your goal. Or, the vague perception of a goal from a distance. Or, a secondary benefit for attaining something.

Almost-golf, *n.* Almost-golf can refer to any golf-like game that does not follow the official rules precisely. It can also refer to this specific hybrid of the two games golf and miniature golf. The advantage is that (together with a golf practice net) most golf shots can be practiced in most backyards. You can set up eighteen "fairways" with corresponding mini-putt "greens," or, you can establish three fairways and holes only, and play six rounds to get a score for eighteen holes. You can be as creative as you want with the features in the mini-putt area, just be sure that a ball can roll onto it easily from at least one direction. (Consider using green-turf carpet on 4x8 boards with pressure-treated 2x4's as the mini-walls.) Each player starts out with three clubs: a putter, a pitching wedge, and a 4-iron. Players can share clubs, because there are usually no great distances to walk in a backyard. Each hole is played starting from the "teeing ground" (with whichever club is most appropriate, actual tees not required), played over the fairways (which may or may not have almost-hazards), and onto the corresponding mini-putt "green" to finish the hole. The player with the lowest score almost-wins (gets to start the next time).

Almost-gone, *adj.* As good as gone. Or, when you can still see them (or their car, or boat) as they leave. Or, not nearly as gone as you would like.

Almost-good, *adj.* That which is pretty good, of high relative-value, or mostly good. If the enemy of the "best" is the "good," then the enemy of the "good" is the "almost-good," and so almost-on. Or, enterprising.

Almost-goodwill, *n.* Kind feelings.

Almost-govern, *v.t.* To regulate so lightly that people wonder if anyone is paying attention. Or, to do nothing and hope for the best (much political theory is about how to *not* meddle too much and still stay in power).

Almost-governance, *n.* The regulating of or by an almost-governmental entity (AGE).

Almost-government, *n.* Collectively, the individuals and adjunct parts of businesses, organizations, utilities, agencies, universities, think-tanks, media conglomerates, and so on that do work almost-for the government at the federal, state, and local levels without being included in the "government payroll" numbers.

Almost-gradual, *adj.* Nearly sudden.

Almost-graduate, *n.* Someone who has passed most of the requisite courses, or who expects to pass their final exams soon.

Almost-grandeur, *n.* When the grandeur is of a small model, or something diminished (as in, the movie version of another world).

Almost-grandstanding, *v.i.* Grandsitting.

Almost-grapeshot, *n.* Grapes.

Almost-graph, *n.* Lines on graph paper, where the axes and values are not labeled.

Almost-grasp, *v.t.* Fumble.

Almost-grateful, *adj.* How you feel when there is nobody around to thank.

Almost-gratuitous, *adj.* When there is actually a small fee (or lagniappe) involved.

Almost-gravity, *n.* The attraction people have for other people (company, parties, crowds, and inhabited planets) because of their almost-aspects. Or, the appeal of almost-stuff, almost-speak, and . . . almost everything almost-really. You can almost feel it.

Almost-graying, *v.i.* What, without modern hair dyes, would be "graying."

Almost-great, *adj.* Good.

Almost-green, *adj.* Yellowish-green, blue-green, or extremely pale green. Now that being "Earth-friendly" is almost-growing in importance, definitions themselves will become more inclusive of the verdant aspects (especially commercially).

Almost-greenhorn, *n.* Not a perfect greenhorn. Someone who has learned "a trick or two."

Almost-gregarious, *adj.* Sociable, affable, amiable, friendly, or talkative.

Almost-grip, *n.* When you can't get a grip, sometimes you can get an almost-grip (and sometimes that's all you really need).

Almost-groan, *v.* Sigh.

Almost-groovy, *adv.* Having very shallow or few grooves. Or, nice or trendy, but not to the extent of inspiring wonder or awe. Almost-almost-hot. [See almost-hot.]

Almost-group, *n.* When one or more members of a group is missing, or asleep. Or, when one or more members of a group is actually a member of an opposing group (a spy, or saboteur). Or, when the makeup of a group changes too quickly. Or, when the members of the group have never met. Or, when some or all of the members of the group don't know they are members of that group. You get the almost-picture.

Almost-growth, *n.* Growth by acquisition.

Almost-guzzle, *v.t.* Drink.

Almost-gypjoint, *n.* With respect to the almost-economic almost-practice of almost-balancing almost-overcharging with almost-undercharging, this type of establishment almost-leans in the direction of the former.

H

Almost-habit, *n.* A tendency in manner or behavior that has not fully settled, and to others is still only almost-predictable.

Almost-habitue, *n.* An occasional visitor.

Almost-hacienda, *n.* A large lot, with an only modest dwelling.

Almost-hack, *v.t.* To almost-prevail over an almost-secure mostly-defensive almost-system (especially while aiming for the soft parts).

Almost-haggle, *v.t.* To attempt to wrangle over price with a sales clerk who is unauthorized to make deals.

Almost-half, *adj., n.* Approximately half. Or, the number 0.4321. Or, one third. Or, even, one over pi. Essentially, unless something is divided so there is an exactly equal volume or molecular count on both sides, each side is just slightly over or under half. The proverbial glass is therefore almost-never half-full or half-empty, but rather it is almost-half full or almost-half empty. To say that a particular glass is half-full or half-empty is therefore to either be unduly optimistic, or extremely idealistic.

Almost-hammer, *n.* A screwdriver handle, or shoe heel, or fist when used as a hammer.

Almost-handkerchief, *n.* A paper tissue, or piece of someone's clothing used in the near-appeasement of a dose.

Almost-happen, *v.t.* Almost-shockingly perhaps, most things only almost-happen. Something usually stops things from going all the way. We only grow almost-up, and almost-learn almost-knowledge from a mostly educational almost-institution (little more than a building with people in it), and eventually settle for a job and career that was not the one almost-in our dreams. Your job probably entails keeping people, and machines, and growth in check; and limiting the effects of certain actions. You boss lets you know that you are only almost-ready for advancement. Your projects sometimes end prematurely. And your efforts — as almost-well meaning as they are — are often thwarted by other almost-as-nearly well-meaning efforts. That's when you go almost-home (to a pub) feeling almost-defeated. Almost-out of frustration you almost-bust almost-out in almost-speak: "We almost-succeeded!" And the next day you wake up and do almost the same things again. Almost-all is for almost-naught. [See almost-knowledge, almost-principle.]

Almost-happy, *adj.* Happiness is almost-always mitigated in some way. We are happy about some things, and not happy about others. And if we think of only the things we just thought we were happy about, we're really only happy about some parts of those things and not happy about others (as we almost-deconstruct our happiness). We might be almost-happy with Junior's grades, or almost-happy with the election results, or almost-happy with our spouse, our house, our lot in life, our level of happiness, and so on. An almost-favorite pastime might be to think of ways to improve one's almost-level of almost-happiness. (But that kind of thinking can wait if the football game happens to be on television.)

Almost-harangue, *n.* A brief complaint. Or, if the almost-passionate words are yours, constructive criticism.

Almost-harass, *v.t.* To almost-persistently disturb someone who almost-enjoys being distracted (probably because a fairly special relationship exists). Children are particularly good at this, and adults find themselves constantly relearning from the younger set how to get what you want almost-nicely.

Almost-harmless, *adj.* Not likely to cause harm, or at least serious harm. In h2g2 parlance, "mostly harmless." In Douglas Adams's series of novels: *The Hitchhiker's Guide to the Galaxy*, the entry for "Earth" in the Guide was updated from: "Harmless," to "Mostly harmless."

Almost-harmonize, *v.* As in: To play a violin well.

Almost-haste, *n.* The kind of agitated bustle that makes it almost-excusable if you forget small details. (I am writing the in almost-haste.)

Almost-hat, *n.* Cap.

Almost-hate, *n.* Dislike. You might hate your job, or some people, but there are probably other jobs and people you hate more.

Almost-have, *v.t.* Whatever is considered *within* some almost-abstract almost-boundary. Nobody fully possesses anything, because possession is merely a social construction. Or, nearly being in almost-possession of whatever is on your shopping list.

Almost-hawker, *n.* A keeper of pigeons, sparrows, or some "lesser" bird than a hawk. Or, someone who sells over the Internet.

Almost-haywire, *adj.* How things get when the almost-method is applied to the otherwise just almost-madness.

Almost-hazard, *n.* A source of some risk or disadvantage, but not really a source of danger. Golf-course "hazards" are really almost-hazards.

Almost-head, *n.* Neck. Or, vice-president in charge of body parts.

Almost-headline, *n.* Subtitle.

Almost-health, *n.* What you have while you await better health. Anyone who says they are completely healthy just hasn't been subjected to the right tests yet. Almost-fire almost-up the almost-machines!

Almost-hearing, *n.* "What did you say?"

Almost-heart, *v.t., adj.* As in: "I almost-heart you." Which means, not in the heart of hearts, but more like in the spleen of hearts. Or, near the middle.

Almost-heavy, *adj.* Between twenty and fifty pounds. Like, if you have a little brother who weighs forty-eight pounds, you could say of him: "He's only almost-heavy, he's my brother."

Almost-hedonism, *n.* The almost-systematic pursuit of almost-fun while still managing to stay out of jail.

Almost-hefty, *adj.* What a phone bill usually is.

Almost-hegemony, *n.* The social, cultural, ideological, political, or economic influence exerted by an almost-dominant almost-group.

Almost-help, *v., n.* What most help is. (It's hard to find good help these days.)

Almost-here, *adv., n., adj.* Near here, but they were running late and then got tied up in traffic. Or, here but on the phone, or in the bathroom. Or, nearly gone.

Almost-heritage, *n.* Something fairly traditional. Or, almost-all of the almost-stuff in the past. Also, the kind of almost-stuff you can almost-pass almost-on.

Almost-hero, *n.* An average person observed to be doing something significantly better than average.

Almost-heuristic, *adj., n.* Learning or problem-solving in an almost hit-and-miss fashion.

Almost-hibernate, *v.i.* To sleep for an unusually long time.

Almost-hierarchy, *n.* Any top-down ranking that is only sometimes relevant. For example, where the usual "pecking order" is temporarily trumped by someone's physical appearance, connections, personality, unique experiences, or specific knowledge.

Almost-hindsight, *n.* Mizzensight. Or, foresight that occurs to you just after the point where it would have been useful to you.

Almost-hint, *n., v.* Almost-beat (circumvent, strike) around some almost-bush (clump, tundra, non-professional).

Almost-hinterland, *n.* Suburb.

Almost-hirsute, *adj.* Hairy, but not too hairy.

Almost-history, *n.* What happened previously, given that we don't know all of it, and that it is misty, deep, dark, and even smelly in places. History is hard to know, because everyone tells it like it almost was.

Almost-hit, *v.t.* Maxwell Smart always just "missed it by *that* much."

Almost-hitched, *adj.* Engaged.

Almost-home, *n.* Your girlfriend's (or boyfriend's) place. Your best friend's place. Your parent's place. Anywhere that is not home that almost-seems like home because you have been there for so long (how you might feel about your hotel room after a few days). Earth, if you are a space-alien getting acclimated.

Almost-homework, *n.* Work that never gets officially assigned to you by your teacher or boss, but if you don't do it your project suffers.

Almost-homogeneous, *adj.* A thing comprised of things that are at least mostly almost-similar.

Almost-honest, *adj.* Tactful.

Almost-hope, *n.* What you have when you've lost hope. Even a no-hope has almost-hope.

Almost-horizontal, *adj.* Not quite level. Perhaps, reclining.

Almost-horse, *n.* Donkey. Shetland pony. Bouvier.

Almost-hot, *adj.* Cool. According to the almost-temperature scale (from almost-top to almost-bottom): **hot** (best if you let someone else handle it), **cool** (or almost-hot, interesting, something your friends will like, and you still won't get arrested for wearing it), **warm** (nearly there, almost-cool), **lukewarm** (tepid, half-baked, almost-cold), **cold** (crisp, uninteresting, uninterested, sick, far away). [See almost-cool, almost-uncool.] [Compare also: Marshall McLuhan's hot (low-participation), cool (high-participation).]

Almost-hour, *n.* Fifty-nine minutes. Or, elevenish. Or, portentously, the hour before the hour you are dreading. [See almost-morning, and almost-afternoon.]

Almost-house, *n.* Apartment. Shack. Double-wide. Or, what's left of your house after a hurricane or tornado hits.

Almost-household, *n.* All the people you are supporting in addition to those that live in your house: ex-wives, kids at college, that parent or grandparent in a nursing home, bartenders, bookies.

Almost-hug, *v.t.* The placing of one arm around someone else's shoulders in a loving, congratulatory, or consoling way.

Almost-huge, *adj.* Big. Large.

Almost-human, *adj.* Anything not completely human, but that still might need to be ruled by human laws (for example: other primates, androids or cyborgs, or extraterrestrials of the almost-nice kind). Or, anything that can sometimes pass for human.

Almost-humanism, *n.* The not particularly radical view that humans are not completely "human" most of the time. They are usually found trying to be something else, including trying to be something other than themselves.

Almost-humdinger, *n.* A person, thing, or idea that is almost-extraordinary, almost-excellent, or almost-striking in some way. You might use the word "humdinger" casually in reference to your favorite new gadget but not to your favorite brand of ice cream, whereas "almost-humdinger" might actually become a brand or flavor of ice cream.

Almost-humor, *n.* Unlike with the more-objective forms of humor, almost-humor only exists if you find "this almost-kind of almost-stuff" funny (because this is mostly a subjective almost-matter).

Almost-hunch, *n.* Women's intuition. Both men and women have hunches, but this is something for which there is no male equivalent.

Almost-hungry, *adj.* Peckish.

Almost-hurricane, *n.* Tropical storm.

Almost-husband, *n.* Fiancé. Live-in boyfriend. Handyman. [See almost-wife.]

Almost-hypermammiferous, *adj.* A mere D-cup size. Having larger than average breasts, but not in a freakish way.

Almost-hypostatize, *v.t.* To treat as almost-real something that may not even almost-exist (like a round square).

I

Almost-icon, *n.* A fairly emblematic sign that is itself vague, or is of something that is vague. (For example, a simple picture of a glass of water that is almost full, or an unlabeled pie chart).

Almost-iconoclast, *n.* A person who doesn't so much challenge the almost-established almost-order, or bust up a frame, as much as suggest almost-aspects and emphasize the almost-principle in such a way that others just go away scratching their heads.

Almost-id, *n.* One of the three almost-divisions of the almost-psyche that is almost-completely almost-unconscious, and is the almost-source from which almost-instinctual almost-needs and almost-desires almost-emerge. [See almost-ego, almost-superego, almost-psyche.]

Almost-idea, *n.* A perception, or sensation. Or, an idea that hasn't completely formed, taken its final shape, or jelled yet (and perhaps continues to morph, and almost-evolve, and stay under the radar of consciousness, waiting to almost-pounce).

Almost-ideal, *n., adj.* Something that is an exceptional version of its type. Or, a close approximation to the ideal. Or, the ideal of anything that is almost-something, or almost-almost. (For example, the almost-ideal child still grows into a more mature version of themselves.) [See almost-something, almost-almost.]

Almost-indefatigable, *adj.* Almost-incapable of being fatigued.

Almost-identical, *adj.* Nearly the same.

Almost-identity, *n.* Any identity that anyone thinks they have, or that another has. [See almost-aspect, Almost-Aristotle.]

Almost-ideology, *n.* An ideology that hasn't completely formed, taken its final shape, or jelled yet (and perhaps continues to morph, and almost-evolve, and stay under the radar of social consciousness, waiting to almost-pounce).

Almost-idiocracy, *n.* A social system where decision-making has become so provisional and irresolute that the net effect is almost the same as it would be in a real idiocracy (where the decisions made are typically unwise or illogical ones).

Almost-idiom, *n.* The idiom of speech that uses almost-words. Verbal or written almost-speak. Or, the application of the almost-method and the almost-way when speaking and writing. Or, an almost-artistic manner or style in applying the almost-method. [See almost-method, almost-speak, almost-way.]

Almost-idle, *adj.* Still fidgeting.

Almost-ignoble, *adj.* At a level not so base, despicable, or wretched that one can't stoop to it on occasion without losing face.

Almost-ignominy, *n.* Embarrassment.

Almost-ignore, *v.t.* Monitor with technology.

Almost-illegal, *adj.* An activity that is so morally questionable or potentially harmful that it is probably illegal somewhere else.

Almost-illegible, *adj.* Incapable of being read, except with the assistance of modern chemistry or technology.

Almost-illuminating, *adj., v.t.* Revealing that something is missing. Or, showing figuratively, or without the use of light. Or, revealing almost-aspects.

Almost-illusions, *n.* Those things you thought you thought you saw.

Almost-ilk, *n.* The likes of the likes of something.

Almost-imagine, *v.* To have vague notions about. Possibly, to be able to describe the box (size, shape), but not the contents (internal structures, behaviors).

Almost-imitate, *v.t.* Trying to imitate and getting it wrong; or, adding just enough of your own originality that you can't be sued for plagiarism, copyright infringement, patent infringement, or the like.

Almost-immaterial, *adj.* Of very little substantial consequence.

Almost-immediate, *adj.* Very close in time or space.

Almost-immigrant, *n.* Second or third generation immigrant.

Almost-immovable, *adj.* Anything deemed immovable.

Almost-immune, *adj.* Possessing a high resistance to disease or contamination.

Almost-impact, *v.t.* Most impacts in the movies. This could be a fake punch (with sound effect), or something more elaborate with special effects.

Almost-impair, *v.t.* Hinder.

Almost-impale, *v.t.* Poke at, perhaps playfully (as with a stick, or Samurai sword).

Almost-impart, *v.t.* To give back. Or, to tender or proffer.

Almost-impeach, *v.t.* To charge (a public official) before a tribunal with misconduct in office, but to *not* succeed.

Almost-imperative, *n., adj.* A hypothetical imperative (a practical necessity, or means to an end), or a categorical imperative (if you still have the choice not to do it), to use Immanuel Kant's distinctions. Basically, everything on your list of things to do that is fairly important, but not essential. Or, everything on your boss's list of things for you to do.

Almost-impersonate, *v.t.* To attempt to impersonate, but to get caught at it. Or, to impersonate in a joking way. [See Almost-Aristotle.]

Almost-imperturbable, *adj.* Almost-cool, almost-calm, and almost-collected, but given to occasional vituperations and unpredictability.

Almost-impervious, *adj.* Will let some things through (typically the wrong things, but not always).

Almost-implacable, *adj.* Pleased or satisfied by exceedingly few things.

Almost-implication, *n.* A meaning that can be denied. (As in: "This almost implies that you're a capitalist, except for all of your socialist leanings.") Or, what is suggested by an almost-statement or almost-theory, especially as it pertains to other almost-stuff.

Almost-imply, *v.t.* When an absence of something is suggestive (because there is nothing there to do the implying).

Almost-import, *v.t.* When all of your stuff gets stopped at the border, or is stolen. Or, when you import almost-stuff.

Almost-importune, *v.t.* To ask nicely once, or twice, or even three times, . . . but not as many as a nine hundred and eighty-seven times.

Almost-imposition, *n.* As seen by the salesman, teacher, or co-worker, an imposition that you *should* welcome. Or, one such situation that you actually do welcome even though you are busy.

Almost-impossible, *adj.* Very difficult. Possible only if a lot of time and other resources were thrown at the problem. Or, possible only with unconscionable cost. Or, considered to be possible if more research were done.

Almost-imprison, *v.t.* To confine under "house arrest."

Almost-improve, *v.t.* To create a "better" next version of something while leaving it as unwieldy or inefficient as the previous version. (Software vendors do this all the time, and then wonder why they lose market share.)

Almost-impudent, *adj.* Both smart and bold.

Almost-inadmissible, *adj.* Through skillfully talking about inadmissible evidence indirectly in front of a judge or jury, a lawyer may sometimes be able to introduce that evidence anyway, and it may even help decide the case.

Almost-inalienable, *adj.* Inalienable (except with attributes). Perhaps, also, variable (inconstant).

Almost-inboard, *adv., adj.* Located on top, under a housing. Or, more noisy than an inboard.

Almost-incapable, *adj.* Someone who needs a kick in the butt.

Almost-inch, *n.* Exactly 0.987654321 inch. Or, 2.5 cm.

Almost-incite, *v.t.* To move to almost-action.

Almost-include, *v.t.* Involve.

Almost-income, *n.* A fringe benefit.

Almost-incommensurable, *adj.* Comparable in profound ways.

Almost-inconceivable, *adj.* Conceivable, just strange or improbable.

Almost-incorporated, *adj.* A partnership or sole-proprietorship with aspirations and rising sales numbers.

Almost-incremental, *adj.* More gradual than incremental.

Almost-indefinite, *adj.* A particular general or generic thing.

Almost-indentured, *adj.* Someone almost-free to go far away.

Almost-independent, *adj.* Seemingly independent when they are with friends, or out until all hours of the night, but not when they ask you for money or need to find that special piece of clothing of theirs.

Almost-index, *n.* A possible alphabetical index for the Almost-Dictionary (almost-pointless, and therefore almost-nonexistent).

Almost-indicator, *n.* An indicator that only indicates in a highly correlated way. (Just because someone is tall that does not mean they are a basketball player.)

Almost-indifferent, *adj.* Somewhat caring. [See almost-listening.]

Almost-indigent, *adj.* Someone not so poor or needy that they can't be taxed more.

Almost-individual, *n., adj.* Any member of a group. Or, a sheep standing almost-up on his hind legs singing: "I gotta be almost-me."

Almost-indoctrinate, *v.t.* When you teach them to be skeptical about what anyone says, including you. Or, to teach someone the almost-doctrine. [See almost-doctrine.]

Almost-indolent, *adj.* Someone who works hard at being lazy.

Almost-induction, *n.* Any amplifying inference that is still considered so indisputable that nobody bothers with how you arrive at the conclusion. Or, a convincing argument for a generality by way of analogy, or anecdote. Or, a "proof" that relies on questionable data. Or, an educated guess about the "big picture."

Almost-industrial, *adj.* What farming, fishing, and forestry are, when they are not completely industrial.

Almost-industrialize, *v.t.* To teach them how to buy fishing trawlers with the relief money, rather than just giving them fish. Or, to introduce only low-tech stuff.

Almost-ineffective, *adj.* Barely effective, and perhaps disappointingly so.

Almost-inefficiency, *n.* All six billion of us competing with each other, and by doing roughly the same kinds of things.

Almost-inelastic, *adj.* Only a little bit elastic.

Almost-inevitable, *adj.* The future is never certain, only almost-certain. (Taxes may be abolished, and aging could be cured, you just never know.)

Almost-infer, *v.t.* Surmise. To jump to a conclusion based on meager or insufficient evidence.

Almost-inferior, *adj.* Maybe inferior in some ways, but superior in others. (Probably mediocre in most ways.)

Almost-infinite, *adj.* Of a finite number so large that you could never reach it by counting (starting at a low number). Or, of a universe so small that people have become bored with it before ever leaving their home planet.

Almost-inflation, *n.* When there has been an increase in the volume of money and credit relative to available goods and services, but prices haven't gone up yet.

Almost-informal, *adj.* Formal, or respecting protocols, but also allowing for humor or lightheartedness.

Almost-informant, *n.* One who sets you on the right path, but doesn't give almost everything away.

Almost-information, *n.* Data with no descriptors (and therefore undeclared meaning). Or, information from a source that is unenlightened or unreliable. Or, when to ask a question is to almost-answer it, and so you don't.

Almost-informative, *adj.* Someone who only tells you part of the information (like what you get on most newscasts). [See almost-news, almost-information.]

Almost-inhabit, *v.t.* Visit.

Almost-inhale, *v.* Breathe wafts in through the nose.

Almost-inhibit, *v.t.* When most is prevented, but something gets through.

Almost-inhuman, *adj.* Lacking in pity or emotion. Or, quite savage or freaky.

Almost-inimical, *adj.* Almost everyone, almost all the time.

Almost-inimitable, *adj.* Inimitable.

Almost-initial, *adj.* Signing your name with an "X." Or, to initial in other than your usual way, so that if that decision boomerangs you have deniability.

Almost-initiate, *v.t.* To start the ball rolling by asking a seemingly-innocuous question (like some executives are prone to do during a review of their own plant). "Let's see what happens if I introduce this subject . . . ."

Almost-initiative, *n.* When the get-up-and-go has got up and left for the kitchen and the refrigerator.

Almost-inland, *adj.* In the tourism industry it is assumed that having your establishment right on the beach is much better than being inland, and, also, better than being almost-inland (three streets back from the beach). When you are almost-inland, flooding may still be an issue. (Being within range of a ship's cannon fire may also be an issue. Almost-arrgh!)

Almost-inmate, *n.* Anyone with a monitoring device attached to their ankle.

Almost-innate, *adj.* A trait that might emerge naturally but that is also enhanced or reinforced by social interaction. Any trait requiring both nature and nurture.

Almost-innocent, *adj.* Not guilty enough to go to jail.

Almost-innovate, *v.t.* To copy ideas in the creating of a new product or service in such a way that they seem novel. [See almost-mutate.]

Almost-innovation, *n.* Maintaining an ever-better status quo without introducing all the risks and disadvantages that accompany real change.

Almost-inordinate, *adj.* Reasonable, but bordering on excessive, undue, unregulated, or immoderate.

Almost-input, *n.* Information that was initially fed into a computer, but then got rejected by a filter program.

Almost-inquire, *v.t.* To bang one's fist down on the counter, then take a good look at the clerk, and the manager, and the condition of the office, and change one's mind about inquiring after all (and just ask for directions or something instead).

Almost-inroad, *n.* A one-way road that only leads out. Or, an almost-journey into almost-abstract thought (and the almost-zone) that leads to where you almost-want to almost-go (in some almost-way) and that ends with an almost-realization.

Almost-insertion, *n.* Hanging around outside, perhaps preventing other things from inserting. (Just what are we almost-talking about here?) [See almost-method.]

Almost-inside, *prep., adj., n.* Perhaps, on the porch or deck. Or, partly outside (perhaps, just talking at the open door).

Almost-insolent, *adj.* A tad impolite or discourteous.

Almost-inspect, *v.t.* What inspectors do, especially if they are in a hurry. What almost-inspectors do when they almost-stick to the almost-method. [See almost-inspector.]

Almost-inspection, *n.* Checking, reviewing, analyzing, or verifying, but to almost-standards. [See almost-standard.]

Almost-inspector, *n.* Someone who almost-performs an inspection. Or, someone who performs an almost-inspection. Or, someone who almost-performs an almost-inspection.

Almost-installment, *n.* How your tenants want to pay you. Or, the installment of almost anything.

Almost-instant, *n., adj.* Time enough for someone to notice, if they are really paying attention. (Each frame of a movie is shown for only an almost-instant.)

Almost-instinct, *n.* A behavior that is attributable more to nature than nurture. Or, a behavior that is attributable to nature and nurture almost-equally. Or, a behavior that is attributable more to nurture than nature (but it took a lot of practice).

Almost-institution, *n.* Institution.

Almost-instrument, *n.* An instrument that is missing a key component.

Almost-insufficient, *adj.* Sufficient.

Almost-insults, *n.* Derogatory remarks meant in a nice way. Or, derogatory remarks meant as constructive criticism. Or, even optimistic constructive criticism made so that others can hear. Or, anything that would be taken the wrong way. Or, any comment at all made about "your relationship" by you. [See almost-meant.]

Almost-insuperable, *adj.* Insuperable.

Almost-insurable, *adj.* When the thing or the situation is changing quickly enough that insuring it would be almost-pointless.

Almost-insurrection, *n.* A failed insurrection. Or, almost any action or speech at all (as perceived by the powers that be).

Almost-integrated, *adj.* Brought together, and forced to get along. Or, lacking enough common interests.

Almost-intentional, *adj.* Of speech or action that is more or less socially unavoidable (like helping the little old lady across the street). People do extraordinary things when they find themselves in situations they can't escape.

Almost-interactive, *adj.* When what you are trying to interact with won't cooperate.

Almost-intercourse, *n.* Very heavy petting. Or, a conversation in almost-speak that almost goes somewhere.

Almost-interest, *n.* Mild curiosity. Or, an interest in almost-stuff, almost-speak, almost-world, . . . or almost-something.

Almost-interested, *adj.* When you start to play with a little doohickey on the coffee table.

Almost-interesting, *adj.* Most of the people, things, and ideas around you most of the time. The space between meanings in a semantic space. [Also, see any entry in an almost-standard dictionary.]

Almost-interface, *n.* A virtual interface.

Almost-interfere, *v.* To show up, but not say anything.

Almost-intermediary, *n.* Informal go-between (such as a kid sister).

Almost-intermission, *n.* Any time you really need to go. (Or, the boring part of the movie or show.)

Almost-internal, *adj.* Up your nose, in your outer ear, or between your teeth.

Almost-international, *adj.* On the Internet.

Almost-interpret, *v.t.* To explain the meaning of something, but not so well that the puzzled looks are gone from their faces.

Almost-interrupt, *v.t.* Put your hand up. (And then if they don't get the hint: cough, sneeze, or drop a book.)

Almost-interview, *n., v.t.* Just asking a few questions. Or, when an interview is interrupted, or for some other reason it is not completed.

Almost-intimacy, *n.* Pillow talk about sports, or work, or pillows. Or, talking about people and events in your life, but not about your thoughts and feelings. Or, "Yes, dear. Whatever you say, dear," and kicking the intimacy-can down the road, where it might be almost-safer.

Almost-intractable, *adj.* Only somewhat easy to manage, or only somewhat unruly.

Almost-intrepid, *adj.* Quite normal with respect to levels of personal fearlessness, fortitude, and endurance.

Almost-introduce, *v.t.* When you just wave your beer bottle alternately at the two people in front of you, but don't speak the introduction because you're eating something.

Almost-invade, *v.t.* Carpet bomb with propaganda messages. Or, approach with threatening military power. Or, trespass. Or, infringe or offend in a small way.

Almost-invent, *v.t.* Re-invent (as in: the wheel, the mousetrap, the phone).

Almost-invest, *v.t.* Spending a lot of time on something, but little money (researching a stock but not buying it). Or, spending a lot of money on something, but little time (gambling on a stock without researching it). Or, investing in almost-stuff (like almost-art), or unfinished projects.

Almost-investigate, *v.t.* What most investigators do (especially those practiced in the almost-method). [See almost-method.]

Almost-invidious, *adj.* What would be invidious if it wasn't done in such a sweet, sexy, fascinating, or ameliorative way.

Almost-invincible, *adj.* Invincible.

Almost-invisible, *adj.* Inconspicuous. Perhaps, something hiding in plain sight. Perhaps, something the same color as the thing behind it. Or, very small.

Almost-invite, *v.t.* When you invite via email (or some other indirect way), and for some reason the intended recipient doesn't receive the invitation in time for the event.

Almost-invoice, *n., v.t.* As is common in the insurance industry, before sending you the invoice they send you information as to your coverage and options (an almost-invoice), so that you can choose to change things.

Almost-Irish, *adj., n.* Non-Irish folk when they dress and act Irish, especially when they wear the color green, and drink copiously.

Almost-irreconcilable, *adj.* Differences that *can* be worked out if certain people are less stubborn or unrealistic.

Almost-irreducible, *adj.* Next to impossible to make simpler or smaller (like an unsmashed atom). Or, easily reducible but not without loss (like the book *Moby-Dick*).

Almost-irrelevant, *adj.* Due to increased interconnectedness, almost-nothing has no relevance.

Almost- irresistible, *adj.* Resistible, but very tempting. Nearly impossible to withstand or contravene.

Almost-irresponsible, *adj.* Responsible, but carefree. Or, responsible, but with multiple allegiances.

Almost-irrevocable, *adj.* The equivalent of really letting the cat out of the bag, . . . but indoors (instead of outdoors).

Almost-island, *n.* A peninsula. A grounding reef that is just below the surface of the water.

Almost-issuance, *v.t.* When the issuance is in the works.

Almost-issue, *n.* A complaint or anomaly that is not a big deal. Or, when someone has the kind of issue that an almost-psychologist can almost-handle. [See almost-psychology, almost-therapy.]

Almost-itch, *n., v.* Twitch. Or, how your skin feels just before it becomes itchy. Any skin sensation that is not an itch exactly, but it wants scratching. Or, an urge to finish something (like when you notice that you missed a spot while shaving, or cleaning the floor).

Almost-itty-bitty, *adj.* Pretty small.

J

Almost-jackpot, *n.* Second or third prize.

Almost-jaded, *adj.* Not so exhausted, apathetic, or cynical from experience that one cannot become significantly more so.

Almost-jail, *n.* Near the jail. Or, in the back seat of a police car. Or, your workplace or domicile, depending on how you feel about those places. Or, wherever you are when you don't want to be there.

Almost-janissary, *n.* An almost-member of an almost-group of almost-loyal and almost-subservient troops, officials, or supporters (perhaps, one who is really just a contractor).

Almost-jejune, *adj.* Having some small nutritive value, significance, or appeal (dull lectures, boring art).

Almost-jeopardize, *v.t.* To expose something (a plan, or real property, or lives) to a minor menace or two, but not to major risk.

Almost-jerk, *v.* To move something quickly, but slowly enough that you don't surprise anyone.

Almost-jester, *n.* A humorist that isn't very funny.

Almost-jewel, *n.* A gemstone not completely cut and polished. Almost-figuratively, someone who still has a few rough edges.

Almost-jiffy, *n.* An indefinite almost-short period of time.

Almost-jittery, *adj.* Nervous, tense, and wary, but still in control (not shaking).

Almost-job, *n.* A sinecure, apprenticeship, charity work, or a part-time job that doesn't pay enough to live on. Or, when you are told you can start work in a week or two. Or, work that is part of an almost-career.

Almost-join, *v.* Hang around.

Almost-joint, *n.* A hole in the wall (dive, honky-tonk). A place where two things don't quite connect.

Almost-jointly, *adv.* When two or more maneuvers or projects are undertaken with combined planning and resources, but the agendas of each are still somewhat at odds with one another.

Almost-joking, *v.i.* When the "joke" makes a fairly serious point. This is sometimes referred to as "half-joking," or "partly-joking."

Almost-jonesing, *v.t.* Craving something salutary or wholesome. For example, the still urge toward exercise, or the next hug.

Almost-journal, *n.* A notebook with no special pre-printed lines. A publication that appears at irregular intervals.

Almost-journalism, *n.* The kind of reporting that is not subject to review before publication (for example, what a blogger does). Or, the kind of reporting that *is* subject to review before publication, so it is "cleaned up" ahead of time, and the final version is a kiss-ass, milquetoast piece riddled with euphemisms, obfuscations, and suspicious omissions. Or, almost-digging almost-deep for something newsworthy to say, and finding more than you can possibly imagine.

Almost-journey, *n.* When you travel to a place in your mind, without actually going there. [See almost-travel.]

Almost-judgment, *n.* An informal, partial, tentative, or very quick educated guess, opinion, or decision. Oddly enough, because life moves so fast, almost-all of what happens depends on these almost-things. [See almost-mutate.]

Almost-judicial, *adj.* Quasi-judicial, or almost-involving almost-judgment.

Almost-judiciary, *n.* An unofficial or temporary body with some judicial powers, but whose decisions may need to be ratified by a more official and less-temporary agency later.

Almost-juice, *n.* A liquid that tastes the way real juice might.

Almost-juicy, *adj.* What could have been more juicy (fruit picked too early). Or, the Censor's cut. Or, when it doesn't name names.

Almost-jumbo, *adj.* Large. But not so large that Mom makes you pay for it out of your own pocket money. Ample.

Almost-jump, *v.* To stretch up or spring just a little with one's feet. Perhaps, not enough to actually leave the ground (like when a wide receiver tries to make a catch before going out of bounds).

Almost-jungle, *n.* Woods, forest, or a large treed backyard. Or, an armpit. Or, the big city. Or, almost-generally, almost-out almost-there.

Almost-junior, *adj.* When someone is temporarily slightly lower in rank only because they are a new-hire, and not because they lack experience or credentials.

Almost-junk, *n.* Something of little value. [See almost-decrepit, almost-discard, almost-garbage, almost-waste, almost-worthless, and most television.]

Almost-jurisdiction, *n.* The scope of an almost-judiciary. Or, a jurisdiction that pertains to almost-stuff.

Almost-jurisprudence, *n.* The consideration and application of fairness, values, practicality, and normative influences in social situations, without appealing to the notions of natural law, positive law, or other often over-generalized almost-under pinnings of actual laws. Or, according to H. L. A. Hart's description of the "open texture" of law: rules have a core of fairly determinate meaning and a fringe of vagueness where they border on other rules and the contexts of particular cases. Or, the use of the almost-method and the almost-way when almost-applying the law.

Almost-jury, *n.* When the jury is not in court, or "hung," or "deliberating," or "eating lunch," and cannot be found anywhere.

Almost-justice, *n.* Justice. [See almost-fair.]

Almost-justification, *n.* When the explanation given seems almost-reasonable or almost-believable. "You need to give me money because I need it."

Almost-just-in-time, *adj.* A little late. A supply chain management strategy wherein parts are produced or delivered only after the customer has called twice and then threatens in writing with legal action.

Almost-juxtaposition, *n.* When the two or more things considered together are found to be different aspects of the same thing.

K

Almost-keen, *adj.* Somewhat enthusiastic, but with reservations.

Almost-keep, *v.t.* When someone lends something to you for an indefinite period, then you may only almost-keep it (because they could ask for it back at any time). [See almost-have, almost-possess.]

Almost-keg, *n.* What's left of the full keg a few seconds after you turn your back.

Almost-kegger, *n.* When a smaller group than expected shows up (perhaps due to rain). Or, when the party is interrupted by a visit by the police department, the fire department, an ambulance, or all three.

Almost-key, *n., adj.* A prop key, or one that isn't really able to unlock the door. Or, almost-important almost-knowledge that is almost-basic to a further almost-understanding. [See almost-understanding.]

Almost-keyboard, *n.* The buttons on a gadget that are other than the full "qwerty" keyboard. Anything you have to peck at to make something happen.

Almost-keynote, *n., adj.* The introductory almost-oration before the keynote.

Almost-kidding, *v.* Being serious in an almost-funny way.

Almost-kill, *v.t.* Render helpless or almost-helpless. Or, when you "kill" a computer program or process you don't really kill it, you just stop it (render it inactive, or almost-kill it). It goes into a latent state, and it can be resuscitated at any time by reactivating it, or starting it, or, ironically, by executing it. There is nothing that really dies.

Almost-kin, *n.* Someone only almost-related (best friend, or ex-brother-in-law).

Almost-kind, *adj.* When you help a little old lady across the street, but she doesn't want to go. Or, something as almost-considerate.

Almost-kindergarten, *n.* Pre-kindergarten. Or, any room containing children—no matter how "well-behaved" they are. Or, any disorderly agitation.

Almost-king, *n.* Prince. Queen. Prime Minister. Tycoon. Someone with a lot of power.

Almost-kinky, *adj.* It has been suggested that when you use a feather it's erotic, and when you use the whole chicken it's kinky. It would follow then that when you use two breasts, a leg, and a wing, it's almost-kinky.

Almost-kiss, *n., v.t.* A kiss where the lips of one are not perfectly aligned with the lips of the other, producing less than optimal effect. Or, a blown kiss.

Almost-kit, *n.* A collection of things that usually go together or should go together, but the kind of collection that is not usually sold in kit form. (For example, all the stuff you take to the beach, or on a picnic.)

Almost-kitty, *n.* A kitty that has just been in a terrible fight and is missing a few bits. Or, an un-weaned kitty. Or, at a stretch, a stuffed animal, or cartoon kitty.

Almost-kleptomaniac, *n.* Someone who steals almost-habitually, but just to keep his or her hand in.

Almost-know, *v.t.* Almost everything that is "known" is only almost-known. (This is almost-epistemic and almost-cognitive.) One needs to be on a constant lookout for lacunae, and new almost-knowledge. [See almost-knowledge, almost-education, almost-history, almost-truth, almost-whole.]

Almost-knowledge, *n.* Incomplete knowledge. We never learn everything we could learn, and we forget details quickly after each exam. There's a gap between what is known about a subject, and everything there is to know about the subject. Likewise, there's a gap between the totality of what is known, and everything that is knowable. Or, the kind of knowledge one gets from considering almost-stuff and almost-speak. [See almost-education.]

L

Almost-labeled, *adj.* Labeled indefinitely (as in: "This box may contain kitchen stuff," or "Panic button").

Almost-labor, *n.* The work of monkeys, cart dogs, sheep dogs, hunting dogs, horses, camels, rodents in wheels, and show tigers.

Almost-lack, *v., n.* When you still have one or two little ones.

Almost-laconic, *adj.* Willing to chat, but out of breath.

Almost-ladder, *n.* Stepladder (especially one with just two or three steps).

Almost-laden, *adj.* When there is still room for one or two more straws on the camel's back.

Almost-lady, *n.* A woman with a somewhat unladylike deportment or standing.

Almost-lag, *n., v.* When one thing follows another chronologically quite quickly. Or, like jet-lag, you experience it when you stop reading or speaking in the almost-idiom and start reading or speaking almost-normally again.

Almost-lamb, *n.* A sheep fetus.

Almost-lame, *adj.* Most, but not all television.

Almost-land, *n.* An almost-real almost-place (not necessarily almost-always almost-surrounded by almost-water). [See almost-noplaceville, almost-real, almost-zone.]

Almost-landed, *adj.* Did not quite land yet, or will soon. For example, on the Apollo 11 mission, of the situation just before Neil Armstrong said the famous line: "The *Eagle* has landed."

Almost-landfill, *n.* Garbage that is still at the curb.

Almost-landlord, *n.* The girl in the apartment-complex office that knows how to use software and answer the phone, but who never seems to be authorized to take action on whatever it is that needs doing. Her favorite phrase: "I sure don't."

Almost-landmark, *n.* A structure right beside a landmark. Or, a temporary landmark (like a circus tent). What a hot-dog vendor tries to be.

Almost-landslide, *n., v.i.* Winning by more than a little, and less than a lot.

Almost-lane, *n.* Cow path.

Almost-language, *n.* An incomplete language, the jargon of a certain profession, or that part of a language that is only almost-separate (such as almost-speak).

Almost-lap, *n.* The lap of a child.

Almost-larceny, *n.* Somewhere between larceny and petit larceny is almost-larceny.

Almost-large, *adj.* Medium. Pretty big.

Almost-last, *adj.* Someone whose last name starts with an "S" or "T."

Almost-late, *adj.* On time.

Almost-lately, *adv.* Recently, . . . but months ago, actually.

Almost-latest, *adj.* The one before the latest. Or the one before that.

Almost-laugh, *v.i., n.* Chuckle. Snicker. Titter. Giggle. Smirk.

Almost-launch, *v.t.* When you decide not to launch immediately but instead to retool or make last-minute modifications before a possible future launch. This could be done because of how the market has shifted.

Almost-laundry, *n.* Two dirty t-shirts and some underwear (not enough for an almost-full load).

Almost-lavish, *adj.* With a few extras.

Almost-law, *n.* A strict but non-binding custom or practice of a community. Or, a recently enacted law that is not yet in effect.

Almost-lawful, *adj.* Something you can get away with because they are not enforcing the law. (This happens often with misdemeanor activity.)

Almost-lawless, *adj.* Creative. Or, destructive.

Almost-layer, *n.* Any imprecisely indicated range within a full spectrum. Or, an extremely thin layer between thicker layers (typically of glue, water, air, fruit filling, or almost-stuff).

Almost-lead, *v.t.* To lead with the permission and oversight of others. [See almost-leading, almost-way.]

Almost-leader, *n.* First mate, vice president, vice principal, cinematographer, supervisor, sidekick, structural engineer, or business analyst.

Almost-leadership, *n.* "Blowing noses," working spreadsheets, calling meetings, and talking on the phone a lot. Most leadership is actually almost-leadership.

Almost-leading, *adj.* Someone who is neither foremost nor providing direction or guidance, but, rather, is doing something more akin to "following from in front." What a business typically finds itself doing after acquiring all of the threatening competitors in the industry.

Almost-leak, *v.t.* Saying something that gets an investigator suspicious.

Almost-lean, *adj.* Just above your "fighting weight."

Almost-learn, *v.t.* To not learn well enough that another lesson on the same topic would not be worthwhile. What somebody who keeps repeating the same mistakes must be doing.

Almost-lease, *v.t.* Rent.

Almost-least, *adj., n.* Next-to-least. Or, nowhere near the greatest.

Almost-leather, *n.* Vinyl.

Almost-leave, *v.t.* When you make like a tree, but don't leaf.

Almost-lecture, *n., v.* Almost-formal instructions given in an almost-informal setting.

Almost-legacy, *adj., n.* Of an outdated computer system that is still vital.

Almost-legal, *adj.* Quazi-legal (being legal in some sense, or to some degree). Or, jailbait.

Almost-legalize, *v.t.* To suspend the enforcement of a restrictive law. (There are many laws that are still "on the books" just in case they are almost-needed.)

Almost-legitimate, *adj.* Ok, as long as everyone you're with agrees not to tell anyone.

Almost-leisure, *n.* Doing something that seems like work during your time off from work (like gardening, or food shopping).

Almost-lemon, *adj., n.* Most cars are not made with so little quality that people return them immediately. (Most of us drive oranges or limes, rather than lemons.)

Almost-lend, *v.t.* When you give money to someone who asks to "borrow" it, but you know there is little chance of them ever repaying it. Or, to consider lending, but then deciding not to lend.

Almost-letter, *n.* A note, memo, or email.

Almost-levee, *n.* The kind that won't withstand the worst storms (hurricanes or tornados).

Almost-level, *adj.* Where the dishes don't slide off the table, but a ball does still roll off the table. A thing that was "level" until some smart-ass decided to check.

Almost-lever, *n.* A software lever, like you might find on a modern slot machine.

Almost-leverage, *n.* The cogency that comes from thinking of almost-angles and speaking in almost-speak. [See almost-angle, almost-speak.]

Almost-liability, *n.* A debt on the balance sheet of a company that is going through bankruptcy proceedings (and so it may not ever be repaid). Or, a child that is now old enough to be able to help out with the farm work (they almost-graduated from "liability" to "almost-liability").

Almost-libel, *n.* Defamatory statements about things that are not legal entities (such as industries, institutions, ideologies, famous historical events, or natural objects).

Almost-liberal, *adj., n.* Ample. Or, a conservative after they've been mugged in such a way that they needed to pay hospital bills.

Almost-liberalism, *n.* Keynsianism.

Almost-liberalize, *v.* To be less conservative.

Almost-library, *n.* A collection of books that is in a room or building mainly used for a purpose other than that of housing books. Or, a collection of media other than books. (An almost-library can be distinguished from a "pile of books" not by weight, but by whether the books are almost-sorted in some way.)

Almost-license, *n., v.t.* When you know the Fish and Game warden personally. Or, when your dad says: "You can do it, but don't tell mom."

Almost-licentious, *adj.* Frisky.

Almost-lid, *n.* A wax seal.

Almost-lie, *n., v.* To tell the truth but not the whole truth, or the truth plus a few little embellishments (from tactfulness or fear, or for selfish reasons).

Almost-lien, *n.* Documented loan.

Almost-life, *n.* The so-called "life" of someone with a desk job. Or, the state of being only almost-conscious (like a newborn, or a real dolt). The life of almost-anything animated without concomitant awareness or sentience (like a tree, or an amoeba). Or, a life that seems to be almost-employing the almost-method in the almost-way. [See almost-method, almost-way.]

Almost-lifetime, *n.* A duration in between a half-life and a life.

Almost-lifework, *n.* Most but not all of the lifework of a writer, an artist, or a composer. (These compilations are often sold with deliberate omissions so that the determined aficionado must then spend more to acquire the rest.)

Almost-lift, *v.t.* When you put you beer down and conscientiously attempt to raise something, but all you do is grunt and swear, and then take another swig of your beer and call your buddy over to help.

Almost-like, *v.* Not overly dislike.

Almost-likely, *adj., adv.* Unlikely, but there's hope, or a considerable but lesser chance than some other outcome. (For example: The quick brown fox jumps over the lazy dog.)

Almost-lime, *n.* Any other citrus fruit.

Almost-limit, *n.* A perceived limit, given that certain things almost-stay the almost-same. [See almost-constant.]

Almost-limpid, *adj.* Almost-clear and almost-simple in style.

Almost-line, *n.* A dashed line. Or, a border, once you get there. Or, a ray (a line that stops somewhere).

Almost-linear, *adj.* Not too curvy. Or, thought of as linear by neurons that go all over the place (for example: straight from here to there).

Almost-lingo, *n.* Language, in almost-speak. Or, almost-speak itself.

Almost-linguistic, *adj.* About language, but mostly about something else (neon signs, for example).

Almost-lining, *n.* Just like most clouds have an almost-silver lining, most clouds also have an almost-lining: that is, a grayish area where there are some cloudlike aspects, and partly just sky. Likewise, there are many things that are only almost-themselves around the edges. Unlike almost-silver linings, almost-linings are not always almost-viewed to be almost-completely positive.

Almost-liquid, *adj.* Something that usually flows slowly, like molasses or lava. Or, assets that have the property of being almost-liquid (bonds, CDs).

Almost-list, *n.* An incomplete list.

Almost-listening, *v.i.* Ah, . . . What? Most of the time we are only almost-listening. There is just too much to focus on (and too much that deserves our ear). Sometimes we have to ask the other person to repeat themselves. (They only ever almost-understand, even though the same thing happens to them.) [See almost-meaning, almost-understanding.]

Almost-lit, *adj.* Too drunk to drive, but still able to speak in complete sentences, your officership.

Almost-literally, *adv.* Virtually.

Almost-literate, *adj.* Subliterate. Only able to read words as long as the word "almost" or shorter. Or, fluent in both the speaking and writing of almost-speak. Aware of the almost-principle. (And, therefore, probably, a little reserved, but otherwise quite a nice person.) [See almost-principle.]

Almost-literature, *n.* Written almost-speak that is also almost-artful (like this sentence). [See almost-art.]

Almost-live, *adj.* Delayed by a few seconds. Or, delayed so they can bleep or cut out almost-all of the almost-speak. According to my almost-conspiracy hypothesis (almost-theory) this happens a lot.

Almost-living, *adj., n.* The famous dead people.

Almost-load, *n.* Carrying a floor lamp, or some other thing that is lightweight but still unwieldy enough to require both hands.

Almost-loan, *n., v.t.* Loan guarantee.

Almost-lobby, *v.t.* When you are hired as a lobbyist to do almost-nothing, just so that you don't lobby for the other side.

Almost-local, *adj.* On the Internet. [See almost-motto.]

Almost-location, *n.* Near or at a place where almost-movies are made. [See almost-movie.]

Almost-lock, *n., v.t.* Secure a latch. Ensure that something is at least childproof. Protect in a way that does not require a key or combination.

Almost-lodge, *n.* Cabin.

Almost-log, *v.t.* To notate in a book in a cryptic way (so only you can almost-understand it).

Almost-logical, *adj.* A scheme that is not well thought-out, or one that sounds plausible but is riddled with inconsistencies.

Almost-long, *adj.* Of medium length, but that is obviously adequate. Or, not as long as you desire. The "long hello" lasts from conception to about middle age, after which there may be a rather lengthy "long goodbye;" but each of these periods in a person's life are really only almost-long.

Almost-longevity, *n.* Almost nothing lasts for as long as it would like.

Almost-look, *v.t.* Glance.

Almost-loose, *adj.* Moving around in an annoying fashion, but still contained (perhaps a tooth, or the change in your pocket).

Almost-loot, *v.t., n.* To plunder only natural resources, not anything man-made (as when returning from the forest with firewood).

Almost-lopsided, *adj.* Two pros vs. two aspiring amateurs on a tennis court.

Almost-loquacious, *adj.* Speaking many words, but when each one of those words needs to be there in precisely that way for legal reasons.

Almost-lose, *v.t.* Quit before the game is completely lost. (Perhaps by throwing a tantrum, or out of concern for the kids back home and how late it's getting.) Or, win by an almost-hair (an uncomfortably small margin).

Almost-lost, *adj.* Not lost, just misplaced. "I know it's somewhere in this closet." Or, if need be, the old standbys of navigating by the sun or stars, using the map, or asking for directions, might be used.

Almost-lot, *n., adj.* More than a few. Or, most of a lot.

Almost-lottery, *n.* Life (the biggest crapshoot of them all).

Almost-love, *n.* Like. Adoration. Admiration. Respect. Loyalty. The various aspects of almost-love can form a basis for a relationship, and can sometimes be more reliable than love. Almost-love can span and conjoin stretches of love. Almost-love can also be frustratingly insufficient if more than almost-love is expected. Almost-love is a almost-splendored almost-thing.

Almost-low, *adj.* When only very tall people bump their heads on it.

Almost-lowdown, *n.* The varnished truth. Or, the way-out lowdown.

Almost-lower-middle-class, *adj.* Someone who owns a boat, even though they still just rent their own home.

Almost-loyalty, *n.* Convenient loyalty. Or, loyalty with limits.

Almost-LPGA , *n.* An association for lady golfers who are not very good at golf, or who are very good at almost-golf. [See almost-golf.]

Almost-lubberly, *adj., adv.* Inexpert at sailing and seamanship, but likes to have friends with boats.

Almost-ludicrous, *adj.* Something laughably absurd, except that it really did happen to you.

Almost-luggage, *n.* A purse. Or, all that stuff that will fit in your pockets or purse.

Almost-lukewarm, *adj.* Not quite as warm as lukewarm.

Almost-lumber, *n.* Uncut timber.

Almost-lump, *n.* Someone who doesn't quite pull their own weight.

Almost-lunch, *n.* Brunch.

Almost-lunge, *n., v.* Step forward unexpectedly.

Almost-lurid, *adj.* Melodramatic or sensational, but not so as to cause shock or horror.

Almost-lurking, *v.i.* Moving inconspicuously, but not furtively.

Almost-luxury, *n., adj.* Nice surroundings, but nothing royal or particularly ostentatious. Perhaps, understated elegance.

M

Almost-machine, *n.* A cyborg. Or, any person that acts machine-like.

Almost-mad, *adj.* Unconventional. Perhaps, of someone approaching one field with the precepts and values from another field. Or, almost-nuts or almost-crazy.

Almost-made, *adj.* Not quite made yet (as with: dinner, or something you have to assemble). Or, made up to some degree (as with: an almost-pack of lies, or an almost-house of cards).

Almost-madness, *n.* Either creative thinking, or silliness (the difference often being determined by how much time you have).

Almost-magazine, *n.* A magazine dedicated to almost-stuff and almost-ideas, almost-naturally. [See almost-vague.]

Almost-magnanimous, *adj.* A gesture or act suggesting nobility of feeling and generosity of mind, but done for all the almost-wrong reasons.

Almost-maiden, *n.* A girl so young that she could not properly be considered a maiden.

Almost-mail, *n.* Email. Or, junk mail. Or, when you get an email that is quickly "retracted." Or, mail that was lost in transit. Or, mail that you are waiting for.

Almost-maintain, *v.t.* To care for in a somewhat poor or ineffectual manner.

Almost-major, *n.* Captain. Or, a medium-sized minor, or miner.

Almost-majority, *n.* Less than fifty-percent, but who's counting? Or, a vociferous one or two.

Almost-make, *v.t.* To almost-produce, or almost-assemble from components.

Almost-male, *adj.* Not male, but possessing traditionally male attributes (relatively large, relatively bossy, or relatively pugnacious, for example).

Almost-malfeasance, *n.* Just about anything a public official might do, from the perspective of their opponents and detractors.

Almost-malfunction, *v.i.* To operate within specification limits, but to still produce an anomaly or irregularity.

Almost-malice, *n.* Recklessness.

Almost-malinger, *v.i.* To claim being "only human" in an excuse to avoid duty or work.

Almost-malnutrition, *n.* The nutrition in a diet coming primarily from almost-fast almost-food.

Almost-mammalian, *adj.* Any non-mammalian vertebrate wearing lipstick or a top hat.

Almost-mammoth, *adj.* Just large, and not very hairy.

Almostman, *n.* The almost-formless, almost-ineffable, almost-unchanging, almost-infinite, almost-transpersonal, almost-omnipotent, almost-ground of almost-existence.

Almost-man, *n.* Teenage male. Immature man. Hooligan. Uneducated man. Girly-man. Tough woman. Cyborg.

Almost-manage, *v.t.* Manage ineffectually. Or, oversee in a dotted-line way (shared accountability). Or, manage like Groucho Marx (in character).

The Almost-Dictionary

Almost-management, *n.* Managing by applying the almost-method, and with an almost-firm almost-understanding of the almost-principle and the almost-way. As every business person knows, if you can't measure it, you can't manage it. So it would follow that: If you can almost-measure it, you can almost-manage it. (Especially with things like: energy, ability, tolerance). [See almost-method, almost-understanding, almost-principle, almost-way.]

Almost-manager, *n.* Supervisor. Someone who instructs others, but does not have authority to hire and fire on their own. Or, someone who almost-manages, or is practiced in the almost-art of almost-management.

Almost-mandate, *n.* A suggestion or recommendation made by an authority figure. An expectation. When doing your due diligence means that you probably should do something. Or, a requirement to at least try to do something. Or, a requirement to include almost-stuff, or use the almost-method. [See almost-way.]

Almost-maneuver, *n.* An act of omission executed in such a slight or subtle manner that it was not noticed. Or, an act executed in such a slight or subtle manner that it was not effective (perhaps, a move that was aborted, like just before you ask a girl to dance you notice her warts and go get a drink instead).

Almost-manifest, *adj.* Hiding in plain sight. Or, not readily perceived by the senses.

Almost-manipulate, *v.t.* Let someone else manipulate.

Almost-manliness, *n.* An anthropomorphism.

Almost-mansion, *n.* Nice house.

Almost-manslaughter, *n.* Childslaughter. Or, mutilation.

Almost-manual, *n.* A manual originally written in a hurry by someone almost-unfamiliar with the product, in a foreign language, at the last minute just before product release, and that is then translated poorly into your language. (Many gadget manuals are almost-manuals.) Or, a process that relies on automation to only a small degree.

Almost-manufacture, *v.t.* When something is made just to suit the immediate need ("quick and dirty," without concern as to longevity of the item, the mass replication of the item, or the sale of the item). When something is "good enough for government work," or is "good enough for now" or when nobody will notice but you.

Almost-manure, *n.* The poop of very small animals.

Almost-many, *adj.* Several. [See the sequence of almost-specific counts at almost-all.]

Almost-map, *n.* A map that changes slower (or faster) than the terrain it represents. A map with insufficient detail (as with a pirate's treasure map).

Almost-marginal, *adj.* Positioned more centrally than in or on the margins. Or, of definite concern, but not of primary concern.

Almost-marine, *adj.* Wet rocks. Sand. Stuff on the beach (like driftwood, or towels). Stuff you find near water (like Tiki bars, or gas pumps). [See almost-nautical.]

Almost-mark, *v.t., n.* To mark in a coded or invisible way that goes undetected (as with invisible ink).

Almost-market, *n.* A forum for exchanging ideas. Or, an impromptu market. Or, a place where almost-stuff is bought and sold.

Almost-marketing, *n.* Viral marketing.

Almost-married, *adj.* Engaged. Or, living together with no intent to get married (like the almost-odd couple, perhaps). In an era where people change jobs, careers, and cities, almost as frequently as they change underwear, it is understandable that a life-long commitment to one person is equally difficult. Welcome to the almost-age of almost-marriage. [See almost-age.]

Almost-marshal, *n.* Deputy marshal.

Almost-mart, *n.* A convenience store that doesn't have what you are looking for, and is therefore also only almost-convenient.

Almost-masculine, *adj.* Feminine.

Almost-masquerading, *v.i.* In a lousy costume.

Almost-master, *v.t., n.* To nearly overcome something. Or, to almost-understand something. Perhaps, almost-adept enough to be very dangerous. Or, someone that is fairly accomplished in almost-dealing with the almost-aspects of life. For those almost-grasshoppers out there, becoming this type of an almost-master involves applying the almost-method in the almost-way. [See almost-method, almost-way, almost-field, almost-therapy.]

Almost-match, *n., v.t.* No two things are exactly alike. No two people are entirely compatible. Get over it! (This would be a good name for an online dating service.)

Almost-matching, *v.t.* What dating services do.

Almost-material, *adj.* Physical.

Almost-maternity, *n.* The quality or state of being almost a mother.

Almost-mathematics, *n.* Numbers. Arithmetic.

Almost-matrix, *n.* An almost-place that is either less confusing than the real Matrix, or so much more of a puzzle that nobody can figure it out (yet).

Almost-matter, *n.* Hard to define matter. Or, stuff that you can only almost-almost-understand. [See almost-understand.]

Almost-mature, *adj.* Callow. Inexperienced. Untried.

Almost-maven, *n.* Maven wannabe. Probably, a very smart person. Or, crackpot (if used disparagingly). Perhaps, someone with a post-graduate degree in bullshit, almost-bullshit, extreme bullshit, very smelly bullshit, or it's-false-and-we-know-it's-false-but-we-like-it.

Almost-max, *n., adj.* Almost-maxi, almost-Maxibillion, almost-maxilla, almost-maxim, almost-maximal, almost-maximalist, almost-maximin, almost-maximizer, almost-maximum, almost-maximus, almost-maxixe, almost-Maxwell, or almost-Maxzilla. Or, jumbo.

Almost-maybe, *adv.* Nearly no.

Almost-mayday, *n.* The all-too-familiar almost-distress call given out when a couch potato is out of beer, pretzels, or pizza.

Almost-meal, *n.* Snack.

Almost-mean, *adj.* Selfish. Or, well within the first standard deviation of the average or expected value. [See almost-meant.]

Almost-meaning, *n.* Meaning. The meaning of "meaning" has a lot of slippery slopes (connotation, denotation, intent, implication, value, purpose, and others). What something means, as far as you know. As close as you can get to the meaning without going over. The gist. Or, implying or suggesting rather than stating. Or, the meaning of an almost-expression.

Almost-means, *n.* A few bucks in the bank.

Almost-meant, *v.t.* When you replay a conversation in your head, you find that you intended to say something slightly different than what you actually said. And the person listening had their own perspective and interpretation of whatever was actually said. People only ever almost-understand what is almost-meant. [See almost-deconstruct, almost-listening, almost-meaning, almost-understanding.]

Almost-measure, *v.t.* When you guess at the measurement (such as height, width, or depth) based on reliable cues.

Almost-mechanics, *n.* The kind of mechanics achievable in an imprecise environment (as in, biochemistry or nanomedicine).

Almost-media, *n.* Much of the almost-estate, and the almost-opposite of that part of the world's almost-social almost-psyche that emanates from the now Almost-only Estate (the sometimes almost-monolithic almost-collective: government, business, the press, and big labor). (They are almost-one quite big almost-happy almost-family now and then). [See almost-estate.]

Almost-median, *n., adj.* Nearly at the middle in position.

Almost-mediate, *v.t.* Almost-acting like a monkey-in-the-middle, and dropping the ball occasionally.

Almost-medic, *n.* Paramedic in training.

Almost-medical, *adj.* Medical research that is in the planning stages and that is not ready for human trials yet. Or, things that are not close enough to "medical" (the plastic pill container, the nurse's shoes, the doctor's golf game).

Almost-medium, *adj.* Medium rare.

Almost-meek, *adj.* Non-violent activist. Or, rowdy pacifist.

Almost-meet, *v.t.* When strangers in the night exchange glances, but don't stop to talk. Or, when they meet online.

Almost-member, *n.* A probationary member. Someone part of a group but not having a card, shirt, or mug to show for it. Or, a member of a group that doesn't require membership per se, as with adherents to an ideology (members of the conservative movement, or the ultra-fit).

Almost-memory, *n.* I did know what I was going write here, but I forgot (unless this is it).

Almost-mend, *v.t.* Fix well enough that you can get to shore, or until you can buy a new one.

Almost-menial, *adj.* A relatively low-paying, uninteresting, and possibly servile task or job that involves considerable risk at times.

Almost-mercantile, *adj.* More like children exchanging toys.

Almost-merchant, *n.* A businessman that has yet to make a sale.

Almost-merger, *n.* When a deal falls through.

Almost-merit, *n., v.* When someone who only unwittingly or accidentally does something worthy of merit they are usually deemed worthy of a smidgen less recognition.

Almost-message, *n.* An incomplete message. Or, when: "This is the message," is the message. Or, a message about almost-stuff, or in almost-speak.

Almost-messenger, *n.* Just a pigeon (with no message). The vehicle by which the message is transmitted.

Almost-metaphor, *n.* Simile.

Almost-metaphysical, *adj.* Of the mental stance of considering things objectively. Or, of some almost-abstract thinking about almost-abstract thought. [See almost-abstract, almost-thing.]

Almost-meter, *n.* Yard (or three feet).

Almost-method, *n.* Not going all the way. Not completing what you start. It works in the prevention of war. It works in birth control. You could try it out on your problem. (Hint: Almost-deeds don't usually get you in as much trouble as actually doing something usually does, and you often get points for making some effort, and for your almost-good almost-intentions.) [See almost-aspect, almost-factor.]

Almost-metric, *adj.* An almost-consideration used to almost-measure or almost-gauge. For example, the politician with the best hair cut *deserves* to win.

Almost-middle, *adj., n.* Close enough to the middle (as in: a bull's-eye in darts or archery). Or, not close enough to the middle.

Almost-miff, *v.t.* To come close to offending someone, or putting them into an ill humor.

Almost-mighty, *adj.* The gun might be mightier than the sword, but the pen is almost-mightier than both. And the keyboard and mouse almost-need to be almost-in almost-there somewhere. Oh, and the gunsmith. And ways of making steel.

Almost-mile, *n.* The distance: 0.987654321 of a mile. Or, at a stretch, a kilometer.

Almost-military, *adj.* Paramilitary. [See almost-rank.]

Almost-mill, *n.* Any processor of metaphorical grist.

Almost-mind, *n.* A mind, when it is not made up. To hesitate is to be almost-minded. Let's see. I'm of an almost-mind to think on this definition some more. Hmmm.

Almost-mine, *v.t., n.* Look. Or, a deep hole with nothing in it. Or, not a very deep hole. Or, an above-ground workplace where you can't see the sky or trees.

Almost-minimal, *adj.* Paltry.

Almost-minimalism, *n.* When there is such a thing as *too* small (as with gadgets), or *too* simple or unexpressive (as with art). [See almost-art.]

Almost-mining, *v.t.* Digging. Or, figuratively, looking for almost-stuff.

Almost-minor, *n.* Fetus (and perhaps: baby, infant, and child).

Almost-minute, *n.* Fifty-nine seconds. Or, not very long.

Almost-miscible, *adj.* Capable of being mixed, but not without separation (like olive oil and vinegar, or Republicans and Democrats).

Almost-misdirected, *adj.* Given confusing directions that are not so much wrong as they are incomplete and unclear (and, perhaps, not well thought out).

Almost-misfire, *v.i., n.* When the firing seems atypical.

Almost-misfit, *n.* Someone who almost-doesn't almost-fit almost-in.

Almost-mislead, *v.t.* To technically or legally *not* mislead.

Almost-mismanage, *v.t.* Almost-everything is at least almost-mismanaged if it is not completely mismanaged. (It's a wonder anything ever gets done.) [See almost-management, almost-method.]

Almost-misogamist, *n.* Someone only mildly biased against the institution of marriage, or who only dislikes some aspects of marriage and not others.

Almost-misogynist, *n.* Someone who has "little time for frivolous things," or who only finds objectionable some things about women and not others. (Or, from her perspective, not a complete asshole.)

Almost-misplace, *v.t.* When you put something in a place so close to the right place that you can easily find it from there (but maybe someone else wouldn't be so lucky).

Almost-misquote, *v.t.* When you repeat words incorrectly, but then immediately correct yourself.

Almost-miss, *v.t.* Think of someone you know, especially after seeing a picture of them.

Almost-missile, *n.* Unarmed projectile.

Almost-missing, *adj.* Someone who left for the bathroom, or they just stepped out for a cigarette.

Almost-mistake, *n.* When an oversight is made, or an aspect ignored, but everything turns out almost-ok almost-anyway. Or, a behavior that didn't achieve the desired results this time, even though it usually does. Or, a choice based on taste that not everyone agrees with. Or, deliberately doing something negative, just to make the point.

Almost-misunderstand, *v.t.* Misunderstand, but not so poorly that one's overall judgment is affected. [See almost-understanding.]

Almost-misuse, *v.t.* Use in an atypical manner (like using a screwdriver handle to tap at something, or using a hammer as a paper weight).

Almost-mix, *v.* Shake up a little. Or, to speak with the other side politely.

Almost-mob, *n.* Gang. Or, class (if it is comprised of teenagers).

Almost-mock, *v.t.* Make fun of, in a nice way.

Almost-mode, *n.* Believe it or not, I'm in almost-mode right now.

Almost-model, *n.* A good-looking person with better things to do than just standing around. (Sitting around being much-preferred by some.) It would then follow that an almost-super almost-model would look good leaping from their office chair in a single bound.

Almost-modeling, *v.t.* Wearing clothes that have the designer's name on the outside. Or, walking up and down airport runways.

Almost-modern, *adj.* Something that is sooooo "last week."

Almost-modify, *v.t.* Make the same. Or, remake.

Almost-mollify, *v.t.* Not mollify. But, nice try.

Almost-moment, *n.* A length of time longer than a second, but just shy of a moment. The duration: 0.987654321 of a moment. Or, that time in your life when you first decided to join the almost-side. [See almost-number.]

Almost-momentum, *n.* When there is nothing really forcing things to go in the same direction other than force of habit, or tradition.

Almost-monetary, *adj.* Involving only Monopoly money (or other currency worth as much).

Almost-money, *n.* Credit. Numbers in cyberspace. Liquid assets. Or, a capital idea.

Almost-monist, *n.* Anyone who thinks there must be some kind of oneness or unity to the universe, but who can't mentally get past the dualities and pluralities everywhere.

Almost-monitor, *v.t.* Keep an eye on, not from an intense interest, but perhaps because of a fiduciary responsibility.

Almost-monkey, *n., v.t.* Child. Or, what your mechanic might be doing with your car when you're not looking.

Almost-monoculture, *n.* A "melting pot" that has not been turned up too high. Or, one that has.

Almost-monopolize, *v.t.* Control. (Really, just almost-control.)

Almost-monopoly, *n.* A situation where one player dominates an industry, but other significant players are allowed to remain, perhaps so that the dominant player is not regulated as strictly or severely, or perhaps so the dominant player can acquire the "best of breed" all the time.

Almost-month, *n.* February. Or, twenty-eight or twenty-nine days.

Almost-mood, *n.* A fleeting attitude, disposition, or feeling.

Almost-moon, *n.* An almost-full moon, or a three-quarter moon. Or, almost anything worth howling at.

Almost-moose, *n.* Elk (*Cervus canadensis*).

Almost-moot, *adj.* Of an issue usually debated or disputed, but in the present context there is little reason for controversy.

Almost-moral, *n., adj.* At least in keeping with middle-class values. Or, close-but-no-cigar when trying to stay true to one's own or the prevailing values.

Almost-moratorium, *n.* A moratorium that is not respected.

Almost-morning, *n.* Just before midnight. Or, when you have to get up to go pee. Or, for people who are not "morning people," the first part of the day that only partially exists and that you need to struggle through in order to get to the afternoon and evening (the more productive parts of the day).

Almost-moronic, *adj.* Callow. Sophomoric. Of someone just smart enough that you don't notice how dumb they are until it's too late.

Almost-mortality, *n.* Indefinite longevity (which is all you can ever hope for, because you never know when an unexpected death may occur).

Almost-mortgage, *n.* A perpetual interest-only property-secured loan.

Almost-most, *adv., adj.* Many. [See the sequence of almost-specific counts at almost-all.]

Almost-mother, *n.* A stepmother. An aunt. A nanny. A babysitter known really well by the family. A significantly more mature sister.

Almost-motion, *n.* A relative lack of motion. Or, a motion to almost-pass almost-something almost-in an almost-committee. (This type of motion is popular at the Almost-Party almost-parties). [See almost-moving, almost-method, Almost-Party.]

Almost-motivate, *v.t.* To prod or move someone, but unconvincingly; not to the extent, or in the way that would make them want to move by themselves.

Almost-motivation, *n.* The motivation for further developing a military is that of "having a better defense," but an almost-motivation might be that of "increasing economic aggregate demand," or "spurring technological innovation."

Almost-motto, *n.* Think almost-globally, almost-act accordingly. For those almost-stuck in one place: Think almost-locally, almost-act like you know what you're doing. For the adventurous and imaginative among us: Think almost-universally, almost-act almost-otherworldly.

Almost-mount, *v.t.* To climb on or over part-way (as in children climbing a tree, or someone standing on a car's running board). Or, to ride sidesaddle.

Almost-mountainous, *adj.* Hilly.

Almost-Mouse, *n.* A mouse with a little black cape that would be feeling almost-mighty, except that his tail was cut off by the farmer's wife, and he was then put in a wheel to exercise until he reduced down to almost-nothing. What do you expect, almost-really?

Almost-mouth, *n.* Gullet.

Almost-movie, *n.* Short movie (between the length of a commercial and the length of a feature film). Or, a series of still pictures presented in movie format with some kind of cohesive narrative (some documentaries, and most computer-based training are like this). Or, a movie without humans as actors (perhaps with computer-generated characters). Or, a movie made about almost-aspects, in the almost-way, or by using the almost-method.

Almost-moving, *v.i.* Jiggling. Shivering. Or, stuck in traffic. Or, whatever one is capable of doing in a microscope slide (perhaps, exhibiting Brownian motion only). [See almost-motion.]

Almost-muddle, *v., n.* Huddle.

Almost-mug, *n.* A coffee mug with an almost-saying on it. [See almost-saying.]

Almost-multiply, *v.t.* Add the same thing over and over the number of times specified.

Almost-multitasking, *n.* Juggling and prioritizing a series of activities successfully — according to observers.

Almost-munificent, *adj.* Characterized by only moderate liberality or generosity.

Almost-murder, *v.t., n.* To wound a person severely, especially if done deliberately. Manslaughter. (Perhaps, some of what goes by the name "euthanasia.")

Almost-muse, *n.* An almost-source of inspiration, but not one that was fixated upon for a long time, or with very intense concentration.

Almost-musical, *adj.* Regardless of our ability to *make* music, we all have an appreciation to some degree of the rhythms and the melodies in life. [See almost-art, almost-euphonious.]

Almost-mutagen, *n.* An agent (chemical, biological, or social) that tends to increase the frequency or extent of almost-mutations. [See almost-mutate.]

Almost-mutate, *v.i.* Change just a little, but not by accident. Mutations change things in an undirected way, and almost-mutations change things in a more directed but still incremental way. (The tiny everyday decisions of almost-no consequence.) Excuse me while I almost-mutate. [See almost-contagious, almost-copy, almost-evolve.]

Almost-mutiny, *v.t.* To plan a revolt or insurrection that is never carried out. Or, to blow the whistle on your superiors for some quite justifiable reason.

Almost-mutual, *adj.* Fairly one-sided or lopsided; as in, when one person is in love, and the other is in like (or almost-love).

Almost-mythology, *n.* Any *modern* epic story, especially one that has both a male and female lead, and where treasure, adventure, values, and symbolism play prominently.

N

Almost-naked, *adj.* Barely clothed, or scantily clothed. Or, not sufficiently protected from the elements (covered).

Almost-name, *n.* Nickname.

Almost-nanites, *n.* Nanotech critters that don't perform their intended function very well.

Almost-narrow, *adj.* Wide enough to get through without someone bitchin' about it already.

Almost-nascent, *adj.* Partially developed, but not yet mature.

Almost-nasty, *adj.* Not very nice. Or, very nice indeed.

Almost-national, *adj.* A phenomenon that exists in many places, cities, locales, or regions.

Almost-native, *adj., n.* One who has lived somewhere for a long time, but not since birth.

Almost-natural, *adj.* Barely artificial (as in: bread, or a fountain made mostly out of rocks, or lipstick on a pig). Or, somewhat ill at ease (like a bull in a dress shop). [See almost-artificial. These two almost-aspects work together almost hand-in-glove.]

Almost-nature, *n.* Nature in its symbolic form (clouds indicating rain, bulls indicating stock market rallies). Or, attribute, especially one with an almost-aspect. Or, almost-stuff out in the almost-wild (on a nature trail).

Almost-nautical, *adj.* Having to do with a harbor, pier, dock, wharf, quay, jetty, or captain's hat. [See almost-marine.]

Almost-navy, *n.* Enough of a navy to do serious damage. Or, the color royal blue.

Almost-neap, *adj.* Neaping. Of a tide when the pull of the sun and the moon are almost-opposed. Or, almost at an optimal place, given all of the influences.

Almost-near, *adv., adj., prep.* Still within range. Or, barely close.

Almost-needle, *n., v.t.* Tease, worry, or annoy.

Almost-needs, *n.* The objects of strong desires for almost everything other than the basics (air, water, food, shelter, clothing, basic cable, cell phone). It is tempting to say to a sales clerk: "I need a —," but what you usually mean is that you "almost-need" that thing.

Almost-nefarious, *adj.* Not very nice or good. Somewhat morally reprehensible. Operating without much conscience.

Almost-negate, *v.t.* An incomplete reversal. Or, what sometimes happens to an idea when it is laughed at and ridiculed.

Almost-negative, *adj.* A negative thing that has an almost-offsetting positive to it.

Almost-neglect, *v.t.* To remember at the last moment. Or, to care for in only the essential ways.

Almost-negligible, *adj.* Something you would ignore if you could.

Almost-negotiate, *v.t.* To talk passed each other in a disagreeable way.

Almost-nerd, *n.* A person that is not so studied, disciplined, and focused that they are not also good company.

Almost-nest, *n.* A few twigs placed close together.

Almost-nest-egg, *n.* What a nest-egg will be over time, especially with compound interest.

Almost-net, *n.* A net that doesn't work for some reason (too small, a rip, or the holes are too big). Or, a net for catching almost-stuff.

Almost-network, *n., v.* Something in the form a of a network, but where some of the connections are problematic, or there is insufficient participation by members.

Almost-networking, *v.t.* Making a few contacts, but always waiting for them to contact you first.

Almost-neurotic, *adj.* Nutty or wacky without going around-the-bend cuckoo (that is, like you see people behave in sit-coms). Look around. This almost-psychological almost-condition is so prevalent now that almost-everyone except you is probably almost-neurotic. (That should almost-tell you something. Maybe.)

Almost-neutral, *adj.* Not quite centered, fair, uncharged, uninvolved, or disinterested.

Almost-never, *adv.* Hardly ever. Or, just when you least suspect it.

Almost-new, *adj.* Used, but in very good condition. Or, recently made or grown. Or, just a tad different from the same old thing.

Almost-news, *n.* A message that does not sufficiently inform. "Tornado headed this way. More at eleven." Almost-news might be an important message that is insufficiently researched, or it might be newsertainment, spin, obscurantism, or unimportant filler. Personally, I only need to know about a fire if it's close-by. I don't *need* to know about your charity bake sale . . . ever, and do NOT consider that news. News organizations have to decide how much of a company's press release is commercial advertizing that should be treated as such. While it is the case that to some extent one man's news is another man's almost-news, probably all news venues would be more attractive to their customers if they tried to more clearly separate the two (and even exploit various types of Almost-News as such).

Almost-newspaper, *n.* A flyer, or bulletin.

Almost-next, *adj., prep., adv.* Coming up very soon, but not immediately.

Almost-nice, *adj.* A little rough. Or, fairly pleasing or agreeable.

Almost-niche, *n.* An almost-place for almost-stuff.

Almost-night, *n.* Dusk. Dawn. Twilight. (Note: the twilight zone and the almost-zone almost-overlap sometimes.) [See almost-zone.]

Almost-nil, *n.* A relatively very low number.

Almost-nimble, *adj.* Somewhat bloated, or somewhat slow, particularly both (such as a runner or swimmer after a large meal).

Almost-no, *adv.* Maybe. Or, probably not. Or, to acknowledge the almost-aspect of what you are saying with the word "no" (as in: "You're *almost-no* better than the rest of us").

Almost-nobodies, *n.* Wannabes with little talent. Or, dontwannabes with considerable talent.

Almost-nobody, *n.* An entity that is not fully a person (at least by some definitions).

Almost-noise, *n.* Data that is barely distinguishable from its surroundings. Or, when a sound you normally appreciate interrupts the sound you would prefer to hear (like when someone's voice interrupts your appreciation of Beethoven).

Almost-nominate, *v.t.* What you do to everyone on "the short list" that you don't nominate.

Almost-nominee, *n.* Someone considered for a position or honor.

Almost-nonplussed, *v.t.* Almost-perplexed, almost-baffled, almost-distracted, or maybe almost-speechless.

Almost-nonsense, *n.* That which almost-makes almost-no almost-sense.

Almost-noplaceville, *n.* Not a very interesting place (especially one that is right next to an even less interesting place).

Almost-normal, *adj., n.* Within the first standard deviation (relative to the rest of the herd).

Almost-normative, *adj.* Of a variable-strength almost-abstract almost-gravitational pull in the direction of almost-stuff (instead of almost-normal) that is mediated socially.

Almost-north, *adv., adj.* Not quite due north. North*ish*. One might point out the almost-north entrance to a building (that wasn't built to align with the major compass headings).

Almost-nosedive, *n.* A steeper than gradual descent (during which time no wigs are flipped, but maybe a little coffee gets spilt).

Almost-not, *adv.* Not precisely not exactly.

Almost-note, *n.* An abbreviated message. The larger part of a dollar bill that has been ripped in two.

Almost-nothing, *n.* Nothing. A real nothing is as elusive in our universe as is absolute-zero. (For this reason many of us almost-believe in almost-something.) Or, very close to the number zero. Or, what you are actually doing when you say you are doing nothing. Or, what is on television most of the time. Or, the almost-opposite of almost-something. [See almost-opposite, almost-something.]

Almost-notice, *v.t.* When you think about a situation after the fact and something new comes to mind, you must have almost-noticed that before (it's just that other things were clamoring for your attention at the time).

Almost-noticeable, *adj.* A phenomenon that is so faint that it tests one or more of the senses, . . . and they fail.

Almost-notify, *v.t.* When you try to notify someone, but they don't ever get the message for some reason.

Almost-novelty, *n.* Something too similar to something else to really be different. Almost-novelty is the single most common thing in the universe. This would include but is not limited to mutations in genes or ideas. It is even possible for types of destruction to be almost-novel.

Almost-noxious, *adj.* Shown to be physically harmful only in higher doses. Perhaps, an effluent that you can keep producing until and if a government agency ever gets on your case.

Almost-nuance, *n.* A tiny difference in meaning that is almost chock-full of traces of other meanings. [See almost-deconstruct, almost-meant, almost-understanding.]

Almost-nuclear, *adj.* Most "nuclear" chicken wings are only almost-nuclear (even the almost-naked ones that pack a lot of muscle). Most non-nuclear countries are almost-nuclear in that it wouldn't take much for them to *become* nuclear — now that the cat is most of the way out of the bag (it probably smells the chicken wings).

Almost-nugatory, *adj.* Having little consequence or force, but not so little as to be called trifling, or inconsequential.

Almost-nuisance, *n.* A pest or annoyance that is either not worth the resources to remove it, or that brings with it enough positive that it should remain. For example, people usually don't complain too loudly when a delivery person interrupts, or when a grandchild calls.

Almost-null, *adj.* Nearly empty. Or, almost-amounting to nothing.

Almost-number, *n.* The number 0.987654321. Or, an irrational number. Or, a rounded number (as in: there were about fifty people at the gathering). Of course, any number that is close to the almost-number would be an almost-almost-number (like 0.987654009).

Almost-numeracy, *n.* The leaning in some species toward the capacity for quantitative thought and expression, but which stops at about the place where one scratches one's head (if they can even do that).

Almost-nurse, *n.* A nurse in training. Or, an orderly.

Almost-nut, *n.* Berry. Or, almost-everyone that doesn't think and behave the way we do. (For some reason, a disproportionately high percentage of high school teachers and electrical engineers seem to be almost-nut cases.)

Almost-nutritious, *adj.* Processed.

O

Almost-obedience, *n.* When someone complies with the important parts of what is commanded or instructed.

Almost-obfuscate, *v.t.* To hem and haw (and speak almost-noncommittally). To muddle. To complexify.

Almost-object, *n.* Something that is almost-identifiable or almost-isolatable. Perhaps, an almost-thing. Or, something that is almost-abstract. [See almost-abstract, almost-thing.]

Almost-objective, *n.* Subjective, while respecting the opinions of others to some extent. Or, as objective as you can be. Or, the collective subjective.

Almost-obligation, *n.* An obligation when there is minimal downside if it is postponed or never met. This could be a promise you made to yourself, or one made to a school teacher after your grades are final.

Almost-obscene, *adj.* Not so repulsive or detestable that it isn't welcome almost everywhere.

Almost-obscurantist, *adj.* Not completely in opposition to the spread of specific information, but careful, or cautious, or waiting for the right time. Or, tactful. Or, being neglectfully vague.

Almost-obsequious, *adj.* Exhibiting just enough servile fawning attentiveness to not lose one's job.

Almost-observation, *n.* Something noticed without it actually being seen.

Almost-obsolete, *adj.* Still useful and desirable even though it has since been obviated or almost-replaced in the marketplace by something superior.

Almost-obstacle, *n.* A run-of-the-mill obstacle. Something that would be an obstacle for someone less-determined. A brick wall, if you happen to have a bulldozer.

Almost-obstruction, *n.* Something threatening to impede. Or, a pathway nearly clogged or blocked. Or, a nuisance.

Almost-obtain, *v.t.* To have within one's sights, and almost-within one's grasp (as a fly ball that seems to be going into the crowd behind you).

Almost-obviate, *v.t.* To anticipate and eliminate the need for something, but it happens anyway.

Almost-obvious, *adj.* Obvious to anyone who has been following the situation closely for a long time.

Almost-occasional, *adj.* Occurring at unpredictable intervals (and often when you least expect it). Almost everything happens this almost-way. [See almost-way.]

Almost-occupant, *n.* The girlfriend or boyfriend of the occupant. Frequent visitor.

Almost-occupation, *n.* Hobby (especially one that generates a little income). Avocation. Or, an occupation in one of the almost-fields. [See almost-field.]

Almost-ocean, *n.* Sea, gulf, or really big lake.

Almost-oceangoing, *adj.* Sea-going, river-going, lake-going, or even canal-going (especially if headed toward the ocean).

Almost-odd, *adj.* Different or strange, but not to the extreme. Lucy was odd, Desi was almost-odd. Jerry was odd, Dean was almost-odd.

Almost-off, *adj., prep.* Still on. Perhaps something only on a tad (as a stove, or a stand-up comedian). Or, still here.

Almost-offence, *n.* If you choose to not back down when someone looks at you the wrong way (you may take almost-offence), you may decide to look at them funny too (go on almost-offence).

Almost-offer, *n.* An offer you can't believe. Or, an offer that is not in writing. Or, an offer that is only almost-enough. Or, an offer that has expired (like one on a coupon).

Almost-offhand, *adj.* A Freudian almost-slip. [See almost-slip.]

Almost-office, *n.* An inadequate office. The size of one's workspace is the subject of one of the most common complaints. Almost-everyone thinks that if they had a larger office, perhaps with firmer walls and a door, more chairs, or more equipment, then they would be able to get more done for their boss; and yet almost-every boss still decides or almost-decides almost-against this. Even before skyscrapers, if someone were seated in an inadequately-appointed cave with too few secretaries, they would tend to almost-gripe.

Almost-officer, *n.* Any senior noncommissioned officer, such as a sergeant.

Almost-official, *n., adj.* Someone or something acting as a surrogate for the official. Or, on the side (as a favor) but with official trappings.

Almost-offset, *v.t.* Where the positive and negatives (or conditions) don't quite cancel each other out by way of counterbalance or compensation.

Almost-offshore, *adj.* Still on land. Maybe, at the beach.

Almost-ogling, *v.* Gazing at with mild interest, but not because you are flirting, but because she moved into view right behind your wife and you can't help but notice.

Almost-oil, *n.* Pardonably-crude oil.

Almost-ok, *adj.* Pretty good. Almost-all almost-right. Would be ok, except for that headache.

Almost-old, *adj.* Middle-aged. Or, somewhat old-fashioned.

Almost-oligopoly, *n.* A market condition where several (instead of a few) producers almost-control a market.

Almostology, *n.* The study of almost-aspects, almost-speak, and other almost-stuff (especially by using the almost-method in the almost-way). [See almost-aspect, almost-principle, almost-world, and the rest of this the Almost-Dictionary.]

Almost-ominous, *adj.* Threatening in a mild or vague way (like when it looks like it might rain).

Almost-one, *n.* The number 0.987654321. [See almost-number.]

Almost-onerous, *adj.* When he ain't heavy simply because he's your brother.

Almost-onion, *n.* An onion that doesn't make you cry when it's cut. (Thanks to genetic almost-engineering.)

Almost-only, *adv.* One of extremely few. There is rarely just one way to do something, and sometimes there are quite a few practical and cost-effective ways to do something (just ask someone who skins cats for a living).

Almost-onomatopoeia, *n.* Words used to suggest the sound of something almost-abstract (that does not make a sound). ("Botch" might be the sound of an architect or artist making a design error.

"Flip" might be the sound of someone suddenly entertaining the opposite idea.)

Almost-onslaught, *n.* A fierce sudden attack by relatively harmless beings (such as a houseflies, or groundhogs).

Almost-onstage, *adj.* In the wings.

Almost-on tap, *adj.* Close at hand. When a bar has an abundance of a particular beer in both bottles and cans, the substance might as well be considered free-flowing or almost-on tap. Figuratively, most people have a litany of swear words almost-on tap.

Almost-onus, *n.* Onu.

Almost-oops, *interj.* What to say when you did it on purpose, but didn't mean to cause what resulted.

Almost-open, *adj.* Ajar. Or, open in ten minutes.

Almost-opening, *n., v.* But a sliver of an opening. [See almost-angle.]

Almost-operate, *v.t.* Make something work to the best of your abilities without reading the manual.

Almost-operation, *n.* Procedure.

Almostopia, *n.* A place where everything has almost-aspects, and nothing is finished, complete, sincere, pure, or perfect. This could almost be contrasted with utopia (with its ideal aspects) and dystopia (with its extremely negative aspects). [See almost-aspect, almost-world.]

Almost-opponent, *n.* Co-worker (or anyone you are being measured against). Partner or boss (or anyone in a position to make demands on your time). Customer (or anyone you need to convince). Supplier (or anyone in a position to reduce your effectiveness). Auditor, referee, or judge (or anyone who is in a position to stop you).

Journalists, and everyone else you know (anyone who may tarnish your reputation). Time itself (you are always racing against it). Yourself (sometimes you can be your own worst enemy).

Almost-opportunity, *n.* An opportunity that will almost certainly disappear before you can get positioned to take advantage of it. As the world moves faster and faster, more opportunities will become merely almost-opportunities.

Almost-oppose, *v.t.* To oppose in a way similar to the way the thumb and forefinger are opposed.

Almost-opposite, *adj.* Something that is an alternative to a thing but is not the reverse of the thing. For example, "left" and "right," and "up" and "down" can be considered opposites; but "chocolate" and "strawberry," "organic" and "inorganic," "capitalist" and "socialist," or "x" (independent variable) and "y" (dependent variable) might better be considered almost-opposites. Likewise, alternative alleles of the same gene can be considered almost-opposites. Other often almost-opposed considerations: "freedom" and "determinism," "the state" and "the individual," "mind" and "body," "universal" and "particular," and "time" and "money."

Almost-optimal, *adj.* Desirable or satisfactory, but not the *most* desirable or satisfactory ways.

Almost-optimistic, *adj.* Hoping for the best possible scenario, but planning for other eventualities in a practical way.

Almost-option, *n.* When you have a choice like a Hobson's choice: you can ride any horse you want as long as it's the one closest to the stable door. Or, the option to select almost-stuff instead.

Almost-orange, *n.* Lemon.

Almost-ordinance, *n.* A pea shooter.

Almost-ordinary, *adj.* Fairly rare, but unremarkable.

Almost-organ, *n.* Piano.

Almost-organic, *adj., n.* Carbon compounds not typically found in living tissue. Or, "organic" by certain standards, but not others (as it relates to chemicals, growth stimulants, antibiotics, and pesticides). Or, socially, quite rigid.

Almost-organization, *n.* An organization that might not be there when you need it. Or, an organization that just isn't very organized.

Almost-organize, *v.t.* To reduce the level chaos in a certain place considerably. Probably, to add structure and process.

Almost-Orient, *n.* The Near East.

Almost-oriented, *adj.* "Object-oriented" means the "object" nature or attribute is dominating; and likewise, "almost-oriented" means that almost-aspects are foremost. It would be almost-oriented of someone to consider this definition as like nearly bang on. [See almost-aspect, almost-almost, almost-speak, almost-stuff.]

Almost-original, *adj.* The second or third version or edition of something. A derivative product. Like the original, but also with a fairly rare or fancy twist. [See almost-mutate.]

Almost-originate, *v.t.* Cobble together. [See almost-create, almost-credit, almost-make.]

Almost-orotund, *adj.* Speaking plainly, clearly, and just strongly enough. Or speaking almost-speak in a bombastic way.

Almost-ounce, *n.* What you might get when you pay for an ounce.

Almost-oust, *v.t.* Ignore. Or, put on a "graylist." [See almost-blacklist.]

Almost-out, *adj., prep.* Someone who has moved closer to the door, but then stopped to talk.

Almost-outcomes, *n.* What happens at almost-events.

Almost-outdated, *adj.* A product on the market now, and especially right after someone has just invented something better.

Almost-outfit, *n.* A skimpy little thing.

Almost-outgoing, *adj.* Not shy. Or, someone who will be leaving soon.

Almost-outlaw, *n.* Someone who is looking for trouble, but hasn't yet found it.

Almost-outline, *n.* A dotted line around something. Or, an almost-abstract boundary.

Almost-outlook, *n.* An in-look that from necessity considers some things outside.

Almost-outlying, *adj.* Something relatively distant that is still included.

Almost-outperform, *v.t.* Close, but no cigar.

Almost-output, *n.* Output that is also input (and that you may never see or handle). The output of an almost-middle step in a process.

Almost-outreach, *v.t.* Side-reach. Or, at a stretch, in-reach.

Almost-outright, *adj., adv.* Something that is out, but not completely.

Almost-outrun, *v.t.* To run nearly as fast as something or someone else. Or, trying to keep up.

Almost-outside, *adj.* Partly inside. Maybe, near a door or open window.

Almost-outsider, *n.* A stranger that looks and/or acts like the rest of your group.

Almost-outsource, *v.t.* When you outsource to one of your own subsidiaries.

Almost-outstanding, *adj.* Outsitting. Or, instanding. Or, out, but on crutches.

Almost-outstrip, *v.t.* When you take your clothes off really quickly, but not as fast as the person next to you.

Almost-outvote, *v.t.* When you vote *and* have a political bumper sticker on your car *and* have a similar sign on your lawn. Or, when your side loses democratically.

Almost-outward, *adj.* Tangentially. [See almost-outlook.]

Almost-over, *adv., prep., adj.* When it's all over but the crying. Or, when the two-minute warning has sounded. Or, before some fat lady sings (and they keep changing who it is, so you never know when it is going to happen). Or, when it's time to rush out to the parking lot to leave before everyone else does the same.

Almost-overall, *adv., adj., n.* Over most.

Almost-overboard, *adj.* Hanging from a line (or rope).

Almost-overcapacity, *n.* Capable of, or actually producing slightly more than enough, just in case.

Almost-overdue, *adj.* Near the appointed time. Or, approaching the state of being more than ready.

Almost-overeating, *v.i.* Eating to what would be excess, except that you know your next meal will be small or belated.

Almost-overexposed, *adj.* Famous, but for some very good reason.

Almost-overhaul, *v.t.* To repair some parts of something, but to not sufficiently modernize, and to not change the deep structure.

Almost-overlap, *v.t.* To become so proximate that there may be problems — with transitioning, jurisdiction, attention, or whatever is in the gap.

Almost-overlook, *v.t.* To not overlook, but also to not mention anything about it (and just wait and see).

Almost-overnight, *adj.* When it gets there in the late afternoon of the following day, or at least fairly quickly.

Almost-overpaid, *adj.* Paid extra for things like risk or hazard, odd hours (night shift or split shifts), being on-call, or because nobody else is willing to do the job. Or, paid minimum wage to do almost-nothing.

Almost-overrun, *adj.* Still standing.

Almost-oversupply, *n., v.t.* Enough.

Almost-overtime, *n.* Extra hours for which you don't get paid, but . . . you might get recognition.

Almost-overturn, *v.t.* Flip on its side. Or, to just make people cock their head to one side questioningly.

Almost-overweight, *adj.* Would probably be considered overweight in different clothing.

Almost-overwhelm, *adj.* Almost-underwhelm.

Almost-owe, *v.t.* How things almost-are when someone does you a favor.

Almost-own, *v.t.* Lease. Or, jointly own.

P

Almost-pace, *n., v.* To set a "fairly steady" rhythm for work or exercise. (If you don't almost-pace yourself, your almost-nature may almost-do that for you.)

Almost-package, *n.* An incomplete package. Perhaps she can sing, but not dance. A software package that when installed needs to be updated over the Internet. A package containing a gadget that runs on batteries that are not included.

Almost-packed, *adj.* Packed to the point that you still need to collect your bathroom stuff. (This is when you almost-think to call the taxi company.)

Almost-pact, *n.* A breakable "agreement in principle." An agreement — maybe even as serious as an international treaty — that imposes a negligible cost for its abridgement.

Almost-paddle, *v.t.* What the person that sits at the back of a canoe sometimes does. What both of you do when trying to sneak up on an almost-jittery animal.

Almost-paid, *adj.* When the check is in the mail. Or, two days before payday. Or, your final status if you don't watch your accountant like a hawk.

Almost-pain, *n.* Pressure.

Almost-pajamas, *n.* Negligee. Boxer shorts.

Almost-pallid, *adj.* Having the humdrum-average amount of color, sparkle, or entertainment value.

Almost-palpable, *adj.* Some social or almost-abstract phenomenon that almost-gives the almost-impression that it is capable of being touched or felt physically.

Almost-paper, *n.* The fabric of an electronic document.

Almost-par, *n.* A bogie, in golf.

Almost-paradigm, *n.* A loosely-defined pattern or framework for thought, especially one that shifts a lot. Or, a very large almost-aspect. [See almost-aspect.]

Almost-paradox, *n.* Paradox (because all seemingly contradictory observations become almost-understandable eventually). Or, an odd comparison that is not entirely contradictory.

Almost-paralysis, *n.* When slow and small movements are still possible to some degree. The nerves might not be severed, but the system took a shock. Executives often see it part of their job to shock their organization out of an almost-state of almost-paralysis (not one of the official fifty states, but the first to be founded on the almost-method).

Almost-paramount, *adj.* Secondary, but still important.

Almost-paramour, *n.* A possible future lover. Someone you don't want your spouse to meet even though nothing has happened yet.

Almost-paraphernalia, *n.* Relatively-small accessories like almost-shirts, almost-mugs, and almost-bags.

Almost-paraphrase, *v., n.* To deliberately make some minor change in the meaning of the original phrasing (and not just deliver the gist). Or, to attempt to deliver the gist of what was said in your own words, but your memory of the original is so poor that you do an almost-bad job of it.

Almost-parasitic, *adj.* Seemingly and mostly parasitic, but partly symbiotic (a not-entirely one-sided relationship).

Almost-parent, *n.* Step-parent. Uncle or aunt.

Almost-park, *n.* A backyard. A "parklet," or "parkule." The stretch of green in the median of a highway. The kind of bench, newspaper dispenser, and trash basket combination that one finds near some bus stops. Some parks are subdivided into many smaller almost-parks (so that they can charge multiple admission fees). "Almost-park" can almost-be an almost-relaxed state of mind, . . . yes.

Almost-parking, *v., n.* Stopping. Or, stopping at the side of the road. Or, leaving your engine running while you and your car are on a ferry. Or, to accidentally leave your car in neutral only to see it later roll down the hill.

Almost-parsimonious, *adj.* Almost-sparing, almost-stingy, almost-thrifty, or almost-restrained. Applying Ockham's razor and then "feathering the nest" a bit. Being both penny almost-wise and pound almost-wise.

Almost-part, *n.* A non-essential part in a movie that may get cut out completely at the editing stage. Or, a bit part.

Almost-participating, *v.* Just listening, but with interest.

Almost-particles, *n.* Almost-waves.

Almost-partner, *n.* A good-time-not-a-long-time partner. Or, a partner that is forced almost-upon you by circumstances. Or, a collaborator in a business venture where the arrangements are very loose.

Almost-parturient, *adj.* Eight-months pregnant, either physically or figuratively.

Almost-party, *v.i.* To have a pretty good time, without getting wild. Or, to party separately together (over the phone or internet, and perhaps in sympathy for a cause).

Almost-Party, *n.* An almost-serious almost-group that almost-together almost-promotes the almost-method (and almost-speak and other almost-stuff) in certain almost-political almost-arenas. There is often an almost-candidate that is almost-running (just jogging) for some almost-position. You might almost-consider almost-joining . . . later, . . . maybe, . . . a little. [See almost-position, almost-way, almost-world.]

Almost-pass, *v.t.* In sports, a thrown or kicked ball that was only almost-caught. Or, when a man says to a woman: "A-hem, . . .," or: "Hey, . . .," or "Hey baby, wanna, . . . you know, ..." And she tries to let him know what language she speaks. And then the balloon he's in takes off.

Almost-passenger, *n.* A stowaway. Someone hanging on for dear life. Or, someone who just missed the boat.

Almost-passport, *n.* Two pieces of identification (neither of which being a passport), where at least one has a picture.

Almost-pass-time, *n.* Something that helps to pass the time, but disagreeably so (like doing the laundry, visiting the dentist, or getting your computer to work properly).

Almost-password, *n.* Your child's name, or your pet's name. Or, that part that is unique in each password and not common to all your passwords.

Almost-past, *adj., prep., n.* The residual and persistent present (no matter how much you wish it would go away, it's still there). For example, whatever has already happened in the room you're in, right up until the time you leave it.

Almost-patchwork, *n., adj.* Incongruous parts that don't fit together all that well.

Almost-patent, *n.* A patent that is pending.

Almost-path, *n.* Any section of the almost-way that is almost-visible, almost-quantum, or in disrepair.

Almost-pattern, *n.* When the pattern changes faster than you can determine what it is. This frustrates many almost-detectives, and almost-shrinks.

Almost-pay, *v.t.* To reach into your wallet in front of the person, and whoops, there is hardly any money there. "How could I have been so forgetful?"

Almost-payback, *n.* Retribution that is insufficiently hurtful.

Almost-payment, *n.* When you pay that part of what you owe that you have on you right now.

Almost-peace, *n.* Just a few decibels lower than almost-war.

Almost-peak, *n.* Near the top.

Almost-peddle, *v.t.* Peddle with only one leg. Peddle when you don't need to (going downhill).

Almost-pedestrian, *n., adj.* Someone walking slowly on a conveyor platform that is moving. Or, something interesting about something commonplace or unimaginative.

Almost-pee, *n.* Apple juice. Beer.

Almost-pejorative, *adj.* Disparaging or belittling words said in a nice way.

Almost-pen, *n.* Pencil.

Almost-penalize, *v.t.* When a punishment does not disadvantage the recipient (as when junior is sent to bed early, but he gets lots of sleep and then aces a test the next day).

Almost-penis, *n.* An artificial penis. She might also say, a flaccid penis.

Almost-penitent, *adj.* Regretful to the extent that one has been caught.

Almost-pension, *n.* Social security payments.

Almost-penultimate, *adj.* The next to the next to last.

Almost-people, *n.* People who are not all there. Or, people who have not yet become all they can be. Or, people who dig almost-stuff. Or, statistics about people who are not right in front of you. [See almost-person.]

Almost-perceptible, *adj.* That which is undetectable via the senses, but may be detectable with the right specialized equipment.

Almost-perception, *n.* When the signal-to-noise ratio is too low for detection to take place. Or, perceiving in "usable and improvable" increments. We perceive as if going through successive idea-bubble stages (or layers) of almost-understanding: first comprehending all of what is available with the technology and data first available, then discovering what is to be found in the next, and then the next bubble, rather that perceiving everything in a certain direction all at once. [See almost-knowledge, almost-understanding, almost-vision.]

Almost-perfect, *adj.* High quality. Probably how you saw your spouse before you got married. Or, almost anything that almost-fits or is almost-appropriate. Things usually don't have to be perfect for us to enjoy them, appreciate them, like them, approve of them, and so on. Only ideals are almost-perfectly almost-perfect, in that temporarily they are taken to be almost-standard. (Of course, another way of seeing things is that everything *is* perfect just the way it is. But that could be almost-nonsense.) Practice makes almost-perfect. [See almost-universals.]

Almost-perform, *v.* Fulfill in an incomplete way. Choke.

Almost-perfunctory, *adj.* Not just done to accomplish the function (as with a dutiful smile), but with a little added interest.

Almost-perigee, *n.* Almost as low in an elliptical orbit as can be.

Almost-peril, *n.* Any visit to the in-laws. Any visit by little nieces and nephews. Or, more generally, the situation in any place where there are children, generals, or almost-things.

Almost-period, *n.* A semicolon.

Almost-peripatetic, *adj.* Having a penchant for mall shopping.

Almost-perishable, *adj.* Everything except food (which is perishable almost by definition).

Almost-perk, *n.* A privilege or benefit in addition to one's regular compensation, but one that is so commonplace, incidental, or unmentionable that it is not listed as a perk (clean air to breathe, no annoying public address system, or a boss that is not ambitious).

Almost-permanent, *adj.* Whatever you think is permanent.

Almost-permission, *n.* Implicit permission. Where it has been decided that there will be no oversight. Or, expected permission. Or, permission in writing to "bend the rules."

Almost-permissive, *adj.* When you let your kids do what other parents don't let their kids do, even if you think the other kid's parents are almost-stupid (because there is still probably some kind of reasoning behind their prohibition). Or, allowing almost-stuff.

Almost-permit, *n.* To permit with deniability. If nobody *sees* you let your dog take a crap on someone else's lawn . . . . Or, if you don't have much choice . . . .

Almost-pernicious, *adj.* Fun.

Almost-perpetual, *adj.* Will go on for quite a while (perhaps repeating), until one day when you least suspect it, . . . something.

Almost-perpetuity, *n.* A long but finite non-specific almost-chunk of time.

Almost-perseverance, *n.* Tenacious pursuit that is abandoned before the realizing of a goal (to pursue an alternative goal, or just to quit — either way being in accordance with the almost-method).

Almost-persnickety, *adj.* Fairly fussy, fastidious, punctilious, snobbish, but not exceedingly so.

Almost-person, *n.* The definition of "human" is a scientific one, whereas the definition of "person" has tended to be both more socially-determined and variable. Once you have defined "persons," some of those candidates that don't meet all of the requirements might still fall into a more leniently-defined category "almost-person." (For your convenience.) Depending on the situation, borderline cases have typically included the yet unborn, minors, the mentally-retarded, pets, corporations, and computer systems. We may need to accommodate space aliens into our social structures in a hurry. Soon we will need to determine how the law should handle artificial intelligences, robots, and cyborgs. For example, Almost-Aristotle might be the almost-spitting image of the old man, and there might be many almost-hims (only almost-identical of almost-course). Will we consider these Almost-Aristotle's to be persons or almost-persons? Will self-improvement ever become illegal? Until then, we need to grapple with the fact that people are constantly and almost-naturally improving themselves. So, almost-all people are almost the almost-people they later become. [See Almost-Aristotle, almost-cyborg, almost-human.]

Almost-personal, *adj.* More than just business. "Did you see the game last night?" "How was your weekend?" "Did you have a good time?" "Would you like another one of those?" "Has your contact information changed?" "We'd just like the information for our files; it's not like we're going to later *use* the information, . . . or sell it."

Almost-personality, *n.* The personality of an almost-person. Or, a personality that has been diminished (as by disease, or self-doubt). [See almost-person.]

Almost-personnel, *n.* Computers, robots, software, foreigners, children, volunteers.

Almost-perspective, *n.* This one (the one presented in the Almost-Dictionary). Or, the perspective of an almost-person in Almostville, Almostland, Almost-World.

Almost-pervasive, *adj.* Almost "in your underwear," and "in your soup." Or, something that pervades just a little bit.

Almost-pessimistic, *adj.* Realistic, in a cynical or gloomy sort of way, but still hopeful and planning in a practical way.

Almost-petition, *n.* Sort of like being "all hat and no cattle," an almost-petition is all signature and no plan (just statements of principle, with nothing actionable, probably phrased negatively).

Almost-petty, *adj.* Not petty enough to overlook and not mention.

Almost-petulant, *adj.* Behavior or speech bordering on insolent or rude in nature.

Almost-PGA, *n.* An association for golfers who are not very good at golf, or who are very good at almost-golf. [See almost-golf.]

Almost-phallic, *adj.* A bit pointy (perhaps, resembling a tall building, a woman's raised arm, or anyone's head).

Almost-phase(s), *n.* The down-time between phases of a project (such as analysis, build, implement) that is usually set apart for management reviews, acquiring funding for the next phase, planning, and re-work). Generally, almost-speaking, the longer the almost-phases, the more problems have developed (and the more serious they are), often indicating that the organization around the project is confused, or distracted.

Almost-phobia, *n.* The fear of almost-aspects. Or, the fear of almost-stuff. This includes but is not limited to: the fear of only almost-high places, the fear of only fairly small enclosures, the fear of speaking to medium-sized groups, and the fear of only getting an almost-pension almost-upon almost-retirement.

Almost-phony, *adj.* Overstated, embroidered, romantic, or . . . normal.

Almost-physical, *adj.* That which exhibits properties of both particles and waves. Basically, everything that is the case. Or, that which is mostly feelings and mood.

Almost-piano, *n.* Harpsicord.

Almost-picaroon, *n.* Any rogue, bohemian, or pirate that you like more than dislike.

Almost-picket, *v.t.* To only picket for the photo-op. Or, to only almost-picket yer dose.

Almost-pickle, *n.* A cucumber that has so far only been almost-preserved in brine or vinegar. Or, a pickle that has had a bite taken out of it. Or, the state you are in before you find that careful wording that is needed to get yourself out of a situation. [See almost-distress.]

Almost-picture, *n.* If a picture almost-says a thousand words, then an almost-picture only almost-says about 987.654321 words (or, almost-roughly speaking, a few fewer words). The almost-picture is also most likely using a lot of almost-speak. (You might even almost-need to squint.) [See almost-number, almost-speak.]

Almost-pier, *n.* A pier too small for your ship or boat to dock at.

Almost-piffle, *n.* Almost-nonsense or almost-idle talk from which a significant or timely fact emerges.

Almost-pigeonhole, *v.t.* When you try to metaphorically pigeonhole someone, and then they almost-wriggle almost-free.

Almost-piggish, *adj.* Not sticking to the almost-diet. Finishing what's on your plate, instead of eating only what you need. [See almost-diet, almost-overeating.]

Almost-piggyback, *v.t.* When one human carries another human on his or her back.

Almost-pilloried, *v.t.* Publicly humiliated without the use of a pillory (just the media, or the almost-media).

Almost-pilot, *n.* Co-pilot. Auto-pilot. Pilot trainee. Back-seat pilot. Remote pilot of a drone or micro-drone.

Almost-pinch, *v.t., n.* When a man reaches over to tweak a woman's backside, and then stops himself.

Almost-pint, *n.* The amount of beer you get in almost-pint mugs.

Almost-piracy, *n.* Having a good time.

Almost-pissed, *adj.* Peeved. Or, almost drunk.

Almost-pitch, *n.* "I will probably be getting and almost-have some almost-stuff to almost-sell (rent) to you."

Almost-pivotal, *adj.* Something that causes a change in attitude or almost-understanding without causing a change in direction.

Almost-place, *n.* Any place other than one on the dry surface of Earth (real-estate). (Examples: a place in cyberspace, in outer space, or deep in the psyche.)

Almost-placebo, *n.* Something ingested instead of a controlled substance that is not inert and that does have its own minor pharmacologic effect (maybe not known at the time), like taking an aspirin instead of diazepam.

Almost-placement, *v.t.* Placement, like a golf ball drop when done on an uneven surface on a very windy day (or near where monkeys live).

Almost-plagiarism, *n.* Rewording what you copy (with due diligence).

Almost-plague, *n.* A disease that descends upon many, without getting anyone seriously ill. (Like the common cold, or complacency.)

Almost-plan, *n., v.* The general idea of a plan. Or, a partial plan. Or, what is left of a serious attempt to plan when things are changing too quickly. One can only almost-plan to win a football game.

Almost-planet, *n.* Moon.

Almost-plank, *n.* If you're on an almost-ship and you almost-annoy the almost-captain, he may suggest that it's your turn to buy at the next tiki bar stop. Almost-arrgh! [See almost-ship, almost-arrgh.]

Almost-planning, *n.* The kind of planning that gets done after people start drinking.

Almost-plant, *n.* Seed. Seedling. Nut. Or, a spy who is nuts.

Almost-plastic, *n.* Anything with plasticity that is not plastic.

Almost-platform, *n.* Bench.

Almost-play, *v.t.* Doodle. Frolic. Exercise. Tour. Joke.

Almost-please, *adv., v.t.* There's just no completely pleasing some people.

Almost-pleasure, *n.* Scratching an itch.

Almost-pledge, *v.t.* When you say you will give, but don't tell them who you are.

Almost-plenty, *adj.* Enough.

Almost-plight, *n.* A curious or somewhat-perplexing non-emergency.

Almost-plunge, *v.i.* Swoop.

Almost-plurality, *n.* Two.

Almost-poach, *v.t.* A minor encroachment.

Almost-point, *v.t.* To indicate with one's nose, or elbow, or eyes.

Almost-poison, *n.* Unhealthy food.

Almost-polecat, *n.* The omnivorous mammal *homo weaseliens*.

Almost-police, *v.t.* Guard. Police cadet. Or, to look in another direction (if it's worth your while).

Almost-political almost-correctness, *n.* What political correctness should be: being considerate, without deliberately numbing discourse.

Almost-politician, *n.* A politician that doesn't have the time to make up his or her own mind on things. Or, a politician that always votes for the status quo position (even if something needs to change). Or, a candidate that has not yet been elected to any political office.

Almost-polluted, *adj.* Polluted. If you're in the polluting business: anything that can be further polluted (as a lake, or stream, or stream of consciousness). Pollution comes in two basic almost-forms: almost-negative and almost-positive. Pollution is an almost-negative if you're choking on it, and almost-positive if you can get paid to clean it up, or describe it, regulate it, or film the people who pollute, clean, describe, or regulate. The both almost-good and almost-bad almost-thing is that there is almost-always almost-room for *more* pollution, and *higher concentrations* of pollutants. There is only "pure pollution" if you define the whole thing as pollution. Still, usually there are some good elements within. The quest for ideal pollution continues. [See almost-pure.]

Almost-pond, *n.* Puddle.

Almost-ponderous, *adj.* Not really that weighty or special.

Almost-pool, *n.* Above-ground pool. Hot tub. Wading pool.

Almost-poor, *adj.* Only relatively poor. Or, middle-class. Or, rich (after taxes).

Almost-popular, *adj.* Liked. If famous, tolerated.

Almost-populate, *v.t.* Walk in, and then out.

Almost-populist, *n.* Centrist.

Almost-porn, *n.* The depiction of only almost-erotic images or behavior (perhaps, somewhat revealing or tantalizing without being overly sexual). There are various forms, but largely the distinction almost-hinges on the skimpiness of the clothing, and the type of setting.

Almost-port, *n.* Anchorage, especially one where there is no nearby military installation.

Almost-portable, *adj.* Something that you wish you didn't need to carry.

Almost-portend, *v.t.* To foreshadow something almost-abstract. [See almost-abstract.]

Almost-position, *n.* The almost-position is typically one less settled than just "sitting over there," "lying down," or "being left right out," and more like "rambling," "stumbling," or "standing and scratching one's head." The almost-professional might assert: "You are going to be almost-fine," or "I'm almost-ok, and you're almost-ok," or "It takes 1.987654321 to tango." (Go figure.) When it comes to politics, there are two ways in which the almost-position is helpful. First, never commit wholeheartedly to any position. Second, it is almost-always most appropriate to apply the almost-method in the almost-way. If the goal of most of politics is to maintain the status quo, then the almost-position would be to fix the status quo only when it breaks—which is a more-tenable position than proposing new ways for things to almost-be. [See almost-method, almost-number, almost-way.]

Almost-positive, *adj.* A mostly negative thing that ain't so bad (has some redeeming attributes).

Almost-positivism, *n.* The rejection of negative vibes, and also illogical, unnatural, outmoded, and non-reproducible vibes.

Almost-possess, *v.t.* Nobody fully possesses anything, that's why we have laws. [See almost-have.]

Almost-possible, *adj.* An opportunity that may have never been tried before, but now is worth a try. Usually, when you see an opportunity it is almost too late, someone else is on their way to beating you to it, or someone is busy "raising the bar," or changing the game, or trying desperately to marginalize your efforts. In short, almost everything is almost-possible, but still it's almost-up to you, and almost-down to business. Almost-hang almost-in near there, almost-baby!

Almost-post, *n., v.t.* A small stick or rod. Or, the publishing of a politically-correct milquetoast version of your thoughts that is so innocuous that it is almost-worthless.

Almost-postmodern, *adj.* Mostly modern, with just a hint of the postmodern thing there. (Not at all the same as post-almostmodern, which is now almost old-fashioned.) Almost-postmodernism is an almost-knee-jerk reaction to postmodernism in the almost-way, and using the almost-method, and it can be almost-applied to almost anything (especially so as to almost-shock almost-little almost-old ladies). (Almost everything almost-shocks them anyway.) [See almost-comprehension, almost-complex, almost-customer, almost-deconstruct.]

Almost-poverty, *n.* The almost-financial almost-position in which one is most likely to buy lottery tickets, movie tickets, football game tickets, fast food, alcohol, and/or cigarettes. Also, the condition of not being so poor as to avoid sales taxes, income taxes, utility taxes, hidden taxes, flat taxes, round taxes, and excise taxes. [See almost-poor.]

Almost-power, *n.* Potential power. The power that comes with knowing who to call. The power that comes with having a better almost-understanding. Knowledge is almost power. Or, the power of almost-stuff, or almost-speak.

Almost-powerful, *adj.* Well-connected. Or, the feeling one gets when behind the wheel of a sports car, or pickup truck.

Almost-practical, *adj.* Most people in most situations.

Almost-practice, *v.* When you try to better yourself at something, and then get distracted. Or, practice in dealing with almost-aspects. Or, improving your almost-speak by talking to that almost-person in the bathroom mirror.

Almost-precarious, *adj.* In a medium-risk condition or situation.

Almost-precise, *adj.* Fairly imprecise.

Almost-precocious, *adj.* Exhibiting exceptionally well-developed intellectual or creative abilities for someone so young, but only when attempting to avoid doing homework or chores.

Almost-precursor, *n.* Something that helped something else get where it is today.

Almost-predatory, *adj.* A growler, a howler, and a seeker of "good deals." Selfish, or hungry.

Almost-predicament, *n.* A quagmire from which one quickly sees an escape or solution.

Almost-predict, *v.t.* Determine and state the most likely outcome.

Almost-predilection, *n.* A mental almost-leaning.

Almost-preemptive, *adj.* An almost-action that doesn't so much decide the course of events before the fact, but more or less precludes certain actions from taking place afterward. [See almost-action.]

Almost-preen, *v.* To duly care for one's outer self and appearance without extravagance.

Almost-prefab, *adj., n.* The materials from which future prefabricated things might be made.

Almost-prefer, *v.t.* When you like two things almost equally, and any choosing between the two depends on what almost-aspect one is considering at the moment.

Almost-prejudice, *n.* One's pre-prejudiced leanings.

Almost-preliminary, *adj.* Something that just-precedes the introductory part of something else, but that is so basic that it is usually taken for granted (like going to the bathroom before delivering a speech).

Almost-premium, *n.* The almost-extra involved with almost-stuff and almost-speak. Admittedly, sometimes it's just a few extra letters and a hyphen, but sometimes it's much more. For example, there's the almost-extra almost-confidence you almost-get when you almost-understand new almost-aspects. [See almost-aspect.]

Almost-prepaid, *adj.* An almost-integral part of almost-accounting almost-where things seem to be almost-free (and, typically, where your name and contact information almost-ends almost-up in almost-every database around the world in seconds).

Almost-prepared, *adj.* I ah, well, I think what this means is that one could have thought about whatever it almost-is more. We are almost-always only almost-prepared. The difference between life and death (or success and failure) almost-always comes down to how we almost-handle the gap between "that for which we are prepared" and "that which we actually encounter." When events happen, we use the almost-method, or we get almost-ambitious. Sometimes we think of what to say just a second too late. It is almost-true that to be a success you have to be at the right place at the right time, but you also need to be almost-prepared. (Also, opportunity usually only almost-knocks, so you have to almost-listen, and almost-seek almost-her almost-out.)

Almost-prerogative, *n.* Any right, power, or privilege a man is almost-left with after a woman exercises her prerogative.

Almost-prescriptive, *adj.* Constructive criticism from your boss. Or, advice that is too general in nature to be helpful with specific details.

Almost-present, *adj., n.* Someone not present, but who would be present if it were not for a more pressing engagement. Or, anyone on the phone or in a "chat room" with you. Or, what is happening right now, but far enough away that it will take time for you to know about it (the distant now).

Almost-presentation, *n.* An almost-complete presentation. Or, a presentation about almost-stuff or almost-speak.

Almost-preservation, *n.* When something like what is present now is perpetuated, but it is allowed to change in small ways over time. This can be almost-evolutionary, and may mean "total elimination" in the long run. Or, the preservation of almost-aspects.

Almost-president, *n.* President-elect. Or, Chief Operating Officer (COO).

Almost-press, *n.* A blogger, or bloggers. Anyone with a camera, recorder, or cell phone. Any member of the law enforcement community. Anyone employed by a mass media company.

Almost-preteen, *n.* Fetus.

Almost-pretty, *adj.* Not pretty ugly.

Almost-prevail, *v.i.* Ultimately, to lose. Or, to get your point across and accepted, even though your point gets trumped by a larger more-significant point.

Almost-prevent, *v.t.* To almost-forestall, but to be ultimately not prevent.

Almost-prevention, *n.* When almost-stuff gets in the way of things actually almost-happening. For example, what strict adherence to the almost-method actually sometimes does.

Almost-price, *n.* The price before you settle on a price. Or, the estimated or appraised price. Or, a value expressed in other than monetary terms. Or, anything you are thinking about while haggling with yourself.

Almost-priceless, *adj.* Something very expensive and maybe also unique, but to which someone can still attach a price.

Almost-prime, *n., adj.* Any natural number that is divisible without remainder by the numbers: one, itself, and just a few other numbers.

Almost-principle, *n.* Almost everything is almost-something, almost something else, or has some aspect of itself that is almost-something. [See almost-almost, almost-aspect, almost-something.]

Almost-print, *v.t.* When you try to print something, but then only get an almost-meaningless almost-error almost-message.

Almost-printed, *adj.* Stuck somewhere inside a machine.

Almost-priority, *n.* Something that should take precedence, but not before other thing.

Almost-private, *adj.* Anything you let someone else know.

Almost-prize, *n.* A reward that doesn't interest you.

Almost-probably, *adv.* Maybe.

Almost-probative, *adj.* An almost-question, followed by a preparatory statement with a squeezed in opinion, then a softball question about the topic almost at hand, then an almost-personal question (perhaps, about favorite color), and then a break for commercial.

Almost-probe, *n.* A serious investigation by the person's own political party.

Almost-problem, *n.* A problem that you can ignore, or a problem that is too insignificant to be considered a problem. Or, someone else's problem.

Almost-pro bono, *adj.* "I'm really quite busy helping the needy already."

Almost-procedure, *n.* A list of some things to do that don't need to be done in precisely the order stated. An almost-procedure for losing weight might be: eat less, exercise more, monitor your weight. An almost-procedure for fixing a flat tire might be: take the nuts off before the wheel, put the other wheel on before the nuts, raise the car up before attempting to take the wheel off, and everything you need is in the trunk.

Almost-proceed, *v.i.* To almost-go where you have not almost-gone.

Almost-process, *n.* Almost-all processes are almost-processes, for three main reasons. First, they can be broken down into smaller and smaller steps until (as with one of Zeno of Elea's many paradoxes) you never actually get almost-something done. (This happens a lot.) Next, the more a process is broken down into steps, the more freedom there is for alternate pathways to develop, and so what would be straightforward is now a web of possibilities. Third, the first thing someone is likely to do when finding out about a "process" is to tweak it for the particular situation (local suitability), so for this reason processes are always in flux (as mimemes, they almost-evolve as they are almost-deliberately made to change or almost-change).

Almost-produce, *v.* Supervise.

Almost-product, *n.* What you have when something is almost-finished, almost-complete, almost-together, or almost-ready for sale.

Almost-production, *n.* The stage of "system test" when all the parts are tested together. Or, when an almost-product is made.

Almost-productive, *adj.* Someone who would be productive if they didn't encounter so many distractions, obstacles, constraints, or regulations.

Almost-profession, *n.* An occupation that relies on advanced learning, technical competence, ethical and other almost-standards, but that also involves innovation and artistry, and that is changing too quickly for certifications to be relevant for very long. In the future, almost every profession will be an almost-profession (today, almost every profession relies heavily on certifications). Or, a professional working in an almost-field. [See almost-field.]

Almost-proffer, *v.t.* Hold something out with arm extended for another to take, then take it back as they go to take it, and when they give up, repeat the tease.

Almost-proficient, *adj.* Someone advanced or skilled just enough to be dangerous. According to the Peter Principle, anyone working within a hierarchy who over time has risen to their own "level of incompetence" (or almost-competence).

Almost-profitable, *adj.* As in, "The business is profitable, until you consider what goes to the suppliers, the insurance companies, the government, and the ex-wife."

Almost-profligate, *adj.* Only profligate on the weekends.

Almost-programmer, *n.* Anyone who thinks computer programming is easy.

Almost-progress, *n.* Chasing one's tail. One step forward, then sliding or getting pushed back. One step forward, and then someone changes the game on you so that you're no further ahead. Or, just having a meeting to discuss what progress has not been made.

Almost-progressive, *adj.* Only promising of progress, and not really delivering a whole lot.

Almost-prohibit, *v.t.* Deter.

Almost-prohibitive, *adj.* A reason for *not* doing something that doesn't quite offset the reason *for* doing something.

Almost-project, *n.* The collection of activities and tasks almost-required to get something almost-done.

Almost-promise, *v.t.* Predict hopefully. Or, say that you'll do something in an earnest tone (without using the word "promise").

Almost-promulgate, *v.t.* To announce/declare on a hard-to-find web page.

Almost-proof, *n.* Inconclusive supporting evidence.

Almost-proper, *adj.* A subject for the sit-coms (actually, the almost-situation mostly almost-comedies).

Almost-property, *n.* In real estate, just undesirable land with no building on it (desert or swamp). Or, all property (since possession is merely a social construction, and, therefore, nobody fully possesses anything). [See almost-have.]

Almost-propose, *v.t.* "Hey! What are you doing next Saturday afternoon?" [See almost-pass.]

Almost-proprietary, *adj.* The rest of the so-called "best things in life" (those things not already proprietary). Who's air are *you* breathing?

Almost-prosaic, *adj.* More factual than stylistic, and bordering on dull or unimaginative.

Almost-prospect, *v.t.* To hunt for almost-stuff in out-of-the-way places.

Almost-protest, *v.t.* To complain under your breath.

Almost-protraction, *n.* To prolong an almost-aspect—especially, to extend it, or make it more pronounced. The more almost-protracted something almost-gets, the more the almost-almost is almost-revealed. Hmmm. This often involves risk. This especially applies to projects. [See almost-aspect, almost-almost.]

Almost-proud, *adj.* How you feel when someone has met expectations. Or, how you feel when someone has almost-met expectations by almost-completing an almost-project through using the almost-method almost-properly. Or, not particularly disappointed.

Almost-prove, *v.t.* Make an argument for a position on a controversial topic by relating several anecdotes that make you sound like you know what you're talking about.

Almost-proven, *adj.* Not proven. (A lot of breath or ink might have been spent in the attempts to prove though.)

Almost-provide, *v.t.* To have waiting but hidden (until the right time comes along). Or, to not provide but keep them guessing.

Almost-provincial, *adj.* Having mostly local or very restricted interests.

Almost-provision, *n.* Something you take with you, but then don't use during the trip.

Almost-psyche, *n.* That almost-aspect of mind which almost-sees itself as being composed of almost-ego, almost-id, and almost-superego. It is the almost-psyche that almost-makes one almost-unique. [See almost-ego, almost-id, almost-superego.]

Almost-psychology, *n.* We are only ever almost-listening, almost-understanding, almost-rational, and almost-satisfied. Everything about our brain is in a state of not quite being where we want it, from the continual molecular transitioning, to the ever-changing and incomplete adjustments to new information. But also, our psychology reflects what is happening in our environment, and *its* transitional nature, which in turn almost-originated with the almost-patriarchal solar influence, and its almost-motherly, almost-earthly almost-counterpart. We all learn to be both active and passive, and our dispositions closely parallel the various extremes and transitions in weather. We are at times energetic, ardent, impassioned, ominous, unforgiving, threatening, harsh, cold, unkind, capricious, warm, effluent, inviting, lazy, dry, gentle, subdued, bland, pliant, and going-with-the-flow (or any such attribute in a mollified, combined, or impure form). Razzle-dazzle still razzle-dazzles. These dispositions are also tribal, military, economic, political, social, and cultural, and those types of entities all copied and learned from each other — at least at the almost-conscious level. Also, we are naturally less-than-maximally extroverted, confident, detail-conscious, tough-minded, and creative. The almost-point: We almost-naturally almost-understand the almost-plain and almost-simple aspects mentioned above, even without being educated in the subject of psychology. [See almost-therapy, almost-think.]

Almost-pub, *n.* A place where people go to drink coffee or juice, shoot darts, and talk. Or, where everyone wears a fake dartboard on the back of their head so that other people can poke at the bull's eye with their finger as a conversation starter.

Almost-public, *adj.* Behind some kind of firewall, but something that many people can still access. A company-wide email warning of a pending audit would be almost-public. Or, more generally, anything not public.

Almost-publish, *v.t.* Say. (Especially of something said into a microphone.) Send via email.

Almost-puerile, *adj.* Not childish, but somewhere between juvenile and sophomoric.

Almost-punch, *v.t., n.* A slap, or jab. Or, a nail. Or, a statement that packs a wallop. Or, a bowl full of booze that is contaminated with just a few drops of your favorite fruit juices.

Almost-punctilious, *adj.* Almost sufficiently concerned about the details and conventions.

Almost-pundit, *n.* Any pundit with whom you disagree.

Almost-purchase, *v.t.* To fill your "basket" online, and then click away from the site before giving your payment information.

Almost-pure, *adj.* Containing impurities. Somewhat impure. Even if something contains one part per million of something else it is not a pure substance.

Almost-purpose, *n.* Not exactly the intended use of something, but close. Perhaps, a secondary purpose.

Almost-pursuant to, *prep.* In near-conformity with, or in some accord with. Or, because I said so, but I found an antecedent event I can blame, and my almost-reasoning from there might seem more palatable to you.

Almost-pursuit, *v.t.* Continuing to follow someone's movements while remaining stationary.

Almost-push, *v.t.* The soft sell.

Almost-pusillanimous, *adj.* Only cowardly or timid when it comes to new and unfamiliar things, otherwise just reserved.

Almost-puzzle, *n., v.* An only almost-difficult situation. Perhaps, something like a paint-by-numbers, or how to get the child-proof container open, or a drunk test if you're not drunk.

Almost-pyramid, *n.* The pyramids in Egypt are now only almost-pyramids in that they have been worn down. Or, perhaps, a triangular pyramid (as opposed to square pyramid).

Q

Almost-quail, *n.* The other birds that you may also hunt with your license during quail season. Or, if the day is almost-over, beer cans.

Almost-quaint, *adj.* Something almost or becoming old-fashioned. Obsolete and uninteresting. Something that has lost its fascination.

Almost-qualified, *adj.* Trained, but with no experience. Or, not legally eligible to perform the riskiest parts of the job.

Almost-quality, *adj., n.* Lacking excellence (having significant intrinsic inadequacies or deficiencies). Or, that which could be improved upon, but serves its purpose adequately. Almost-quality is what you get when you improve something or make it more useful, but at the same time keep costs down by cutting corners. Almost-quality is the result when you purposely make something less robust than it could be so that you will be able to also sell replacements (as with light bulbs, or automobiles). The "future of quality" borders on a lot of gray areas.

Almost-quantity, *n.* Nearly as much (as the quantity just mentioned or desired). Or, a wildly imprecise guess at a quantity (such as: "a *lot* of people," "*much* wealth," or "there are probably *over a million* ants on the planet").

Almost-quantum, *n., adj.* A quantity or amount that is insufficient or less than expected. Or, related to an insufficient amount of energy to have any effect whatsoever (for some unknown, or for some almost-understandable reason). Or, responses that are not so much a gradual but more of an incremental nature. (And, possibly, where there is leaping and jumping with no legs).

Almost-quarrelsome, *adj.* Someone who insists on vocalizing their version of an almost-understanding just made by someone else, even though they agree. Or, quarrelsome in or about almost-speak.

Almost-quarry, *n.* Anything that could be hunted, would be hunted, or might be hunted. Therefore, almost anything identifiable as an object. Or, almost anything not yet identifiable as an object.

Almost-quarter, *n., adj.* A fifth. Or, two dimes. Or, four nickels. (I don't believe in pennies.)

Almost-quarterly, *adv., adj.* Something that can't be counted on to occur every three-month (because of problems in the supply-chain, no doubt).

Almost-queen, *n.* Princess.

Almost-quell, *v.t.* To almost-overwhelm and almost-reduce to almost-passivity or almost-submission. Or, to diffuse or disperse.

Almost-quench, *v.t.* To almost-extinguish by substantially satisfying, damping, cooling, or decreasing.

Almost-query, *v.t., n.* To raised one eyebrow questioningly.

Almost-question, *v.t., n.* When you repeat a statement as if you are thinking about its implications. "The boat is going to smash into the dock." Or, when you make your question sound like a statement to see if anyone is going to refute it. "So you slept so soundly that you didn't hear the train." Or, when you think about something as being not quite right, but you don't say anything right away. "Hmmm." Or, the question: "Can it be improved?"

Almost-questionnaire, *n.* A poorly-designed questionnaire, and one that does not permit conclusive results to be drawn from the feedback. (Such a questionnaire might ask: "What is the price of peanut butter in your city?" or "How often do you listen to music?")

Almost-queue, *n.* A fickle and impatient queue.

Almost-quibble, *v., n.* When quibbles are mixed with bits (as on the Internet) in such a way that there is no pure or complete quibble.

Almost-quick, *adj.* Much faster than a tortoise, yet much slower than a hare. (In that one of those two are probably going to win the race, it's almost-amazing that almost-everyone takes the almost-quick route.)

Almost-quid pro quo, *n.* When the motive or kickback has not yet been found, but you almost-suspect that something is almost a foot.

Almost-quiet, *adj.* Just loud enough to keep you awake.

Almost-quilt, *n.* A crazy-quilt. Anything patchwork.

Almost-quintessence, *n.* Almost the most perfect embodiment of something. You know it can be improved upon, but that would be unnecessary. For example, we usually stop shopping when we have found something adequate.

Almost-quiver, *n.* A cup or mug that you can keep darts in.

Almost-quixotic, *adj.* Almost-impractically almost-chivalrous, almost-romantic, and almost-visionary. Said another way: of *the* most common almost-outlook.

Almost-quiz, *v.t., n.* When you come home late and your spouse tries to find out what you've been up to through indirect means.

Almost-quorum, *n.* Only almost-enough for a quorum.

Almost-quota, *n.* An informal quota. A floating percentage or range describing a proportional part or share.

Almost-quotable, *adj.* An awkward phrase, or long harangue. Or, the gist. Perhaps, what was said, but not recorded precisely.

Almost-quote, *v.t., n.* To misquote or paraphrase in a still-recognizable way. "Two bees or not two bees, that is the almost-question."

R

Almost-race, *v., n.* A considerably safer way of having fun. Racing often encourages people to venture beyond almost-safe activities into more dangerous behavior, and should usually be avoided. Almost-racing typically rewards people for participating and finishing, and diminishes the importance of being first or almost-first.

Almost-rain, *n.* Drizzle.

Almost-raisin, *n.* A very ripe grape.

Almost-rally, *v., n.* To almost-gather almost-together almost-around an almost-common almost-cause.

Almost-rampage, *v.i., n.* Any spree or binge that involves shopping, particularly one that involves running.

Almost-random, *adj.* Recklessly non-selective.

Almost-range, *n.* The place where you go to practice-fire blanks.

Almost-rank, *adj., n.* Just stinky. Or, in the Almost-Military, the approximate (or shady) positions of social secretary, admirable, almost-major almost-general, almost-senior almost-chief almost-petty almost-officer, almost-double agent, talent scout, lance corporal, flag waver, flag folder, tenderfoot, nurse's aide, breakfast cook, horse, hey you, who me, and left-right-out.

Almost-rapacious, *adj.* Excessively grasping or covetous, but no more than what almost-anyone else would be doing in the same situation.

Almost-rare, *adj.* Seemingly rare, until you try to sell one.

Almost-rat, *n.* Mouse.

Almost-rational, *adj., n.* Cloudy or vague thinking, or only somewhat-logical thought. Or, possessing a better than average almost-understanding on the subject at wrist. An attribute found to some degree in most humans (but don't expect anyone to be completely rational all the time, especially those closest to you). [See almost-abstract, almost-understanding, almost-real, almost-empirical.]

Almost-raven, *n.* Crow.

Almost-raw, *adj.* Very rare (as in, it might still almost-moo).

Almost-reach, *v.t.* Reach out, but not far enough.

Almost-read, *v.t.* Peruse, scan, flip through, browse, or even speed-read. Also, even if we read every word in the book, we don't remember all of it. [See almost-understand.]

Almost-ready, *adj.* When you don't yet have your keys in hand, your watch on, or your hair combed. (For women and clowns, this is to describe a state later in the process than when makeup has not yet been applied.)

Almost-real, *adj., n.* Not yet seen, or discovered, or invented, or imagined. Or, virtual. Or, a prototype, or scaled-down model. [See almost-abstract, almost-something.]

Almost-realize, *v.t.* When you have inklings about something, but the penny hasn't dropped yet. (Perhaps you should take up the practice of almost-talking to yourself.)

Almost-reason, *n., v.* Excuse. Or, lame excuse. Or, lame version of sophisticated thinking. Or, a kind of post-facto weak justification for a fortuitous intuition.

Almost-recall, *v.t.* When a loophole in the legal proceedings allows for there to not be a recall.

Almost-receipt, *v.t.* When it really is in the mail.

Almost-receivable, *n.* An IOU with no signature. Or, a verbal IOU.

Almost-receiver, *n.* The guy that was supposed to catch the ball.

Almost-recent, *adj.* Long enough ago that it might be worth doing again.

Almost-recession, *n.* The economic condition of being close enough to a recession that you might as well start calling it something. That's it. It's that simple. The technical definition of the word "recession" seems to be so esoteric or disputed, and it's use is so unavoidably defeatist that we very much need this new term.

Almost-reciprocate, *v.t.* Monica: Your hair looks exquisitely beautiful. Linda: I like your hair too, Monica.

Almost-recondite, *adj.* Almost-deep, and maybe almost-obscure (of the non-obvious parts of a subject).

Almost-reconsider, *v.t.* To feign or curtail a reconsideration: "Let's see. Hmmm. Ok, still no. Take a hike."

Almost-record, *n.* What you think of as one record might exists physically as related records, probably as updateable or partially updatable information. If this is the case, then each piece would be an almost-record.

Almost-recording, *n.* Sound bite. A brief catchy comment or saying, especially one deliberately taken out of a larger context (perhaps to almost-spin almost-it).

Almost-recover, *v.t.* To regain most of the ground lost.

Almost-recreational, *adj.* For fun, but also for profit.

Almost-recruit, *n.* A recruit that leaves only days after being hired because the job he or she really wanted came through.

Almost-recurring, *adj.* When you've been in a similar situation before, again and almost-again. When history only almost-repeats itself.

Almost-red, *adj.* Orange, pink, or maroon.

Almost-redirection, *n.* When your call doesn't get transferred correctly.

Almost-reduction, *v.t., n.* Reduction, absent emergent properties.

Almost-redundancy, *n.* An alternative but inferior near-duplicate process of making near-duplicates. (For example: A bank's theoretical ability to keep track of accounts on paper in emergencies might work for a few minutes, but not for very long.)

Almost-redundant, *adj.* An alternative but inferior near-duplicate definition about ways of making duplicates with almost-mutations that you might almost-like better. [See almost-contagious, almost-copy, almost-mutate, almost-redundancy.]

Almost-refer, *v.t.* Allude.

Almost-refined, *adj.* You can dress them up, but you can't take them out.

Almost-reflection, *n.* Almost-you, when the mirror-mirror-on-the-wall gets confused (or foggy).

Almost-refund, *n., v.t.* When you know that some of your money is coming back to you, but you haven't received it yet.

Almost-region, *n.* That almost-gray almost-area where almost-everything that almost-exists almost-resides (this is an almost-place, almost-unlike almost any other). [See almost-abstract, almost-ideal, almost-zone.]

Almost-regret, *v.i.* When you do regret some things (like the collateral damage), but don't regret taking the action.

Almost-rehabilitate, *v.t.* When you are not quite the same afterwards. Today, still, when recovering from most things that would require "rehabilitation," the improvement is rarely completely restorative.

Almost-reify, *v.t.* Hypostasize. Or, reify.

Almost-reject, *v.t.* Marginalize.

Almost-relate, *v.t.* To not tell the whole truth. To make a long story short (telling the whole truth usually takes hours, so we are often almost-satisfied with the summary version).

Almost-related, *adj.* Anyone, and their ex-spouse. The mother of the bride, and the mother of the groom. An unmarried couple. Perhaps, a deceased person, and the person visiting their grave.

Almost-relationship, *n.* The kind of relationship that is shallow or tenuous (such as with acquaintances or people you meet only on the Internet). Or, the kind of one-way relationship you have with people you know *of* but don't know personally (people on television or in the movies, historical figures, artists or authors). This works the other way too: you have an almost-relationship with strangers to you that already know much about you, and might feel they have the right to interrupt you; hence, caller-id. [See almost-friends.]

Almost-relative, *n.* Not a blood relative, but a DNA relative (someone of the same species).

Almost-reliable, *adj.* Likely to let you down at just the wrong time. Almost everything "reliable" is only almost-reliable. That's why we fret so much. Reliability is usually not left open-ended, but defined to be within certain parameters. A hammer is reliable when hitting nails. The more complicated a thing (the more degrees of freedom), the more room for less reliability. You almost-don't want to bet your life on computer software, or hardware, but you do every day.

Almost-ironically, the computer revolution was initially driven by the desire to get the unreliable human out of the system, but then quickly the reliability of software and data became even more problematic (and now the humans are all doing a "quality" job trying to keep the computers from going haywire). Our world itself is only almost-reliable in many ways: volcanoes may erupt, hurricanes may form, economic disasters may just spring out of nowhere, and what lurks behind the next corner is anyone's guess.

Almost-remark, *n.* A remark under the breath.

Almost-remarkable, *adj.* Something that would be remarkable if not for the fact that many others have already done it successfully many times.

Almost-remedy, *n.* Treatment. Song and dance.

Almost-remove, *v.t.* To turn off, or otherwise leave in an ineffectual state. To bind and gag. Or, to marginalize.

Almost-renewable, *adj.* Theoretically renewable, but practically non-renewable.

Almost-renown, *n.* What you have when you're quite famous.

Almost-rent control, *n.* Rent control (because it only works under certain conditions, for short periods, and to a certain degree).

Almost-repair, *v.t.* To try to repair, and fail. Or, to find out which parts need replacing.

Almost-repay, *v.t.* To pay back most of what is owed.

Almost-replace, *v.t.* When a trainee take over someone's position, they only partially replace them at first, until they "get up to speed," and "hit the ground running," and make almost-all of the almost-same mistakes easy-over again.

Almost-reply, *v.t.* To just echo (but at least the sender knows the message was received in its entirety).

Almost-report, *n.* An insubstantial report (one that might only be accurate at the thirty-thousand foot level, or does not include the right kinds of numbers, or is not timely enough). Or, any report that indicates the condition of certain almost-aspects or almost-stuff (perhaps, an Almost-State of the Almost-Sphere report).

Almost-represent, *v.t.* To act as an agent for someone else, but in the same way a purchaser's real estate agent (who gets paid by the seller), or a lawyer (who must respect the law first) does.

Almost-representational, *adj.* That which almost-obscures while it almost-reveals. While a realistic-looking portrait might be considered representational art, an impressionistic or cubistic version of the same scene might be considered almost-representational. [See almost-abstract.]

Almost-repress, *v.t.* To nearly subdue others, or one's self.

Almost-request, *v.t., n.* When you keep asking about the subject or "beating around the bush" until the other person gets the hint.

Almost-require, *v.* Crave. Ask. Entreat. Importune.

Almost-requisite, *adj.* Optional, but regarded as necessary by almost-everyone.

Almost-rescue, *v.t.* To throw someone a life jacket, and hope for the best.

Almost-research, *v.t., n.* A quick Internet search on the subject. Or, research that is done by someone else (when, if you want it done right you must do it yourself). Or, research purposely done with an insufficient sample size (rendering inconclusive results), so that when you are finished you will be asked to continue your research using a more appropriate sample size.

Almost-reserve, *n.* Where almost-whines are kept until the time is almost-right. Or, your refrigerator. Or, when you say too much.

Almost-reserved, *adj.* Just reserved enough that you don't get almost-bounced.

Almost-resident, *n.* The girlfriend or boyfriend of the resident.

Almost-resignation, *n.* Joking with your boss that you don't really want to work there anymore. Or, showing up but not doing any work. Or, going absent without leave.

Almost-resolution, *n.* A partial or temporary resolution.

Almost-resolve, *n.* When you try your best to determine that a certain thing will happen (like getting more sleep, or more exercise), but there are other things acting to wear on that resolve, or that trump that resolve.

Almost-resource, *n.* The part-timer, Mr. Sleepy-head, Mr. Never-shuts-up, the Sick-leave Diva, and other such characters.

Almost-respond, *v.t.* The way Mr. Poker-face puts on that blank stare.

Almost-response, *n.* "I'll get back to you on that."

Almost-responsible, *adj.* Not fully in control. Or, someone who shares responsibility. As responsible as a member of a group making a collective decision can be (juror, legislative assembly member).

Almost-responsive, *adj.* Responding in unsatisfactory ways (only speaking in clichés, or trying to respond immediately after a general anesthesia).

Almost-rest, *n.* Cat nap. Or, whatever you get to do when you boss claims that a change is as good as a rest. Or, not the full complement.

Almost-result, *n.* A preliminary result. Or, those parts of the outcome that can't easily be hidden.

Almost-retail, *adj.* Wholesale. Internet sales, perhaps straight from the manufacturer. Or, "I just happen to have one in the trunk of my car."

Almost-retired, *adj.* Working at a well-deserved sinecure. Or, more likely, after leaving your high-paying job, working at a lower-paying job with longer hours.

Almost-retrieve, *v.t.* To locate and bite at to make sure it's dead, and then just sit there and whine.

Almost-return, *v.t.* When you return to the same place and almost-know it for the almost-first time — but both you and the place have changed, so really a significantly-different self only almost-returned.

Almost-revenue, *n.* Accounts receivable.

Almost-review, *n.* A review, just in almost as many almost-words.

Almost-revise, *v.t.* Say the same thing almost-differently.

Almost-revolution, *n.* A calm and unhurried revolution. The transition to almost-speak might almost-be one.

Almost-ribald, *adj.* Not so lewd or obscene that it can't be on prime-time television.

Almost-rich, *adj.* Comfortable. Still working, but with a staff.

Almost-rig, *v.t.* Coming close to completely setting up a sailing ship or theater with the basics of support equipment.

Almost-right, *adj.* Not right enough that there is not some mistake, misrepresentation, or only almost-understanding evident.

Almost-rights, *n.* Those privileges that you think are yours until someone takes them away.

Almost-ring, *v.i.* When your gadget is set to vibrate, or flash, or shock you, or crawl up your nose, or get your attention another way.

Almost-risk, *n.* When there is a safety net. Or, when there is no significant exposure. When there is an almost-complete backout plan (or a Plan B). Or, when you have an angle.

Almost-risk-management, *n.* Keeping your resume up-to-date.

Almost-risky, *adj.* Getting up in the morning.

Almost-river, *n.* Creek. Stream. Brook.

Almost-road, *n.* Lane.

Almost-robot, *n.* Human (especially one doing piece-work for a living). Or, cyborg (especially one doing piece-work for a living).

Almost-rock, *n.* Soft rock.

Almost-rocket, *n.* Large bullet.

Almost-role, *n.* Cameo. Bit part. Non-speaking part. Or, when your role is to *not* do something. Or, when your role is to almost-do something.

Almost-roll, *n.* Rock.

Almost-room, *n.* Walk-in closet.

Almost-rope, *n.* Thick string.

Almost-roust, *v.t.* An unsuccessful attempt to drive (as from bed) roughly or unceremoniously.

Almost-route, *n.* Detour.

Almost-routine, *n., adj.* Something that has been done two or three times before. Or, a routine with minor variations.

Almost-rubber, *n.* Plastic.

Almost-rule, *n.* Rule of thumb. Or, any rule that was made to be bent (almost-broken).

Almost-ruler, *n.* An almost-straight edge with no measuring units marked.

Almost-run, *v.i.* Jog.

Almost-runway, *n.* A walkway, especially one used by models to show off almost-fashionable shoes to potential renters of evening footwear. Or, that part of the airport where planes get together to sniff each other's butts before taking off on a long trip.

S

Almost-sacrifice, *v.t.* When you give up something you didn't much want anyway.

Almost-safe, *adj.* Safe. No person or thing is completely safe, the best you can hope for is almost-safety and almost-security.

Almost-sagacious, *adj.* Almost-knowledgeable and almost-wise in an almost-sophomoric way.

Almost-sail, *v.i.* What you say you do in a sailboat when there is no wind. Or, getting ready to leave port.

Almost-salacious, *adj.* So serious a situation that the licentious imagination doesn't go very far.

Almost-salad, *n.* A mixture with too few items or types (as in, when a tomato and a head of lettuce are placed in a bowl).

Almost-salary, *n.* When you stop getting paid for the overtime you do (perhaps for a slightly higher hourly wage and a better title), but you still don't get the benefits that the salaried people around you get.

Almost-sale, *n.* A discount from a previously-raised price (a practice which makes the job of almost-policing price-fixing more difficult).

Almost-salient, *adj.* Most talk. Or, the mouse in the china shop, right after the bull enters.

Almost-saloon, *n.* Tavern. Tiki bar. Any restaurant with a bar.

Almost-salutary, *adj.* A placebo.

Almost-sample, *n.* A sample that is so small or unrepresentative that only almost-conclusions may be inferred about the population as a whole.

Almost-sanity, *n.* Sanity. The words "completely" and "perfectly" do not belong next to the word "sane."

Almost-satellite, *n.* Projectile.

Almost-satire, *n.* Real life. Any story involving humans that is not actually satire. Or, any story involving almost-stuff, especially when the almost-stuff is used to expose and discredit corruption and near-folly.

Almost-satisfied, *adj.* Rarely is someone completely satisfied, . . . about anything. Usually, being satisfied is a matter of degree. Being satisfied about the various relationships we have with people is also a matter of degree, and we seek what we don't get from one in another. If you've had your almost-fair share of almost-abuse, and you almost-try by using the almost-method but still just get only some almost-satisfaction, you just might find that you do still get most of what others think you almost-need.

Almost-saturated, *adj.* Where there is still room for more. Nearly full of something that fills in the gaps between other things.

Almost-savage, *adj.* Very unruly. Or, childlike. Or, like an almost-garage almost-rock almost-band.

Almost-save, *v.t.* What someone does when they set money aside, because of inflation.

Almost-savvy, *adj.* Using almost-speak in cool almost-ways. Or, using almost-speak when it is almost-inappropriate (in medical journals that almost-ban almost-speak). [See almost-hot, almost-way.]

Almost-say, *v.* Think something that is too blunt or tactless to say.

Almost-saying, *n.* An almost-catchy, almost-pithy, or fairly provocative sentence or statement in almost-speak. Possibly, an almost-slogan. [See the Introduction for a few examples.]

Almost-scale, *n.* A scale good enough for home use, but not good enough for commerce. Perhaps, your two outstretched hands.

Almost-scarce, *adj.* Something not worth hoarding. Or, something that just might be worth hoarding.

Almost-scare, *n.* A surprise that didn't make you jump, or spill your drink.

Almost-scary, *adj.* The future, on a good day. The fragility of life, on any day.

Almost-scene, *n.* What you see when you're hanging out in Almost-World. That which is in an almost-frame, especially those things that are almost-almost in almost-nature. [See almost-world.]

Almost-schedule, *n.* A tentative list of things to do.

Almost-science, *n.* Technology. Science fair science. If science is what we do when we don't know something, then almost-science is what we do when we confirm or repeat what we already almost-understand — in other words, something not even as adventurous as Kuhnian "normal science."

Almost-scoop, *n.* Less than a full scoop (like some "scoops" of ice cream).

Almost-scope, *n.* What you thought was the scope before you started the project (and before the scope got almost-creepy).

Almost-score, *v.t.* Get to third base.

Almost-scout, *v.t.* Look.

Almost-scramble, *v.i.* When you manage to work diligently behind the scenes (paddle hard, like a duck) but to not let people notice the level of difficulty (and to look good doing it).

Almost-scraper, *n.* Something that almost scrapes, like a sky almost-scraper (a thirty-story building). Or, someone who tries to just scrape through at school, but has failed at least one year.

Almost-screen, *n.* A prototype of what might appear on a screen (a mock up, where none of the values are real). Or, a filter that doesn't work (like a mosquito net with holes in it).

Almost-screwball, *adj.* Amiably unpredictable.

Almost-script, *n.* A first-draft of a stage play or screenplay.

Almost-scrutinize, *v.t.* Speed-read or scan quickly with intent to get the general gist.

Almost-sea, *n.* Lake.

Almost-seal, *n.* Baby seal.

Almost-seamless, *adj.* Barely noticeable. The ideal for transitions is that they are as almost-seamless as possible.

Almost-search, *v.t.* Glance. Browse. Or, seek, but with an interest in *not* finding.

Almost-season, *n.* The year can be thought of as being subdivided into eight parts: winter, almost-spring, spring, almost-summer, summer, almost-fall (or almost-autumn), fall, almost-winter, and then back almost-around (up a bit). Any one of the four "transitional" parts of the year; or, collectively, all of them. It is during almost-season when people are most at a loss for what to wear, and, coincidentally, when wearing almost-wear is most appropriate. [See almost-wear.]

Almost-seat, *n.* Stool. An uncluttered spot at the corner of a desk. Or, an uncomfortable "perch" on a racing-style bicycle.

Almost-seaworthy, *adj.* Most boats are only almost-seaworthy (even in fair weather), but most ships are only almost-seaworthy in exceedingly stormy weather.

Almost-secluded, *adj.* May be hidden from view, but not from satellite surveillance.

Almost-second, *adj.* Third.

Almost-secrecy, *n.* When it seems everyone knows but you.

Almost-secret, *adj., n.* When you are at liberty to tell a few close friends as long as you ask them not to repeat what you say.

Almost-secretary, *n.* Blonde secretary.

Almost-security, *n.* A racket, almost-like most others. Nothing is completely secure, so people and institutions only have almost-security at all times. However, there is an industry that runs almost parallel to the almost-security industry, the minimum-security industry, and it is often just as profitable. The minimum-security industry just puts out weaker, more frivolous, or less-reliable products: white picket fences instead of tall razor wire fences, lawn sprinkler systems instead of moats, door knobs instead of dead bolts, little yappers instead of pit bulls, regular windows instead of bullet-proof glass, bicycle helmets instead of military headgear, login ids and passwords instead of top secret clearances, kitchen utensils instead of rifles and cannons, passive surveillance and night watchmen instead of armies and fighter jets.

Almost-seek, *v.t.* To look for in your spare time. Feigning a search. [See almost-search.]

Almost-seems, *adv.* Of a vague impression. When you're really small it almost-seems like you parents are giants.

Almost-seepage, *n.* When something is seeping out so slowly that it doesn't present a problem.

Almost-segregate, *v.t.* To merely allow cliquishness or disproportionate assemblies.

Almost-segue, *n., v.i.* A connecting phrase that nearly gets you to the next subject, but not quite. Or, connecting verbiage that contains almost-words. Like almost-every infant (as almost-explained by Freud), when I was a child I almost-hated my father, and others who were competing with me for resources, but I was almost-ambivalent about my mother because she fed me; then later, I figured out that almost-everyone was both almost-good and almost-bad, and mostly trying their almost-best, and so that's almost-how I came to write the Almost-Dictionary, and therefore, how I got to almost-define almost-words like the one after this one. [See almost-gap, almost-self.]

Almost-self, *n.* A significant part of one's self.

Almost-sell, *v.t.* Rent out, or lease out.

Almost-semantics, *n.* The almost-superficial study of almost-meanings (like this one). [See almost-aspect, almost-deconstruct, almost-definition.]

Almost-semicolon, *n.* Comma.

Almost-seminal, *adj.* Of the almost-origins of almost-new almost-stuff.

Almost-semiotics, *n.* The study of partial signs or almost-signs (perhaps, those things that you are not quite sure are signs) like a broken tree limb in the forest, or someone just coughing once. Almost-semiotics is also that part of semiotics that is almost-focused on the almost-aspects of signs. [See almost-aspect, almost-eme, almost-sign.]

Almost-senior, *adj.* More senior than the rookies.

The Almost-Dictionary

Almost-sentence, *n.* Clause. Or, a commuted sentence.

Almost-sententious, *adj.* Given more to clichés and platitudes than pithy remarks.

Almost-separate, *adj.* Distinct but joined (like the four wheels of a car, or a person's lips, or nostrils). Maybe, connected in vague ways or through culture (like farming and healthcare).

Almost-sequentially, *adv.* First in, first out (unless there are almost-special circumstances).

Almost-sergeant, *n.* Corporal (especially one with healthy lungs and good diction).

Almost-serious, *adj.* Joking in a way that makes sense. Or, serious but also tipsy.

Almost-service, *n., v.t.* Service with a snarl. Or, the kind of service you get from a new-hire, or someone that doesn't know what they're doing.

Almost-set, *n.* In a tennis match, when the players get to the beginning of a tiebreaker. Or, when one or two things in the set are broken or missing, but the other components of the set are still useful.

Almost-settle, *v.i.* Mentally plan for a change. Or, to almost-gradually almost-reach the bottom.

Almost-several, *adj.* A few. [See the sequence of almost-specific counts at almost-all.]

Almost-sex, *n.* Any of the various kinds of intimate relations that do not produce children.

Almost-shade, *n.* The kind of protection you get from a single palm tree on a bright summer day.

Almost-shaky, *adj.* Anything having to do with the stock market.

Almost-shallow, *adj.* Just over your hip waders.

Almost-shape, *n.* An approximate shape (as in, the approximate shape of the Earth is spherical). Almost-everyone almost-cares about the almost-shape you're almost-in. [See almost-athletic, almost-bra, almost-fit.]

Almost-share, *n., v.* Less than your share. Less than a share. Or, a sample. When you give someone only a taste of the whole.

Almost-sharp, *adj.* Blunted from use, but still menacing.

Almost-shelter, *n.* Tent. Or, a rough foliage refuge with a lean-to roof.

Almost-shift, *n., v.* Like a paradigm shift, but in the almost-almost direction. It's just an almost-jump to what's left, and an almost-step to the right.

Almost-ship, *n.* Boat. Sailboat. Yacht. Or, ship with a big hole in the hull.

Almost-shipment, *n.* When you get most of your shipment delivered, rather than having to wait for your supplier to send all of the order at once. (This happens mostly with almost-large orders, with growing supplier companies, in volatile industries, and in tight just-in-time supply chains.)

Almost-shirt, *n.* A halter top. A muscle shirt. Or, any shirt that has an almost-saying on it. [See almost-saying.]

Almost-shit, *n.* Poop. Or, a poor presentation. Or, a poor presentation of an almost-aspect. Or, a shitty way of referring to almost-stuff.

Almost-shitload, *n.* Nearly a full shitload.

Almost-shiver, *v.i.* When you are cold enough to want to jump up and down to keep warm, but you resist the urge to shake and quiver.

Almost-shock, *n.* Surprise. Or, future shock, after you get used to it. Anything you may initially find disconcerting about almost-speak or almost-stuff.

Almost-shoddy, *adj.* What is sometimes referred to as "good enough for government work." (Something that pretty much or almost-serves its purpose without being commercial grade.)

Almost-shoes, *n.* Sandals. Flip-flops.

Almost-shop, *n.* A trading post. An online shop. Anywhere with a cash register that isn't ringing. Any shop that sells almost-stuff.

Almost-shopkeeper, *n.* Sales clerk, especially one who is entrusted to close.

Almost-shopper, *n.* Someone who is just browsing.

Almost-short, *adj.* Still within the first standard deviation in height (or length).

Almost-shortcut, *n.* A route that is shorter than the usual one, but that is so slow that it doesn't significantly reduce travel time.

Almost-shortlist, *n.* The list that is shorter than the long list, and longer than the eventual shortlist.

Almost-shortly, *adv.* Longer than you're prepared to wait (unless you are waiting for medical assistance, in which case you almost-must be almost-patient).

Almost-shorts, *n.* Capris. Skorts. Bermuda shorts. Boxer shorts.

Almost-show, *n.* An almost-short single online video (maybe one made by amateurs). Or, an extemporaneous effort at entertaining.

Almost-showy, *adj.* When you can see "above the knee," as it were.

Almost-shrill, *adj.* An almost-loud, almost-annoying, high-pitched sound. (The kind of noise kitchen appliances make.)

Almost-shrinkage, *n.* When something is growing slower than comparable things around it (as with economies, or populations).

Almost-shutdown, *n.* When production is allowed to go "underground."

Almost-shuttle, *n.* A shuttle that can't go anywhere without external boosters.

Almost-sibling, *n.* Close cousins. Or, a stepbrother or stepsister.

Almost-sick, *adj.* Not sick enough to take a sick day (you'd rather save it for when you're not sick), or getting better but still contagious enough that you'd rather get out of bed and infect everyone (and take drugs to make you seem less sick).

Almost-side, *n.* Profile showing front and side. Or, the side where almost-stuff and almost-speak are appreciated. If you've looked at life from two or three sides now, you still may not be fully appreciating the almost-side. [See almost-aspect, almost-principle.]

Almost-sideline, *n.* Something you wish was a sideline thing or issue, but it just jumped out in front.

Almost-side-step, *v.* While attempting to evade or avoid, you step right in it.

Almost-siesta, *n.* Daydream. Catnap. Power-nod.

Almost-sight, *n.* Blurry vision, or uncorrected vision.

Almost-sigma, *n.* Pretty good quality. (Just less than one sigma.) The kind of quality that just comes naturally from everybody doing their job in such a way that they don't get fired. When it's more important that it be done quickly, than that it be done optimally. Sales before sigmas. [See almost-number.]

Almost-sign, *n.* Most of a sign. Or, perhaps, something you're not sure is a sign, so you keep it as a clue to see if together with other almost-signs it adds up to something. Or, that part of a sign that has almost-aspects. [See almost-eme, almost-icon, almost-semiotics, almost-principle.]

Almost-signal, *n.* A tell, or unwitting disclosure.

Almost-signature, *n.* The signature you use when you're not signing important financial documents. Perhaps, one where you leave out a few letters on purpose.

Almost-signify, *v.* When there is a bit of a mismatch between what is signified and what is meant.

Almost-silent, *adj.* Any house, after the kids have gone to sleep.

Almost-silicon, *n.* Aluminum (one proton less).

Almost-silk, *n.* Nylon (nearly as nice).

Almost-silver, *n., adj.* Gray. Or, pewter. Or, bronze.

Almost-similar, *adj.* Occasionally comparable (perhaps, only when they play tennis). Or, comparable only with respect to certain aspects (a chair and a table). Or, similar with the exception of small but important differences (men and women, human and ape genomes, or sedans and sports cars).

Almost-simple, *adj.* Something with almost-hidden complexity, but that is usually comprehended easily.

Almost-sing, *v.i.* Hum, or whistle.

Almost-sing-along, *n.* A gathering of people with too much time on their hands when they let their lips almost-flap in almost-unison (usually informally, and especially when they don't know all the words).

Almost-single, *adj.* What people are almost-naturally almost-like when they are not with their spouse.

Almost-sink, *v.i.* To partly submerge, and then stop.

Almost-sister, *n.* Sister-in-law. Longtime female friend.

Almost-sit, *v.i.* When you are leaning on a railing or a fence with your bum.

Almost-site, *n.* A web site that is about almost-stuff or almost-speak.

Almost-situation, *n.* A situation wherein almost anything can happen.

Almost-size, *n.* The scope of something almost-abstract (like a problem, or a calculation, or an idea). Solving all of the world's problems is an almost-sized enterprise. Or, bite-size, or pocket-size.

Almost-sizeable, *adj.* Of a size now that even those not in the industry are starting to take notice.

Almost-skeptical, *adj.* Someone who looks at you askance, but doesn't have the time or inclination to ask the questions.

Almost-sketch, *n., v.* Doodle. [See almost-art.]

Almost-ski, *v.* When you fall down too much on skis. [See almost any Warren Miller film for a few almost-creative ways to do this.]

Almost-skill, *n.* Aptitude. Cunning. Dexterity. Or, ability and experience gleaned from a related field or endeavor.

Almost-skin, *n.* Scar tissue. Or, an incomplete covering.

Almost-skip, *n., v.* A temporary and "happy" style of walk.

Almost-skirt, *n.* Miniskirt.

Almost-sky, *n.* That huge volume of air underneath the blue at the top.

Almost-slack, *adj.* Neither loose nor taut.

Almost-slander, *v.t., n.* Defamatory but factual statements.

Almost-slang, *n.* Words or phrases that have been slang for so long that they are listed in the almost-standard dictionaries. Or, strange new words or uses for words that would be slang if more people used them.

Almost-slap, *v.t., n.* To physically threaten and get ready to slap, perhaps with hand up (with children, this is usually enough for them to almost-understand).

Almost-slashed, *adj.* Prices that are just said to be "slashed," but were really just tickled.

Almost-slave, *n.* Employee. Child. Younger sibling.

Almost-sleep, *v.i., n.* Catnapping. Dozing, or nodding off for a few minutes. Or, nearly asleep.

Almost-sleepy, *adj.* How almost-everyone often feels in the early afternoon.

Almost-slender, *adj.* Not fat. Or, one's post-postpartum look. (You can have as many babies as you want and still *almost-keep* your girlish figure.)

Almost-sleuth, *n.* A nosey parker, or busybody.

Almost-slip, *n., v.* A deliberate Freudian slip. [See almost-Freudian slip.]

Almost-slogan, *n.* An almost-expression or almost-saying, particularly in advertising. A slogan that is in almost-speak.

Almost-slow, *adj.* Moving at a deliberate pace. Not really all that slow. Or, quite fast.

Almost-slump, *v.i., n.* What would be normal if it were happening in January or February.

Almost-small, *adj.* Between medium and small. Or, not small, but relatively small compared to something else.

Almost-smash, *v.t.* Strike. Hit. Chip. Ding.

Almost-smidgen, *n.* Nearly a full smidgen.

Almost-smile, *v., n.* Smirk. Grin. A reserved smile, perhaps one with no teeth showing. An attempted smile while there is a cigarette or thermometer in the mouth.

Almost-smooch, *v., n.* Kiss gently.

Almost-smuggle, *v.t.* To import or export something that is not illegal to move; but, something that would need explaining. (Like when your teenager sneaks a dictionary into the house.)

Almost-snitch, *v.i., n.* Someone who reveals something that they didn't know was a secret.

Almost-snow, *n.* One of the almost two hundred different terms for snow that Eskimos have. This one refers to the fake white stuff used to help decorate shopping malls at almost-Xmas time.

Almost-soak, *v.* Wet. Spray. Sprinkle.

Almost-social, *adj.* How you act when you can't completely be your unguarded self in a group (as with co-workers, or where you are expected to be extremely polite).

Almost-society, *n.* A loosely defined association or group, maybe where most members don't even know that the association exists.

Almost-sociology, *n.* The study of the almost-aspects of groups of people. Or, the study of groups of people as individuals from the perspective of psychology. Or, the study of almost-people in groups. [See almost-people.]

Almost-sodden, *adj.* Heavy with moisture, but not to saturation. Or, too drunk to drive.

Almost-software, *n.* Vaporware. Software that might be released, or was never released (maybe because a competitor just released something better). Software still containing design flaws and bugs to the extent that it can't be released or used. Or, software that needs to be frequently updated or patched over the Internet (when you least expect it, for your convenience).

Almost-soil, *n.* Dirt in which nothing will grow.

Almost-sold, *adj.* After the handshake, but before the exchange.

Almost-soldier, *n.* Boot camp trainee. Or, mercenary. Or, bootlicker.

Almost-solo, *adj.* With someone else.

Almost-solutionist, *adj., n.* Anyone who is for intermediation, subscription-based treatments, and perpetual "further study," but shies away from the deliberate *creation* of problems to fix.

Almost-solved, *adj.* When you know most of the following six things: who, what, when, where, why, and how. Or when you already know someone had ability, motive, and opportunity. Or, when you have no idea who did it, but there's only fifteen minutes until the end of the show.

Almost-solvent, *adj.* Able to pay most debts (definitely not "investment grade").

Almost-somebody, *n.* A person that doesn't *feel* like a somebody today. Or, a nobody (euphemistically). Or, a nobody (objectively). Or, an entity that possesses only some of the traditional aspects that a person would have, or where those aspects are structured or manifest in unusual ways (or something not completely personified).

Almost-something, *pron.* Nearly that thing (a statue just before the sculptor is finished, a tree when it was smaller). Or, something else quite like the thing (a different brand of beer). Or, anything not meeting a criteria or threshold (a room that is almost-tidy, a race that is almost won). [See almost-aspect, almost-ideal, almost-stuff.]

Almost-somewhat, *adv.* Just a tad less than what would otherwise be almost-almost. [See almost-almost.]

Almost-somewhere, *adv., n.* A place very close to somewhere. Nearly somewhere. Right next door to somewhere. In the neighborhood of a landmark or important place. In the mail, or stuck in traffic. Or, when you really do almost-travel, . . . almost anywhere. [See almost-travel.]

Almost-soon, *adv.* At a time in the future that is uncertain enough that you don't want to hold your breath and wait.

Almost-soporific, *adj., n.* Something that promotes lethargy without causing sleep. (For example: sports, games, drugs, sex, books, television, classes, exams, or anything else we throw at teenagers to slow them down.)

Almost-sort, *v.t.* A partial or incomplete sort (as when books are arranged on a shelf, or clothes in a closet). Or, when you sort by one criteria, the list is then almost-sorted by a different but highly-correlated criteria (for example, "height of child" and "age of child").

Almost-sound, *adj.* Fairly risky, and probably without enough planning.

Almost-soup, *n.* That time just before a meal when you first start to salivate.

Almost-sour, *adj.* Seemingly unpleasant or moody by disposition a lot of the time.

Almost-source, *n.* The surrogate or agent of the real source.

Almost-Southern, *adj.* Anyone living in the South that doesn't like grits.

Almost-space, *n.* The stratosphere. That place that is sky-high. Or, somewhere that is too limited or small. Or, a space for almost-stuff. [See almost-sky, almost-zone.]

Almost-spare, *adj.* Anything you hardly ever use but that you might use, even though you only have one of it. Or, the third one, that you have just in case the primary and the spare both fail.

Almost-speak, *n., v.* A subset of the English language that includes the word "almost," almost-words, and other words that suggest the concept of being nearly or approximately something. Almost-especially, paragraphs, whole texts, or orations made using a relatively high percentage of almost-words. (Almost-paradoxically, almost-speak usually *adds* precision to speech.) [See almost-word, almost-expression, almost-angle, almost-aspect, almost-method, almost-principle, almost-something, almost-stuff, almost-think.]

Almost-special, *adj.* Something atypical, but nothing to write home about. Or, something just a little bit more special than average. Or, what "special" things become to you, once you become familiar with them.

Almost-specialize, *v.* The more you specialize the fewer people need your services, and you don't want to specialize so much that nobody needs your services. Also, the less you specialize the less your services will be worth. For most people in most situations the best almost-choice is to almost-specialize.

Almost-species, *n.* Whatever types of beings we create from now on.

Almost-specious, *adj.* Showy or sophistic, but bordering on unsound or unresearched. Or, only having the appearance of false genuineness.

Almost-spectacular, *adj.* The sight of something a little less than astoundingly impressive (especially visually).

Almost-speculation, *n.* An educated guess. Hunch.

Almost-speech, *n.* Mumbling. Or, an extemporaneous utterance of sufferable duration. Or, speech (or writing) in the almost-idiom, especially that which includes specific reference to the approximate nature of the subject. [See almost-speak.]

Almost-speed, *n.* A relative lack of stillness that must be overcome.

Almost-speeding, *adj.* Barely over the speed limit, but still going with the flow of traffic and not passing everyone.

Almost-spelling, *v.t., n.* Writing without a spell-checker or dictionary. Creative Spelling as an almost-art form. [See almost-art.]

Almost-spend, *v.* Allocating money in a fund, or budget for a particular purpose. Often, when you don't spend money you almost-need to spend time instead (or vice versa).

Almost-sphere, *n.* An almost-abstract "cloud" that includes and excludes with no physical lines being drawn. For example, a person's sphere of influence is really an almost-sphere of mostly indeterminate influence. Or, whatever is "finite yet unbounded."

Almost-spiel, *n.* A few words.

Almost-splendid, *adj.* Pleasing. Nice.

Almost-split, *v.* What parents often do, just to scare the kids into behaving.

Almost-spoken, *adj.* Non-verbal communication (gestures, winks, or other facial expressions). Not spoken. Or, soft-spoken. Or, spoken in almost-speak. [See almost-speak.]

Almost-sponsor, *n.* Someone who contributes advice, a meal, or materials like cardboard and markers to an almost-good cause. (Often, a friend or relative, especially a parent.)

Almost-sponsored, *adj.* Love is a many-sponsored almost-thing.

Almost-sport, *n.* Active games people play that don't have set rules yet.

Almost-spot, *n.* Dot.

Almost-spouse, *n.* Fiancé or fiancée. (Both words almost-spelled like "finance.") [See almost-husband, almost-wife.]

Almost-spread, *v.* To not completely or evenly spread (as in: to give only most of your samples out, or very quickly load the peanut butter on the bread). To spread as with marbles, or grapeshot, or lies.

Almost-squalid, *adj.* Not so filthy or degrading that someone is not proud to call it home.

Almost-square, *adj., n.* Rectangle (especially where the short sides are almost as long as the long sides).

Almost-squeeze, *v.t., n.* Grab or hold firmly. Or, soon-to-be girlfriend or boyfriend.

Almost-stable, *adj.* Uncertain. Stable for some purposes perhaps, but not for a few important other purposes. Or, a place where donkeys live.

Almost-staff, *n.* Contract staff. Outsourced staff. People you have little control over. [See almost-employee.]

Almost-stage, *n.* An in-between stage. Also, a part of a process that is not well-defined, especially one that is only almost-distinct from the other parts of the process (not yet a "natural type"). Or, a living room, garage, or wherever performers first almost-perform.

Almost-stand, *v.i.* To stand while bending over a bit (perhaps only to sit down again and out of courtesy, or to brace oneself with straight arms and hands on knees).

Almost-standard, *n.* A level or condition that one might expect, but that is not actually required. Or, vague, incomplete, or subjective criteria or specifications. Or, not so standard that that others of the same type might not also be useful (for example, a so-called "standard of living"). No almost-standard dictionary is considered to be the very last word about a language. [See almost-inspection.]

Almost-staple, *n.* Small nail.

Almost-star, *n.* Character actor.

Almost-start, *v.* Get ready to start.

Almost-starved, *adj.* Very hungry.

Almost-state, *n.* Being in transition between two stable conformations.

Almost-statehood, *n.* The condition where the structures of an advanced society are nascent.

Almost-statement, *n.* The ramblings of someone after a journalist's microphone gets placed in front of them (before they have time to think of what to say). Or, the ramblings of the journalist, if they didn't do their homework. Or, the statement in almost-speak of someone following the almost-method of speaking about—. [See almost-method.]

Almost-stationary, *adj.* Moving very slowly relative to something else.

Almost-stationery, *n.* The background of an email.

Almost-statistics, *n.* The surrounding approximations, inexactness, estimating, abnormalities, disturbances, questionable data, and confusion that accompany the formulas and specific variables of statistical work. Or, very sloppy statistical work. [See almost-aspect.]

Almost-status, *n.* What the status will almost-certainly soon be. (As in, "the almost-bride is almost-pregnant.")

Almost-status quo, *n.* So close to normal that you can reach over and hang your hat on the status quo from there.

Almost-stay, *v.* What a dog does when you tell it to stay. (He might even have that special "I'm going to almost-stay, just watch me," look on his face.)

Almost-steal, *v.* To go there and take, and then give back before anyone notices. Or, when the asking price for something is much lower than what the things is actually worth.

Almost-steel, *n.* Iron.

Almost-steep, *adj.* Steep enough that the road or train tracks don't go straight there, but not so steep that you will need to go the rest of the way on foot. Yet.

Almost-stemmed, *adj.* Very short stemmed (especially for cut roses). This style is becoming very almost-popular, because there are even fewer prickles.

Almost-step, *n., v.* A baby step, or half-step. What to most people would be less than a step. Both "add water" and "stir" are almost-steps.

Almost-stepchild, *n.* A child of the person with whom you are cohabiting (someone you have not yet adopted).

Almost-stiff, *adj.* Not so inflexible that you can't get back on the tennis court for another game (but you are going to be feeling it worse tomorrow).

Almost-stifle, *v.t.* When you stick a sock in it, but it keeps on talking.

Almost-still, *adj.* Still breathing.

Almost-stock, *n.* An equity interest in a private company that you don't control.

Almost-stop, *v.t.* To slow down enough so that you can, if you need to, stop in the right place. Or, for those only almost-fortunate drivers, especially at a completely barren but only almost-unattended intersection, a way to demonstrate that you are both a menace to society, and willing to contribute to the municipal coffers.

Almost-storage, *n.* The kind of place where you don't really want to leave things because they are usually gone before you get back. (Like a "Lost and Found.")

Almost-store, *n.* An almost-place online where you can really buy almost-stuff. [See almost-world.]

Almost-storm, *n.* A strong gale (wind having a speed of 47 to 54 miles per hour, as indicated by the Beaufort Scale).

Almost-story, *n.* A story with a surprise ending, and where the surprise is that it isn't there. Once almost-upon a time the ending to this story just vanished. Or, a story outline only. Once almost-upon a time they needed some information about me for their files, and for my convenience, so that we could almost-all live almost-happily thereafter for a while.

Almost-stow, *v.t.* Keep on your lap.

Almost-straddle, *v.* One foot on the dock, and the other foot almost-on the boat as it is leaving, and then . . . almost-trouble (splash).

Almost-strange, *adj.* Unconventional. Curious. Singular. This might apply to most things, people, and ideas that you have not yet encountered.

Almost-stranger, *n.* Most people you have encountered.

Almost-strategic, *adj.* Tactical. Or, something that would be strategic if it wasn't so flaky.

Almost-strategy, *n.* A design strategy to quickly get things into near-final form, and then to more-meticulously improve from there.

Almost-stream, *n., v.* Trickle.

Almost-street, *n.* Alley. Dirt road. The parts of a parking lot marked for driving rather than parking.

Almost-strength, *n.* Sheer existence, or mere endurance. Or, related to one's ability to almost-wield almost-speak.

Almost-stress, *n.* Tension.

Almost-stretch, *v.* Clasp your hands behind your head.

Almost-strict, *adj.* Not very lenient.

Almost-strife, *n.* Arguing.

Almost-strike, *n., v.* Spare. Near-miss. When a group of bowlers threatens to almost-leave.

Almost-striking, *adj.* Something very, very normal.

Almost-strip, *v.i.* To take off most of your clothes (as at a doctor's office, or at the beach, or to get into bed). Or, to not remove any clothing, but to playfully reveal a little more leg.

Almost-stripper, *n.* Someone who doesn't quite take it all off. A tease.

Almost-structure, *n.* A real plan for a physical structure. Or, an almost-abstract structure. Or, a social structure. Organization charts are almost-structures.

Almost-strudel, *n.* A fairly attractive woman. Or, at a stretch, almost any pastry that is not a strudel (especially if you're not fussy).

Almost-struggle, *n.* The almost-biff and almost-pow of almost-everyday almost-life. [See almost-strife.]

Almost-student, *n.* A person that attends school or classes but doesn't study much. Someone who is just "auditing."

Almost-study, *n.* Study amidst distractions.

Almost-stuff, *n.* Anything that has almost-aspects. Or, any almost-thing: almost-matter, almost-energy, almost-substance, or almost-abstract thing. Anything almost-almost (which is almost everything). "I think about what it almost-is, therefore it is almost-stuff." Or, stuffed stuff. [See almost-aspect, almost-abstract, almost-almost, almost-ideal, almost-something, almost-thing.]

Almost-stuffed, *adj.* Full or satisfied (especially as with a meal). Or, just a stuffed shirt.

Almost-stunt, *n.* A trick that is neither surprising nor difficult, and almost-not meant to attract attention or publicity.

Almost-stupid, *adj.* Sometimes neglectful, or erratic. Or, of someone out of their element.

Almost-style, *n.* This is the almost-wave of the almost-future. Pretty soon almost-everyone will be almost-doing almost-it (whatever that almost-is). Perhaps, something almost-akin to cafeteria-style, or almost-free style. [See almost-art.]

Almost-subaltern, *adj.* Someone almost-holding their own. (Not just an apprentice, or lackey.)

Almost-subject, *n.* A vaguely articulated subject, or a vague subject. Or, a noun that is stuck in a predicate *clause.*

Almost-subliminal, *adj.* Something above the threshold of consciousness, but below the threshold of attention.

Almost-subscribe, *v.t.* Allowing yourself to get notifications for free (like, for when it's time to get your oil changed). Or, when you get a few months worth of a magazine for free while they hope you get hooked enough to pay the subscription fee.

Almost-substance, *n.* That which would almost-be by definition. Or, a hard to define substance. Stuff you can only almost-understand. [See almost-abstract, almost-real, almost-thing.]

Almost-substandard, *adj.* Something extremely useful and very high-quality that is made to fail-safe, break, deteriorate, or weaken in predictable ways relatively quickly. (Sometimes said of the almost-jewels in the crown of capitalism.)

Almost-substantiate, *v.t.* Lend credence to. Or, almost-embody.

Almost-substitute, *v.t., n.* An almost-poor substitute.

Almost-success, *n.* The achievable part of success. Or, the next best thing to success. Or, if you are using the almost-method, it is what you can almost-achieve if you almost-try. [See almost-method, almost-way.]

Almost-successor, *n.* Someone being groomed as a successor.

Almost-succulent, *adj.* How the steak *you* get almost-inevitably almost-turns almost-out to be or not to be. That is almost a question.

Almost-sudden, *adj.* Not unexpected. Or, slow. Or, protracted.

Almost-suggest, *v.t.* Hint.

Almost-sum, *n.* When you quickly add up a series of numbers paying attention only to the high-order digits (perhaps, to check that you were not overcharged egregiously).

Almost-sun, *n.* What you see on the horizon when the sun is almost-set. (By almost-contrast, when the sun is overhead it almost-beats almost-down with its rays.)

Almost-sunk, *adj.* Losing fast, in a battle with the almost-elements (chemicals).

Almost-sunlight, *n.* That which exposes or makes clear those almost-things that add to social and mental insight.

Almost-super, *adj.* Almost-faster than a speeding bullet, almost-able to leap over almost-high almost-rises, and almost-as powerful as a horse. Anyone who almost-fights for provisional truths, justifiability, and the almost-way. (My almost-kind of almost-hero.) [See Almost-Wonder.]

Almost-superego, *n.* One of the three divisions of the almost-psyche that is only almost-conscious, but is almost-sufficient to almost-impose on the rest of almost-thinking the almost-rules and almost-values almost-considered almost-important. [See almost-ego, almost-id, almost-psyche.]

Almost-superior, *adj.* Superior only in some ways (and not all of the important ways).

Almost-supervisor, *n.* One who supervises half-heartedly, or in a distracted manner. Or, an older, wiser, or taller attendee.

Almost-supplier, *n.* Your supplier's supplier, or your supplier's, supplier's supplier. But not your supplier's, supplier's, supplier's supplier (that would not be almost-enough).

Almost-supply, *v., n.* Engender hope in eventual supply.

Almost-support, *v.t., n.* The kind of assistance you get *after* you purchase something.

Almost-suppress, *v.t.* Quell, but not remove or eradicate.

Almost-supreme, *adj.* The next-to-highest in ranking. Subordinate. The almost-supreme machine *wants* to get better.

Almost-sure, *adj.* Pretty sure. Or, pretty and sure.

Almost-surge, *v.t., n.* A surge in name only. A few keeners out skylarking. When almost-something almost-swells or almost-overflows.

Almost-surplus, *n.* More than ample, maybe.

Almost-surrender, *v.* Give up a battle or some ground, in order to perpetuate a war or larger cause.

Almost-surrogate, *v.t., n.* To act as surrogate, but in an insufficient or "only as needed" way.

Almost-survey, *v.t., n.* Take a few photos of the place.

Almost-survival, *n.* Survival of the almost-fittest, . . . until the almost-end. Or, the survival of almost-stuff.

Almost-suspect, *n.* Regardless of the evidence presented, the surviving spouse, the butler, and the pool-boy are almost-suspects until the end of the show.

Almost-suspense, *n.* The degree to which a movie can be suspenseful if it is riddled with commercial advertising.

Almost-sustain, *v.t.* Almost-keep almost-going for almost as long as almost-necessary.

Almost-swallow, *v.* When you pretend to swallow, and instead keep the pill hidden in your mouth.

The Almost-Dictionary

Almost-swamp, *n.* Anywhere, after a good long rain.

Almost-swanky, *adj.* Almost-fashionably almost-elegant almost-without being almost-ostentatious, almost-pretentious, or almost-too energetic or loud. A great place to go on a first date. (Definitely good enough for the "almost-in" crowd.)

Almost-swap, *v.t.* Exchange looks.

Almost-swarthy, *adj.* Of a tanned complexion, and almost clean-shaven. Apparently, women almost-go for this almost-look on a man.

Almost-swear, *v.* To use almost-words in an almost-vain way (perhaps while reflecting, after almost-hitting your thumb with a hammer). Or, to indicate in a court of law that you will very likely almost-speak as objectively as you can of your almost-understanding of the situation as presented.

Almost-sweet, *adj.* Bittersweet. Or, just not very tasty.

Almost-swell, *v.* To slightly enlarge or distend.

Almost-swill, *n.* The worst kind of food that you are willing to put up with before deciding to go out in the rain to eat at a better place.

Almost-swim, *v.* Tread water. Or, drown.

Almost-swindle, *v.* When you try to swindle someone who has heard of your kind of scam, or who doesn't trust you, or who doesn't have any money.

Almost-swing, *v.* In baseball, when the batter doesn't "break" their wrists. Or, just rock gently.

Almost-sympathetic, *adj.* It's too bad, but it serves you right for trying to do that.

Almost-synchronous, *adj.* Occurring at nearly the same time. Sometimes events are coordinated but synchrony is not the primary concern, and other times the near-synchrony is of utmost importance (in order for things to almost-work almost-properly, or in an attempt to make things seem less contrived).

Almost-syndicate, *n., v.* An almost-group, especially in the periodicals racket, or in television. [See almost-group.]

Almost-synergy, *n.* Combined almost-action that in almost-operation goes almost-haywire.

Almost-synonym, *n.* A word that means roughly the same thing. A near-synonym, or cognate. Or, a word used just for its segue potential.

Almost-synthesis, *n.* A collection of cobbled-together concepts and ideas that together quite-convincingly explain how certain seemingly incompatible almost-opposites can co-exist. [See almost-thesis, almost-antithesis, almost-opposite.]

Almost-system, *n.* What most systems are. Nobody is happy with it just the way it is, every stakeholder has hopes for it improving or changing in certain ways. The gap between what is and what might be is sometimes called "opportunity." If you build it, somebody is going to want it modified.

T

Almost-table, *n.* A very small table (like a flimsy tv-dinner table, or short-legged breakfast-in-bed tray). Or, almost any surface other than a table (even that of a chair, or sidewalk, or the top of someone's head), especially if used as a table.

Almost-taboo, *n.* Things you can do or talk about only with almost-special permission. Or, certain topics or things that are not included here in the Almost-Dictionary because they are decidedly unworthy of mention.

Almost-tacit, *adj.* An implied but indefinite indication. When someone's silence could mean agreement or disagreement, guilt or innocence, amusement or boredom, or whatever, all you know is that it means something. If the bear doesn't attack, that might be a tacit signal that he doesn't feel threatened, but it is only an almost-tacit indication that he likes being interrupted.

Almost-taciturn, *adj.* Disinclined to speak on most subjects, but loquacious about some things. Or, disinclined to use almost-speak.

Almost-tackle, *v.* Block.

Almost-tacky, *adj.* Unrefined.

Almost-tactful, *adj.* Tact-almostfull. Fairly sensitive and skillful in relations with others, and usually not offending others to an egregious extent. Or, including in one's conversation only that which wants to be said really badly (instead of needs to be said).

Almost-tactics, *n.* Operational devices for almost-accomplishing almost-ends. Or, fumbling. Or, using the almost-method in almost-employing most of your forces in almost-combat (pillow fighting, paintball, and the like).

Almost-tail, *v.t.* Following surreptitiously to see whether they go North, South, East, or West, but not all the way to where they are going.

Almost-tailgate, *v.i.* When you go to a football game in a sedan or convertible and have a picnic before the game.

Almost-tailor, *n.* The guy in a department store Men's wear section that tells you that the suit that only almost-fits you does fit you.

Almost-take, *n.* A glance (the almost-opposite of a double-take where you stare at someone conspicuously twice).

Almost-take off, *v.i.* What a plane does before it crashes after reaching the end of a runway.

Almost-talent, *n.* When you are not yet good enough at something to make money at it.

Almost-talk, *v.t., n.* Whisper. Or, twaddle. Or, baby talk (oversimplified speech or writing). Or, giving a speech almost-entirely in almost-speak. An almost-talk on finance might start like this: Money almost-talks, but it actually has almost-nothing to do with making the world go round. [See almost-speak.]

Almost-tame, *adj.* Probably ready to strike at something. Or, almost-wild.

Almost-tangible, *adj., n.* Feelings about certain software assets.

Almost-tangle, *n.* An ensnarling twisted web or mass of stringy stuff that is easy to deal with (spaghetti, or your limbs and the embracing limbs of your children).

Almost-tank, *n.* Sport-utility vehicle (SUV).

Almost-tantamount, *adj.* Nearly equivalent in value, significance, or effect.

Almost-tardy, *adj.* Not late, but late enough that people were starting to worry about whether you would be on-time.

Almost-target, *n.* An empty beer can, an old toaster, or a cactus.

Almost-task, *n.* Subtask.

Almost-tasteful, *adj.* Somewhat deficient in taste.

Almost-tax, *n.* A fee so indirect or hidden that few people know of its existence, let alone how it might benefit the government.

Almost-team, *v.t., n.* The opposite of double-team, where less than one-on-one coverage is appropriate. Or, less than a full complement of players. Or, a team that hasn't gelled yet.

Almost-tease, *v.t.* To begin to annoy, provoke, or arouse desire, but then to immediately desist.

Almost-technical, *adj.* Easy enough that a child could do it.

Almost-technician, *n.* An apt technician with no credentials. Or, a bumbling idiot with credentials.

Almost-technique, *n.* An imprecise procedure, expressed by someone who only almost-knows it. "Well, first you do this, then that, then after that—. Excuse me while I take this call." Or, a personalized version of the almost-method. [See almost-method.]

Almost-technology, *n.* Common sense. Or, anything useful that has been around for more than a few years.

Almost-teenager, *n.* Tween.

Almost-telephone, *n.* Beeper. Or, a telephone that is not the latest model of telephone.

Almost-teleprompter, *n.* A guy at the back of the room sending semaphore signals.

Almost-television, *n.* Videos, like you might see on the Internet. [See almost-movies.]

Almost-temporary, *adj.* As permanent as you can get. Will probably outlive you (or your tenure, or your patience). In software development, you may think you are writing quick-and-dirty code that will only be used once, but then someone will want to keep it.

Almost-tenant, *n.* The girlfriend or boyfriend of the tenant.

Almost-tend, *v.i.* To be almost-predisposed.

Almost-tendentious, *adj.* Only pretending to have a tendency or bias in favor of a particular point of view.

Almost-tennis, *n.* Ninenis. Or, badminton. Or, table tennis. Or, squash. Or, racquetball. Or, "smashed doubles."

Almost-tenor, *n.* Baritone.

Almost-tense, *n.* In almost-speak, this almost-refers to the almost-past, the almost-present, and the almost-future. The situation as it relates to the almost-aspect of time (when people are often almost tense). Not being fully in any of the other tenses, and far from perfect.

Almost-tentative, *adj.* Less tentative than one would expect. Or, tentative about almost-stuff. Or, to almost-start into the decision-making process with just one foot, as it were (by using the almost-method). And that is probably the way this definition is going to stay. Yes. To be, or not to be almost-tentative, that is the question. Which makes almost-sense.

Almost-tenure, *n.* Often the last step before tenure; but, as always, still just one major blunder away from the unemployment line. [See almost-unemployed.]

Almost-terminal, *n.* Toll booth. Where you have to stop for a bit, and then move on.

Almost-terminology, *n.* What you are looking at now.

Almost-terminus, *n.* A terminus that just goes on and on.

Almost-test, *n.* Determining the ratio of almost-words to other words to see whether almost-speak is at play. Or, any test that allows for an inconclusive outcome (such as making up your mind about a person solely by the kind of car they drive, or how they are dressed).

Almost-testify, *v.* To attest that one is unsure about something.

Almost-thank, *v.t.* To express gratitude in a partly sarcastic way.

Almost-theft, *n.* When something that belongs to the owner is hidden on the owner's premises such that the owner can't find it easily (usually as part of a practical joke).

Almost-theory, *n.* A popular hypothesis. Some cobbled-together facts, measurements, and anecdotal evidence that have not yet come together in the form of a proper and cohesive theory.

Almost-therapy, *n.* Psychosocial assistance in the use of the almost-method, and in following the almost-way. The therapy could take a while, and cost an almost-sorrowful sum, but ordinarily this is not the case because people discover that they already use the almost-method and live the almost-way, and so they just return to whatever it was they were trying to do before they considered going to see someone to talk over issues that would probably just go away by themselves anyway. [See almost-method, almost-master, almost-way.]

Almost-there, *adv., n.* Somewhere else.

Almost-thesis, *n.* When you're not yet even at the first stage of a dialectic, and the antithesis might still be one of any number of things. [See almost-antithesis, almost-synthesis, almost-theory.]

Almost-thing, *n.* An idea, or concept, or almost-abstraction (something that a brain does, especially anything that remains between vague and almost-concrete). Or, a thing that is almost as described (nearly the way it is talked about), or is almost something else (it has other aspects or uses, or it is moving or developing into something else, or it has components that could have other uses). [See almost-abstract, almost-principle, almost-something, almost-stuff.]

Almost-think, *v.* Quickly surmise. What the brain does in a knee-jerk reaction. Or, to just to allow ideas to waft through consciousness without letting them rest or change any other ideas (as when a brain is almost-made up). Or, what the brain does in between bouts of cogitation. Or, what dumb animals do. Or, what you pthink (with a silent "p"), which is not what you think so much as what you think you are allowed to say you think. Or, thinking in almost-speak, or about almost-stuff. Almost-focusing on the inner aspects of the almost-method, or the almost-way. If I think and suppose that therefore I am, I may still almost-think and consider that maybe I am almost a lot of different things (if you almost-catch the almost-way I've almost-drifted). [See almost-method, almost-therapy, almost-way.]

Almost-third, *adj.* Fourth (and maybe also fifth if they were neck and almost-neck).

Almost-throng, *n.* Three or four people almost-together.

Almost-through, *prep., adv., adj.* When you can see the light when you near the almost-end of the tunnel. Through like Pooh (after eating a pot of honey), or like Zeno of Elea (trying to leave a room and getting through the door). "Could somebody give me a push, please?"

Almost-throw, *v.t.* Toss. Or, win (and confound the bookies).

Almost-throwaway, *adj.* A keepsake. Something throwaway that you will get brownie points later for having kept.

Almost-thumb, *n.* Forefinger (especially when hitting the space bar when almost-typing).

Almost-thwart, *v.t.* To anticipate, and make a serious yet ultimately unsuccessful attempt to exclude, hinder, or prevent.

Almost-tidy, *adj.* When there is nothing on the floor except furniture.

Almost-tier, *n.* A tier that includes almost everyone. Or, a tier that doesn't include anyone.

Almost-time, *n.* Not a particular time, but rather of those nondescript and meaningless durations between events. If you are early for an appointment, or between the fun and challenging occasions in your life, it is then that you almost-notice the almost-passing almost-plainness of almost-time. When you are not sure what the time is, you just might be on almost-time (or a redneck). In almost-time, events are only almost-synchronous (for your convenience). In order to insert something into your schedule, you almost-need to almost-carve almost-out the almost-time as well as the time (planning for the delays and the downtime as well as the work). Or, the time in imprecise terms (as in: "dinnertime," "next week," or "whenever"). Like the "time" in "space-time continuum," almost-time is relative to the observer (in almost-space-almost-time). [See almost-travel.]

(If you are reading the Almost-Dictionary almost cover-to-cover, it may be nearly almost-time for you to almost-take an almost-break.)

Almost-timely, *adv., adj.* One or more seconds too late to be any good. What a different world this would be if everyone immediately thought of the very best thing to say in every situation. What a different world this would be if everyone was always ready for what was about to happen.

Almost-tired, *adj.* Tired enough that you consider the possibility of taking a break. Somewhat fatigued. When you can still go another round.

Almost-tits, *n.* Almost-almost-boobs. [See almost-boobs, almost-breasts.]

Almost-tizzy, *n.* Nervous anxiety or confusion, not quite rising to the level of having a fit, or being goofy.

Almost-together, *adv., adj.* At a place and/or time that is slightly different.

Almost-toilet, *n.* Potty. Almost anywhere in the great outdoors.

Almost-tolerance, *n.* When you *could* care less. Or, when something is passed a threshold or breaking point. Or, one's ability to tolerate almost-speak and other almost-stuff.

Almost-tone, *n.* A tone you can almost detect in someone's voice, that is akin to an instrument being slightly off pitch. It is also possible to almost detect almost-tone in writings. In other words, not quite a full tone or intonation.

Almost-tool, *n.* A handy linguistic device for separating the real world from the one that is only almost-there. "Does it have a handle?" you ask. "Almost," I would say, which is to be neither almost-here nor almost-there.

Almost-top, *adj.* Top drawer.

Almost-total, *n.* The total before tax. Perhaps, the total before your lawyer adds on his or her fee. Or, the quickly-estimated total.

Almost-touch, *v.* When things are close but there is still something fluid between them. Or, if a story is so almost-earnest that it makes the listener almost-feel almost-something, then it might be almost-touching.

Almost-tough, *adj.* All leather jacket, and no cattle.

Almost-tour, *v., n.* An online tour. Flipping through a picture book. A slide show. A travel show on television. [See almost-travel.]

Almost-towel, *n.* Hand towel. Tea towel. Face cloth. Rag. Paper towel. Someone else's t-shirt. You own overalls. (This is the almost-official "Order-After-Towel.")

Almost-town, *n.* Village.

Almost-toxic, *adj.* Unsavory. Displeasing.

Almost-trace, *v., n.* To follow (as a line) through something that is almost-not there (transparent, vague). Or, more generally, to look for almost-evidence. Or, that which is even smaller than a very tiny bit. Or, perhaps, that part of the "trace" in deconstruction that has not yet been considered — because it is so fantastic, or "far out." [See almost-deconstruct.]

Almost-trade, *v., n.* An almost-complicated scheme whereby one country incentivizes another to buy its goods (therefore, mostly one-way trade).

Almost-tradition, *n.* Something that we have always done in situations like this, since at least last week.

Almost-traffic, *n.* The relatively-few vehicles on the streets at three o'clock in the morning.

Almost-train, *v.t., n.* To almost-teach someone almost-something. Or, just an engine pulling a caboose. Or, a gravy train. Or, a wave train.

Almost-tranquility, *n.* Relative tranquility. The condition in any home once the kids have gone outside to play.

Almost-transaction, *n.* When the transaction is not quite completed before it is aborted, or when it gets reversed or backed out immediately for some reason.

Almost-transhuman, *adj., n.* Someone who is not completely transhuman.

Almost-transient, *n.* One that should be passing quickly in and out, but for some reason they grow roots.

Almost-transit, *v.t.* The passage of something only most of the way across (the sky, or a river). From the riders perspective, public transit is usually only almost-transit (you still have to walk after you almost-get there).

Almost-transition, *n.* An improvement or change that is under-funded or lacks energy (and, possibly, is *meant* to fail).

Almost-transitive, *adj.* While you're almost-busy trying to get some transitive verb up and running, almost-something almost-intransitive almost-takes its almost-place such that you just almost-think about almost-it.

Almost-translation, *n.* One of the many uses for this dictionary. Or, when someone acts out what they find difficult to articulate (as when a tourist indicates to a foreigner that they need to find a phone).

Almost-transmit, *v.t.* When *you* hit SEND, but *they* don't receive (because of a glitch).

Almost-transport, *v.t., n.* Moving as "the system" moves. You are transported by the bus, but you are almost-transported around the Sun with Earth's orbit. A fossil is almost-transported as that layer of rock that it's in moves. Unlike "active transport," or "supersonic transport," almost-transport is more passive. Or, transported in your imagination (an almost-place where our whole universe might be almost-transported). [See almost-tour, almost-travel.]

Almost-travel, *v., n.* The next best thing to being there. There are many ways to almost-travel: that is, to not travel, but to gain almost-all of the benefits of travel. Your almost-trip can start sooner, is over faster, and you don't need as many suitcases. When you think technology, think almost-travel. Almost-travel is almost-always almost-good enough. (When it comes to the five sense, they usually have the same relative importance as almost-always: you might miss the smell of the place, but not as much as you miss the sight of the place.) If you are in the present-day United States watching a documentary about the days of the Roman Empire, you are then almost-traveling in almost-space-almost-time. Likewise, observing distant stars almost-involves time-travel, because you are seeing things the way they were years ago. [See almost-tour, almost-transport.]

Almost-travesty, *n.* An almost-debased, almost-distorted, or almost-grossly inferior imitation — especially once you discount incompetence and the usual lack of attention to detail — where the situation was as to be almost-expected (so what's the problem?).

Almost-treatment, *n.* "Treatment," or whatever is guaranteed (in writing on the package) to absolutely positively have no chance of *curing* the said ailment, but what may help you *feel* almost-better. Or, more generally, almost anything used to get almost-relief.

Almost-tree, *n.* Bush (especially a large one). Or, a particular tree when it was smaller (check a photo album containing pictures of your backyard).

Almost-trend, *n.* A trend that is already over before you notice that it is a trend.

Almost-trespass, *v.* When you set foot on someone's property accidentally, and with no intention to go further.

Almost-trial, *n.* A sham trial. Or, a monkey trial.

Almost-trick, *n., v.t.* An obvious trick that everyone should know (the way to continue reading a book once you get to the bottom of the page is to turn the page, the best way to almost-impress a woman is to almost-ignore her).

Almost-tricky, *adj.* Quirky enough that you write a note for yourself as to how to do it a second time, but not so difficult that you inform everyone you know.

Almost-trifle, *n.* A trifle that is a little off. Or, a trifle that is missing an ingredient. Or, an even smaller serving than what's left of the trifle. Or, an even smaller part of almost anything else.

Almost-trifling, *adj.* A pretty big deal.

Almost-trillion, *n.* The number: 987,654,321 thousand.

Almost-trim, *adj.* How they both look two years after the wedding.

Almost-trip, *v., n.* When your foot catches on something for a second but you recover before falling.

Almost-trivial, *adj.* It is so unimportant or ordinary that you don't care, and neither does anyone else, except just one person who's opinion you care about.

Almost-troglodyte, *n.* Anyone who lives *near* or *above* a cave.

Almost-trouble, *n.* Not serious trouble. Or, anyone who busts out in almost-speak at an inopportune time (especially at an otherwise almost-somber occasion).

Almost-truce, *n.* A welcome respite in the natural horse-and-monkey-play of children when they know there is an adult watching (marked by merely tepid squabbling and less-severe injuries). Or, a good time to plan the next assault.

Almost-truck, *n.* A full-sized pickup truck. A scaled-down version is obviously an almost-almost-truck.

Almost-trucking, *n.* Whatever is done with, in, and around full-sized pickup trucks. (This differs from "trucking" in at least three respects: tailgating is done *more* frequently, stopping at coffee shops is done *less* frequently, and the loads are typically much smaller.)

Almost-truculent, *adj.* Self-assertive.

Almost-true, *adj., adv.* A very reliable model, or very reliable information. The latest scientific model (until a better one comes along), or the best almost-understanding (in certain ways, to the best of someone's recollection, or beyond a reasonable doubt). Or, less than the whole truth. Or, the varnished truth. Or, a statement expressing verisimilitude or truthiness. Sometimes the rest of the so-called truth is beyond the edge of the knowable, so don't worry about it (unless you have the time). [See almost-knowledge, almost-mutate, almost-understanding.]

Almost-trust, *n., v.* Trust but verify. Or, almost-keep on an almost-short almost-leash.

Almost-trustworthy, *adj.* Human. (Which is more than we can say about some of the other species.)

Almost-tube, *n.* A place to see almost-movies.

Almost-tuition, *n.* What gets paid at the Almost-Academy.

Almost-turbid, *adj.* Just a little cloudy.

Almost-turn, *v.* Just a turn of the head, or a twist at the waist.

Almost-twaddle, *n.* The kind of almost-silly almost-idle talk that does actually contain within it an important message (even if it is just said to pass the time in an elevator, at bus stop, or in a cafeteria lineup).

Almost-twin, *n.* Look-alike.

Almost-type, *n., v.* Of a kind in-between established types — neither one nor the other. A blend, hybrid, or mutant, perhaps. Or, when one haphazardly uses the wrong fingers on the letters of a keyboard.

U

Almost-ubiquity, *n.* The presence of a thing or idea in many places, but, too often, not where you almost-need to find it. (Examples: the almost-ubiquity of the rule of almost-fair almost-play, or the almost-ubiquity of the comfy chair).

Almost-ugly, *adj.* Something that takes a little getting used to.

Almost-ultimate, *adv.* The penultimate. Or, something near the farthest point, or acme. Using "almost-ultimate" instead of "ultimate" would be more suitable in many circumstances, especially in pop culture.

Almost-ultimatum, *n.* A technique used in negotiating where a supposed "final" proposition is offered, but if it is rejected yet another seemingly final one will be offered, and so on.

Almost-umpire, *n.* The guy sitting next to you in the stands with the big mouth.

Almost-unabridged, *adj.* Missing stuff that could be there. For example, even almost-standard dictionaries that claim to be unabridged are missing most of these almost-words.

Almost-unadvised, *adj.* Somewhat risky, unless you know what you're doing.

Almost-unanimous, *adj.* When there is just one guy who won't "get with the program."

Almost-unattached, *adj.* Encumbered by weak bonds, but not by overly-restrictive physical or financial ties.

Almost-unbalanced, *adj.* Self-balancing. Or, almost-weird, and a bit of a loose cannon. Or, when the credits and debits are so irregular that the integrity of the accounting is suspect.

Almost-unbelievable, *adj.* Puzzling. Or, when you know some of the information, but not the particulars, so there is not enough to go on to be able to believe wholeheartedly.

Almost-uncertain, *adj.* As certain as you can be in those circumstances.

Almost-uncool, *adj.* Would be cool, but is either a little ahead of, or behind the times. [See almost-hot.]

Almost-under, *adv., prep., adj.* When the anesthetist asks you to start counting backwards from a hundred, and while you can still hear yourself count.

Almost-underdog, *n.* The contender that would probably lose if it were not for an almost-special advantage they have.

Almost-underfund, *v.t.* To under-fund only to the extent that scope, reach, capability, operational effectiveness, efficiency, quality, morale, and customer satisfaction all suffer, and to the extent that most of your most highly-skilled people go elsewhere, but not to the extent that deadlines are missed.

Almost-underline, *v.t.* To mark underneath with a dashed line.

Almost-undermanned, *adj.* Not undermanned, unless you consider all of the unpaid overtime that will be required.

Almost-underpaid, *adj.* Someone with plenty of potential and energy that will be "underpaid" at that same rate as soon as they get a little more experience under their belt.

Almost-underpriced, *adj.* At the goldilocks price (competitive but not self-defeating).

Almost-underrated, *adj.* Possessing possible niche appeal.

Almost-understanding, *n.* A partial understanding that is expected to be improved upon (of a proto-truth or provisional truth, or a proto-thought of any new development). Or, a somewhat-confused or merely general understanding. How you understand something complicated after hearing someone explain it in a sophomoric way. Or, a comprehension of anything still only hypothetical or theoretical. (Science would be out of almost-business if we understood everything. No wonder they write those scientific papers in such qualified, skeptical, tentative, almost-abstract, and barely-readable ways.) Sometimes it seems like we almost-enjoy (or almost-suffer) the occasional lacuna or fuzziness within a full field of total awareness; but more often it's the reverse, where our splotchy areas of almost-understanding form the "fairly reliable" parts in an almost-terrain of quite profound ignorance. [See almost-knowledge, almost-true.]

Almost-undertake, *v.t.* To plan an activity to the *n*th degree, and then to only almost-do some of it.

Almost-underwater, *adj.* Floating precariously. Or, sinking. Or, on land where a tsunami is about to hit.

Almost-underwhelm, *v.t.* Almost-overwhelm.

Almost-underworld, *n.* Those otherwise good and decent folk who steal from their employers.

Almost-undo, *v.t.* To try to, but to *not* undo. Or, to *mostly* loosen, negate, ruin, unsettle, or seduce.

Almost-unemployed, *adj.* Everyone who is employed (because they are just one major mistake away from being unemployed).

Almost-unexpected, *adj.* Disasters are almost-always almost-not expected.

Almost-unfair, *adj.* Almost-all is nearly fair in almost-love and almost-war (or so they might almost say), but when deception or impatience creep in things can almost-end almost-up almost-being almost-unfair.

Almost-unfinished, *adj.* Declared to be finished, but with potential for a lot more. Almost every only almost-creative expression can be seen as almost-unfinished. Or, a sloppy job.

Almost-unfit, *adj.* Fit (but could work out more regularly). Or, just barely meeting specifications.

Almost-unified, *adj.* Almost-together, but almost-not.

Almost-uniform, *adj.* Fairly consistent or even.

Almost-union, *n.* When two or more things come together, but you can still see light between them. Marriages are only almost-unions. Or, when coworkers start discussing each other's wages.

Almost-unit, *n.* The only loosely-defined "attention span" can be considered the common base of many more-precise measures. We stop reading a book, change the television channel, change subjects when talking, stop exercising, and take a coffee break, all when our interest has waned; therefore, such things as book length, movie length, the size of a piece of paper, the number of words in an email, the number of words in a slogan, and the length of a business meeting are all largely determined by this almost-unit.

Almost-universals, *n.* Generalizations. Ubiquitous almost-abstract particulars. [See almost-abstract, almost-embody.]

Almost-universe, *n.* A subset or sample that contains almost-all of the elements. Or, that part of a universe that you know about. Or, everything that has almost-aspects. Or, the consideration of just the almost-aspects. [See almost-aspect.]

Almost-unknown, *adj.* Partly known.

Almost-unnoticed, *adj.* Noticed.

Almost-unofficial, *adj.* Official.

Almost-unprofessional, *adj.* In the style of "business casual."

Almost-unqualified, *adj.* The majority of people you are likely to encounter in a business or professional setting (either because they just barely qualified, or because they are now doing something other than that for which they qualified).

Almost-unreliable, *adj.* Almost-everyone (unless they are almost-completely unreliable).

Almost-unrest, *n.* A ruckus in which no bones are broken, no gunshots are heard, and no one loses any sleep.

Almost-unsatisfactory, *adj.* Satisfactory.

Almost-unscrupulous, *adj.* Principled.

Almost-unskilled, *adj.* Young.

Almost-unsound, *adj.* Almost everything of a musical quality. Or, almost anything someone else says is sound.

Almost-unspecialized, *adj.* Non-professional. Or, abecedarian. Or, dilettantish.

Almost-unstable, *adj.* Someone of a usually stable temperament in an unstable situation (in between jobs, or as a tourist).

Almost-unsure, *adj.* Pretty certain.

Almost-untenable, *adj.* Barely defendable.

Almost-unthinkable, *adj.* Whatever is *this* side of unthinkable.

Almost-untrue, *adj.* Containing a grain of truth (in farm country), a gram of truth (if you are using the metric system), a bit of truth (if you are a computer programmer), a dollop of truth (if you are in the food and beverage industry), an iota of truth (if you are Greek or Semitic), a modicum of truth (if you speak Latin), a scrap of truth (if you work in manufacturing), a particle of truth (if you are a physicist), a morsel of truth (if you snack a lot), a speck of truth (if you are an ophthalmologist), a whoop of truth if you are an ornithologist), or a smidgen of truth (if none of the above ring a freaking bell).

Almost-unusual, *adj.* As of this writing almost-speak might be considered almost-unusual.

Almost-unwell, *adj.* Someone who seems like they are healthy, but their condition could deteriorate.

Almost-up, *adv., adj., prep.* Above the horizon, but not overhead.

Almost-upbeat, *adj.* Many down-beats are almost-upbeat.

Almost-update, *v.t., n.* When someone tells you something you already knew, as if it were new news. Or, when you find out more about almost-stuff.

Almost-upgrade, *n., v.t.* A "bug fix" only (a repair, rather than improvement).

Almost-uplift, *v.i.* Support.

Almost-upon, *prep.* Nearly on. Perhaps, hovering over. Or, close in some sense in at least one type of space.

Almost-upper-middle-class, *adj.* The almost-forgotten middle-middle-class.

Almost-uppermost, *adv., adj.* Nearthetoppermost. Or, top-drawer.

Almost-uppity, *adj.* Almost-snobbish, but in a nice way.

Almost-uprising, *n.* Anything that mostly goes sideways, especially political movements.

Almost-upscale, *adj.* Wherever you live.

Almost-upset, *adj.* Bothered, or disquieted.

Almost-upsetting, *adj., v.* Something that would normally be upsetting, except that this time you bet the right way and made money.

Almost-up-to-date, *adj.* Alive, but not watching CNBC.

Almost-urban, *adj.* Suburban.

Almost-urbane, *adj.* Almost-sophisticated, almost-suave, and almost-cosmopolitan; perhaps also showing many of the almost-refined qualities and manners of almost-polite almost-society. Or, conscientious.

Almost-urge, *v.t.* Suggest.

Almost-urgent, *adj.* Almost every request (by the time it makes its way to your desk).

Almost-useful, *adj.* In the way.

Almost-usurious, *adj.* Your own mortgage rate.

Almost-utility, *adj.* A utility that delivers in an unreliable way.

Almost-utter, *v.t.* Mumble. Mutter. Stutter. Splutter.

V

Almost-vacant, *adj.* Nearly empty. Perhaps, abandoned. Or, soon to be unoccupied.

Almost-vacation, *n.* Any vacation from work when you don't leave home and go somewhere special. Or, just an afternoon off, a long weekend, or any vacation you consider to be too short. Or, a vacation that is curtailed unexpectedly.

Almost-vacuum, *n.* Space.

Almost-vagina, *n.* An artificial vagina.

Almost-vague, *adj.* Clear enough that they get the almost-picture, or general gist. (Almost-Vague would be a great name for a magazine about almost-stuff. Of course, so would Almost-Stuff.)

Almost-vainglorious, *adj.* Confident and self-assertive.

Almost-valid, *adj.* Credible.

Almost-valuable, *adj.* Something you don't need but that would be difficult or costly to replace (so it could be almost-priceless).

Almost-value, *v.t.* To estimate a ballpark value. Or, to undervalue (as in, to deliberately appraise low). Or, to not values as much as an alternative (as in: we sometimes need to make tough choices).

Almost-variable, *n.* A variable that stays essentially constant where you are (like the boiling point of water). (When doing calculations, sometimes it is simpler to just assign these variables specific values.) [See almost-constant.]

Almost-variance, *n.* The kind of variance you get almost-naturally. Or, the kind of variance almost-introduced by considering almost-aspects. [See almost-aspect.]

Almost-variety, *n.* When the available choices are all too similar to each other.

Almost-vault, *n.* A small fireproof lockbox. A room or compartment for the safekeeping of *non*-valuables.

Almost-vegetarian, *n.* Part-time vegetarian. Someone who only occasionally eats meat.

Almost-vehicle, *n.* A vehicle that is so slow or so precarious that it is not worth taking (a pogo stick, or a dilapidated ski lift).

Almost-velocity, *n.* The mere perception that something is moving.

Almost-venture, *n.* A venture that never gets beyond the initial planning stages.

Almost-verbatim, *adv.* A copied citation where typos are introduced, or where the meaning is slightly altered. One example: The almost-quick almost-brown member of the species *Vulpes vulpes* (essentially, a fox) almost-jumped almost-over (ran straight into) the almost-lazy (sleeping) mongrel of a dog. Or, almost-word for almost-word.

Almost-verbiage, *n.* Lots of almost-speak.

Almost-verify, *v.t.* To check too superficially or uncritically, or like you want it to pass the inspection.

Almost-versatile, *adj.* Someone with a wide range of skills in a narrow area. Or, someone with very few but ubiquitous skills.

Almost-version, *n.* The state of a product just before the next release (and when everyone is in a rush). A test version of something (or working prototype).

Almost-vertical, *adj.* Leaning slightly.

Almost-very, *adv.* Quite.

Almost-vexatious, *adj.* Causing concern. Or, something that would be annoying or troublesome except that it doesn't affect you.

Almost-viable, *adj.* Something that may be viable in the future, or was viable at one time, or might *seem* viable, but that right now is *not* viable. Maybe, something that would be viable if fresh ideas were introduced.

Almost-vicinity, *n.* The surrounding area of the surrounding area. Close enough that you can swing by after work on the way home.

Almost-vicious, *adj.* A ferocious Chihuahua. Some weather.

Almost-view, *n.* The perspective that almost nothing is absolute or complete. Or, an almost-expression made about almost-stuff. Which is to almost-say: An almost-expression of almost-understanding almost-about or consistent with the almost-principle. [See almost-aspect, almost-principle.]

Almost-vigor, *n.* What you get in addition to flavor with your coffee or tea (and/or by using the right brand of shampoo).

Almost-vindication, *v.t.* The justification for a much lighter sentence.

Almost-VIP, *n.* Someone who thinks you should have heard of them.

Almost-virion, *n.* An incomplete virus (consisting of some but not all of its RNA or DNA and protein).

Almost-virtual, *adj.* Mostly real.

Almost-vision, *n.* Echolocation.

Almost-visit, *v.t.* Make a phone call. Visit a web site.

Almost-vituperate, *v.* To berate, scold, or censure, but in a nice way.

Almost-voice, *n.* The whisper voice. Or, the sound of almost-speak. Or, the tone and style of the way someone uses almost-speak.

Almost-vote, *v.* When you vote with your feet.

Almost-voyage, *n.* When you read about a voyage, or view pictures of places. Almost-voyages are safer, and almost-travel generally is a lot less time-consuming than real travel. [See almost-travel.]

Almost-vulgar, *adj.* Mildly crude or rude. If someone were to create a list of "borderline" or "almost-vulgar" words that you can still say on cable television, it might include "poop," "fuzz," "work," and "taxes" for starters.

Almost-vulnerable, *adj.* When you have "an angle," and are therefore not as open to attack as one might suspect.

W

Almost-wacko, *n.* Kook.

Almost-wage, *n.* Less than the minimum wage. Minors often work for almost-wages for babysitting, helping to paint a fence, and the like. Or, perhaps, what you get paid during a trial period. Or, the appropriate wage for almost-work.

Almost-wail, *v.i.* Whimper. Polite wailing.

Almost-wait, *v.i.* When you say you'll wait, and you act like you'll wait, but really you are doing something other than waiting.

Almost-waiter, *n.* The male server that makes you wait on him, rather than the other way around. Then he doesn't get a tip—but whines about that because he is working as fast as he can and therefore thinks he deserves one.

Almost-waitress, *n.* The waitress that is auditioning for a different role while she is serving food (actress, girlfriend, therapist).

Almost-waive, *v.t.* When a rule is not applied in a particular case, but because the related information is public those involved suffer anyway. Or, when you get sentenced to "time served." Or, to take a small bribe to forego pressing or enforcing a claim or rule.

Almost-wake, *n.* Slipstream.

Almost-walk, *v.i.* Saunter. Stroll. Limp. Or, when you are on a horizontal mover at an airport and you don't walk at your normal speed but at a pace that would normally be slow for you.

Almost-wane, *v.i.* Not to decrease in size, extent, or degree, but to seem to be doing so relative to things around that are increasing. A common reason for people to change jobs is that salaries tend to almost-wane (with inflation eroding spending power over time).

Almost-want, *v.t.* When you have reasons for *not* wanting something as well as wanting it. Many people only almost-want an almost-ship, because they are expensive to maintain and keep. [See almost-ship.]

Almost-wanted, *adj.* Wanted, but not enough for there to be a poster and a reward for capture. (As in: Almost-Wanted for Jaywalking.) Or, babies that are almost-accidents.

Almost-war, *n.* We know what a hot war is, and a cold war, a guerrilla war, an on-again off-again war, and an all-out war. When weapons became too powerful, all-out war became "mutually assured destruction" (or MAD), and we had to learn to fight the almost-way. Almost-war has become the almost-norm now (in many arenas). Almost-war can be described as any serious dispute other than all-out war, especially a lukewarm or halfhearted war. [See almost-method, almost-way.]

Almost-warehouse, *n.* Garage.

Almost-warn, *v.t.* Caution. When you hint at danger, or vaguely suggest that a path of action might not be the best choice.

Almost-warped, *adj.* Twisted enough to be dangerous, but sane enough to hold a job.

Almost-warranted, *adj.* To give almost-adequate grounds or reason for something. To declare with near-certain justification.

Almost-warrantee, *n.* An assurance by a manufacturing company that is now no longer in business.

Almost-washing, *v.t.* Wiping. Or, cleaning. Or, wetting. Or, soaking. Or, scrubbing. Or, sandblasting. (Somebody could make a song out of this one, and then sing it in the shower with the water turned off.)

Almost-waste, *n.* Anything extra.

Almost-wasteful, *adj.* What happens when getting something done quickly is more important than getting it done economically.

Almost-watch, *v.t.* Watch in a distracted way. You might only be almost-watching the show if you are also preparing dinner, or playing darts. You might only be almost-watching the road if you are also fiddling with some gadget.

Almost-watchdog, *n.* Watchcat. Watchbird. Confused puppy.

Almost-water, *n.* Tap water.

Almost-waterlogged, *adj.* Waterboarded.

Almost-waterproof, *adj.* Leaky, or potentially leaky. Or, water-resistant but not pressure-proof. Almost-all watches are only almost-waterproof.

Almost-wave, *v., n.* Wave, but in such a way as to conserve energy (like the Queen does). Or, when people start doing "the wave" in a stadium, but then the game continues and the wave dwindles into less than a full wave before it stops altogether.

Almost-waves, *n.* Almost-particles.

Almost-way, *n.* It is the almost-way to almost-lead, almost-follow, or almost-get out of the way. If you choose either of almost-lead or almost-follow then you might also almost-run (jog) or almost-walk (saunter). Another way to almost-lead is to almost-inspire (just inform). If you decide to almost-get out of the way then please try to do it before almost everyone almost-gets almost-confused. Where things are uncertain and the signs vague, the path is probably most iffy, and then you will probably be approaching almost-something almost-borderline. That's when the clouds set in. But almost-no-hopes are found there. You spin your wheels. Almost-life is not so much about some "almost-journey," as it is about almost-leaving, watching someone else go there on television, and then mowing the lawn. Then later, talking about your almost-trips for almost-ages anyway, and otherwise almost-using the almost-method quite a bit as you wait for . . . whatever. [See almost-factor, almost-method, almost-follow, almost-lead, almost-travel.]

Almost-wazoo, *n.* The almost-thing that other almost-things sometimes go almost-up.

Almost-weak, *adj.* Strong enough for you to perhaps worry about.

Almost-wealthy, *adj.* Healthy.

Almost-wear, *v., n.* Put on (like a nametag). Or, tie around the waist over your clothes. Or, almost-shirts or other clothing with almost-sayings on them. [See almost-sayings, almost-season, almost-shirts.]

Almost-weather, *n.* Weather has its notorious forms: a bright sunny day, a dark and stormy night, a blizzard, or a hurricane. But the more muted almost-weather also deserves recognition: a fairly cloudy day, a breeze, snow flurries, or that time just before it stops raining when the leaves on the trees are still dripping.

Almost-wedding, *n.* Engagement party.

Almost-week, *n.* Six days. Or, the number of days spent working (typically five). The workweek in general. Or, the number of hours spent working (typically forty).

Almost-weekend, *n.* The day before the weekend, just before quitting time.

Almost-weigh, *v.t.* To just look at an object and guess the weight. "He's a lightweight." Or, "That there is one heavy piano."

Almost-weight, *n.* A person's optimistic guess at their own weight. Or, any weight that is entered on a form at the spot that asks for weight.

Almost-weird, *adj.* Unconventional. Curious. Singular. This might apply to most things, people, and ideas that you have not yet encountered.

Almost-welfare, *n.* Unemployment insurance (still a government hand-out, but more temporary in nature).

Almost-well, *adj.* When you feel much better, but still have an occasional cough, or still occasionally blow your nose.

Almost-wet, *adj.* Damp.

Almost-whack, *v.t.* Hit.

Almost-whatever, *pron., adv.* Whatever, but definitely not certain things.

Almost-wheedle, *v.t.* To look with the eyes at another person in a provocative or suggestive manner.

Almost-whimsical, *adj.* Almost-something almost-capricious or almost-eccentric.

Almost-whipping, *v.t.* Whipping with a wet noodle. Or, a tongue-lashing.

Almost-whisper, *v.t.* To speak softly enough that it sounds like you are intimating a secret, but loudly enough that others can hear what you say.

Almost-whistle, *v.i., n.* The sound you make when you try to whistle, but the attempt is ineffectual.

Almost-white, *adj.* Off-white. Any very light pastel color. Pork is an almost-white meat.

Almost-whole, *adj.* When most of something is together.

Almost-wholesale, *adj.* An extraordinarily inexpensive retail price (really).

Almost-wide, *adj.* More wide than slim. Or, ajar.

Almost-wield, *v.t.* Handle but not hold. Or, swing awkwardly. Or, to control a group like one is herding cats. Or, to know someone who knows someone who can push the button for you.

Almost-wife, *n.* Fiancée. Live-in girlfriend. Or, microwave oven. [See almost-husband.]

Almost-wild, *adj.* Almost-tame. Or, carefree. Or, daring. Or, sporty.

Almost-will, *n.* A frivolous wish. A mental impetus, but only in a hypothetical sense. Or, the inclination to sidestep an issue. Or, a disposition or choice that is not goal-oriented. Or, what someone else or society wants for you, not what you want yourself. Or what you want only because it is medically prudent. The almost-will to almost-power is very much a part of the almost-way. [See almost-way.]

Almost-willful, *adj.* Intentionally not preventing something, but hardly stubbornly prompting it.

Almost-win, *v.* Come in second, as the runner-up (or jogger-up). Perhaps, to temporarily hold the upper hand in a no-win situation.

Almost-wind, *n.* Breeze. Zephyr. Intestinal gas.

Almost-windfall, *n.* An unexpected, unearned, or sudden gain or advantage, but one that is so insignificant that it is hardly worth mentioning.

Almost-windmill, *n.* Something that resembles a windmill (like a giant, perhaps).

Almost-window, *n.* Porthole. Tent window.

Almost-wine, *n.* Grape juice.

Almost-wipe, *v.t.* Smear. This is how children clean up after themselves. It's not a pretty sight.

Almost-wire, *n.* Greetings. Stop.

Almost-wired, *n.* When you thought it was wired correctly, but the lights don't go on.

Almost-wireless, *adj.* Having a few wires.

Almost-wisdom, *n.* Sophistry. Insight. Shrewdness. Cunning. Or, going with the gut (impulsively foregoing the risk analysis) before taking action.

Almost-wish, *v., n.* When you wish almost-upon a planet, moon, asteroid, or space station.

Almost-wispy, *adj.* Fairly thin.

Almost-wit, *n.* A talent for banter.

Almost-with, *prep.* When you ditch your chaperone upon finding someone more interesting (you were only ever almost-with the chaperone, according to you).

Almost-withdraw, *v.t.* Move to just stand off at a safe distance.

Almost-within, *adj.* On the almost-side.

Almost-without, *prep., adv.* With.

Almost-withstand, *v.t.* Withsit.

Almost-witness, *v.t.* To see something happen on television or via some other filtered media (that can be almost-doctored to almost-leave the almost-right almost-impression).

Almost-witticism, *n.* Words that are picked from the field of thought before they are ripe. Or, a repeated joke. Or, almost-sayings that are both clever and concise.

Almost-wobbly, *adj.* A little tipsy.

Almost-woes, *n.* Misadventures that turn out quite well.

Almost-wolf, *n.* Dog, coyote, dingo, jackal.

Almost-women, *n.* Minor teenage girls.

Almost-won, *adj.* Close to winning. Or, came in second.

Almost-Wonder, *n.* An almost-super almost-hero in the almost-world, and in almost-speak almost-lore. He is made up almost-entirely of almost-stuff. Aside from this scant almost-evidence here, he is almost-invisible and almost-forgettable. Sometimes he almost-flies almost-round and almost-saves people from having to do their various tasks completely, but usually he's almost-too busy three that. He almost-performs almost-great almost-deeds as well as almost-all of the almost-normal day-to-day almost-wonder almost-working (like brushing his teeth, and taking out the garbage). What an almost-guy! [See almost-method, almost-super.]

Almost-wonderful, *adj.* Of note. Swell. Nifty. Keen. Peachy. Nice.

Almost-wondering, *v.i.* Hoping the speaker will elaborate more on the subject of your almost-interest.

Almost-wood, *n.* A very sparse growth of trees or shrubs. Or, a wood veneer over some lesser material.

Almost-woof, *n., v.i.* A yap, yep, yip, yop, yup, and sometimes yyp (when you accidentally step on its paw). The almost-warpen woof is even more almost-goofy.

Almost-word, *n.* A hyphenated word (for example, a compound-noun, such as this one) that has the word "almost" as a prefix.

Perhaps, such a prefixed word that is only almost-appropriate given the context. Or, a word or phrase that is not quite understood. [See almost-expression, almost-speak.]

Almost-work, *n.* Extremely light work, easy work, or enjoyable work. Or, work almost-done using the almost-method. [See almost-job, almost-method.]

Almost-workable, *adj.* A situation that calls for a little schmoozing.

Almost-workaholic, *n.* A "workaholic" that also finds time for family, sports, and the community. Or, someone who is not very "hard-core."

Almost-worker, *n.* Someone who does not do much when at work. This could be someone who is paid to cover a base regardless of whether or not they become busy (forest ranger, lighthouse keeper, or receptionist).

Almost-work-out, *n.* Five push-ups, a couple of stride jumps, and a little elbow-bending (preferably with a beer).

Almost-world, *n.* The almost-world includes everything that is almost the case. Almost-World is also a web site where you can see more almost-definitions, almost-speak, almost-sayings, and other almost-stuff. [See the Introduction for the URL.]

Almost-worldwide, *adj.* In the English-speaking world. (Translator: please adjust the language as appropriate for your planet.)

Almost-worth, *n.* Some value in between your "net worth" and some gross exaggeration of what you are worth that your mother is likely to consider more appropriate. The bank calculates your "net worth," but that doesn't fully account for your education, intelligence, appearance, health, self-confidence, experience, connections, potential, celebrity, achievements, and prestige. As a ball-park figure, and normalizing for all of the above, the almost-worth might be the fairest way to compare individuals.

Almost-worthless, *adj.* Everything in the garage except the car.

Almost-worthy, *adj.* Having almost-sufficient merit or importance.

Almost-wrap, *v.t.* To partially wrap. To place in a bag.

Almost-wreck, *v.t.* To partially destroy.

Almost-write, *v.t.* To scratch or finger-paint the letters.

Almost-writing, *v.t.* Thoughts considered while staring at the paper or screen (that might later become part of a letter to someone). Or, writing in the style or idiom of almost-speak.

Almost-written, *adj.* Words that that are not written down yet. Perhaps, stories passed on in the oral tradition. Or, what would have been almost-famous last words, except that there was nobody there to hear them. (Like Aaaaaarrrrrrrrgggghhh!) Or, writing that is not yet finished, or that was abandoned.

Almost-wrong, *adj.* Not entirely false or erroneous. A statement that may inadvertently misrepresent, mischaracterize, confuse, obfuscate, or omit thereby leaving the wrong impression.

Almost-wussy, *n.* A "sleeping giant," perhaps. Someone you don't want to mess with even though they might appear vulnerable at first. Or, someone weak but respectable. Or, someone who wisely feigns incompetence or powerlessness.

X

Almost-xenophobe, *n.* Someone who almost-fears or almost-hates some of the foreigners some of the time, but not all of the foreigners all of the time.

Almost-Xmas, *n.* Any celebration held on December 25th that is somewhat disappointing (perhaps because someone forgets something important, or someone only almost-attends, or because almost everything you get you either didn't want or already have). Or, the evening before Xmas. Or, the entire shopping season. Early in December you could wish people: "Almost-Xmas almost-greetings!" Or, any time you give the kids just enough to shut them up.

Almost-xylophone, *n.* A xylophone with one or a few of the wooden bars missing.

Y

Almost-yacht, *n.* A personal watercraft that has a head but no bath, seats but no furniture, a radio but no television, storage but no wet bar, and a captain but no crew.

Almost-yard, *n.* A very small yard, perhaps of a house in the city. The balcony of an apartment. If you live in an igloo, the great outdoors is your almost-yard.

Almost-yawn, *n., v.i.* A stifled yawn, like the ones that occur in important business meeting.

Almost-yawp, *n., v.i.* A cry, yelp, or squawk uttered by such a small animal that you barely hear it.

Almost-year, *n.* Three hundred and sixty-four days. Or, any of the three out of four years that is not a leap year.

Almost-yearly, *adj., adv.* Not quite every year, or on a periodicity somewhat shorter than a year.

Almost-yellow, *adj.* Off-yellow ever so slightly. An exceedingly light pastel yellow. (A pretty good color for kitchen walls.)

Almost-yes, *adv., n.* Probably. Tomorrow. Or, "Let me see if I can think of a reason why not."

Almost-yesterday, *adv., n.* The day before yesterday, or the day before that.

Almost-yield, *n.* When you haven't seen any return on your investment yet, but you've got a lot of positive feedback from friends and relatives.

Almost-yoke, *n.* When the yoke is on a ewe.

Almost-yoo-hoo, *interj.* Hey.

Almost-yoot, *n.* A tween hoodlum.

Almost-young, *adj.* Anyone between the ages of thirty and thirty-nine. Or, anyone between the ages of forty and forty-nine. Or, anyone who thinks young. Ok, you too.

Almost-yuppie, *adj., n.* An almost-member of the almost-group that disjunctively almost-includes old urban professionals, young rural professionals, and young urban non-professionals. Or, a young urban professional that speaks almost-speak. Almost-everyone is an almost-yuppie at some point in their lives. This is one almost-thing that almost-unites most of us.

Z

Almost-zany, *adj.* Not so ludicrous, exaggerated, or unprincipled that it can't command a mainstream audience. Most sit-coms have almost-zany characters. Actors are encouraged to be almost-zany in their personal lives too, but not so zany that they become almost-unemployable.

Almost-zeal, *n.* Somewhat-fickle interest.

Almost-zenith, *n.* Somewhere near the top.

Almost-zephyr, *n.* A gentle breeze that is so mild that you don't notice it until someone else almost-points it out.

Almost-zero, *n.* Very nearly zero. Or, a few. Or, not enough to worry about. Or, just a circle with a hole in it.

Almost-zillion, *n.* An indeterminately large number close to but definitely not over that other playfully-gargantuan number being discussed (zillion).

Almost-zirconia, *n.* A less-expensive alternative to cubic-zirconia (like clear plastic).

Almost-zone, *n.* Where your mind goes while you are thinking of almost-words and speaking in almost-speak. Or, where the mind almost-goes when using the almost-method to almost-think. (This is also where your mind almost-is while waking up or drifting off to sleep.) Or, the inside of any store that sells almost-stuff. [See almost-think, almost-mug, almost-shirt.]

Almost-zoo, *n.* A classroom. Or, an enclosure containing pictures of the animals that would be there if the lions didn't eat them all.

Almost-zoom, *v.i., n.* Magnify so that the needed detail is clear, but no further (and not to clarify what is then of interest).

Almost-zygote, *n.* A fertilized egg cell that has been almost-unnaturally altered in its biochemistry or genetic almost-makeup.

Of course, there could be more here. Some almost-new almost-words could be added to a subsequent edition, some other almost-words may remain almost-ineffable (let's almost-see, hmmm), and then there is just . . .